S0-BZO-919

Learn C#

Includes the C# 3.0 Features

Sam A. Abolrous

Wordware Publishing, Inc.

Library of Congress Cataloging-in-Publication Data
Abolrous, Sam A.
    Learn C# / by Sam A. Abolrous.
    p. cm.
    Includes index.
    ISBN-13: 978-1-59822-035-3 (pbk.)
    ISBN-10: 1-59822-035-7
    1. C# (Computer program language)   I. Title.
    QA76.73.C154A416 2007
    005.13'3--dc22   2007024261

ISBN-13: 978-1-59822-035-3
ISBN-10: 1-59822-035-7
10 9 8 7 6 5 4 3 2 1
0708

All inquiries for volume purchases of this book should be addressed to Wordware Publishing, Inc.,
at the above address. Telephone inquiries may be made by calling:

(972) 423-0090

To Camelia, my love and my wife.

Contents

Foreword

Some people express themselves by speaking loudly and waving their arms about. If you don't understand, they just yell at you louder and louder until you give in and pretend to understand.

Then there are people like Sam, who takes the opposite approach.

When I worked with Sam on the Microsoft Visual Studio C# documentation team, there was always an aura of calm and concentration emanating from his office. Calm, concentration, and about 90° F heat, because Sam liked to keep his office hotter than a sauna in a desert. Of course, when I sat in his office and asked him to explain some subtle point of a C# application to me, it's possible that I just imagined his superior intellect because the heat made me stupid and drowsy, but I doubt it. Sam knows C#, and that's all there is to it.

While I was working on the documentation, the refrain "Ask Sam" was something I heard a lot. The good news is that now, thanks to this book, you too can ask Sam anything you like about C#, and you'll find the answers here. Just remember to bring some water.

John Kennedy
Senior Content Project Manager, Microsoft

Preface

When the first version of the C# programming language was released with the .NET Framework in 2002, it achieved great success and became the preferred programming language for many programmers around the world. C#, as an evolution of C++, simplified many features of C++ but retained the power of C++. In fact, the power of C# and the easy-to-learn syntax persuaded many developers to switch to it from C++ or Java.

The C# 2005 version (also referred to as C# 2.0) added even more powerful features to the language such as generics, partial classes, and much more. The new features of C# 3.0 that were released in the Technology Preview introduced programmers to a new era called *functional programming*. C# 3.0 focused on bridging the gap between programming languages and databases.

This book covers all the language features from the first version through C# 3.0. It also provides you with the essentials of using Visual Studio 2005 to let you enjoy its capabilities and save you time by using features such as IntelliSense.

Target Audience

This book targets:
- Beginners with no prior programming experience
- C++ programmers who want to switch to C#
- Advanced C# programmers

Beginners can start with the basics of the language covered in the first eight chapters, which do not require any previous programming experience. C++ programmers who want to switch to C# will find many similarities between the two languages and can begin by reading Table 1-1 in Chapter 1, which presents the differences between C++ and C#.

Advanced programmers who are looking for the new features of C# 2005 can start with the table of the new features in Chapter 1, Table 1-2, then go directly to the topics referenced in the table. Although the new features of C# 2005 are introduced in several chapters, Chapters 11 and 12 concentrate on the most important features of C# 2005, namely collections and generics. The new features of C# 3.0 are introduced in Chapter 14 along with ready-to-run examples.

Features of This Book

This book teaches the C# language and provides an introduction to using Visual Studio 2005. The book does not cover web and Windows applications, although it introduces them briefly in Chapter 13. All the programs in this book, except those in Chapter 13, are *console applications*, which means that even if you don't have Visual Studio, you can still write these programs in a text editor and compile them in the *command-line* environment. (Section 1-5 discusses how to get a free C# compiler.) To use the C# 3.0 examples, you must install the new compiler features as explained in the introduction of Chapter 14.

One important feature of this book is that it gives beginners with no prior programming experience a quick start to writing code in C#, beginning in Chapter 2.

The Structure of This Book

Each chapter of the book contains:

- Complete examples that are ready to run. The output of each example is shown in the Output or the Sample Run sections that follow the example. The source code of the examples is included in the companion files, which can be downloaded from www.wordware.com/files/csharp.

- Drills on each topic to help you test yourself. The answers to the drills are listed in the appendix and are also included in the companion files.

- Tips on C# programming as well as special notes for C++ programmers. A comparison of the two languages is given in Table 1-1.

- Syntax blocks using most of the C# statements.

- A summary at the end of each chapter to summarize the major skills you have learned in the chapter.

In general, with this book you can learn the essentials of the C# language and delve quickly into its depth. The book also answers most of the questions frequently asked by programmers since the release of C# 1.0 in 2002.

Acknowledgments

I would like to thank John Kennedy for his time and effort spent reviewing this book and to ensure that it answers most of the readers' questions.

I would also like to thank my family, Camelia, Hazem, Pille, Sally, and Craig, for their support during the writing of this book.

Conventions

Throughout the book different text styles are used to indicate the following:

- *Italics*: to emphasize the first occurrence of an important word or phrase that will play a role in the sections to follow. It is also used in the syntax blocks to indicate text other than keywords. For example:

```
if (condition)
    statement(s)_1          // The original result
else
    statement(s)_2          // The alternative result
```

- **Bold**: to distinguish reserved and contextual keywords of the C# language, elements of the .NET class library, and menu options, except in notes, tables, lists, and code examples. For example:

  get, **set**, **yield**, **value**, **partial**, and **where**

Chapter 1

Introduction to C# and .NET

Contents:
- Introduction to object-oriented programming
- C#, the OOP language
- The .NET Framework
- C# and IL
- How to get a free C# compiler
- Comparison of C# and C++
- The features of C# 2005
- The new features of C# 3.0

1-1 Object-Oriented Programming

Object-oriented programming (OOP) introduced the concept of classes and objects in the early '90s. This methodology is based on the scientific classification principles of ordering and naming groups within subject fields. For example, the Mankind class represents all humans. This class possesses *characteristics*, such as the body parts and senses, and exercises a *behavior*, such as the ability to speak. From this class come the Man class and the Woman class. Each of these classes *inherits* the characteristics and behavior from the Mankind class and adds to it specific characteristics of the Man or the Woman. The Man class is actually an abstraction of the behavior and characteristics of a Man, from which you can create instances or objects such as Craig and Dylan. From the Woman you create objects such as Isabella and Angelina.

In programming, you divide your data into classes. You can, for example, represent the elevators by the class Elevator, which contains the data *fields* that represent the characteristics (the elevator number, the number of floors, and the floor number) and the *methods* (or *functions*) that represent the behavior (going up or down). From the Elevator class, you can create

1

objects such as elevator1, elevator2, and so forth. In fact, you don't have to write the Elevator class yourself in order to use it. It might be created by another programmer or another company, and you just use it in your code, without even seeing the source code.

The OOP principles are summarized in the following list:

- **Abstraction:** The ability to create abstract data objects (classes) that can be used to create instances. (Explained in Chapter 5.)

- **Encapsulation:** Protecting some data members by hiding the implementation and exposing the interface. (Explained in Chapter 5.)

- **Inheritance:** Reusing the code by specializing classes and adding features to them. (Explained in Chapter 5.)

- **Polymorphism:** Changing the behavior of the methods of the inherited class. (Explained in Chapter 6.)

1-2 C#: The OOP Language

Although the C++ language is object oriented, it is in fact a mixture of both methodologies, the traditional and OOP approaches. This means that you can create an object-oriented program consisting of objects that contain the fields and the methods together, or you can write the same old code with global variables scattered in the program file and exposed to accidental changes by other programmers. With small applications, it might be okay to use the traditional method, but with complex programs that are shared by a large number of programmers, the need for OOP arises.

C# was built from the ground up as an OOP language. That means you cannot create a program without building your classes first and having the fields and methods (the *class members*) inside their classes. C# was an evolution of C++, and solved a lot of issues that have always faced C++ programmers. For example, it got rid of pointers that wasted programmers' time and effort in resolving associated problems such as memory leaks. It also got rid of multiple class inheritance, which caused more problems than benefits. In addition, the *generics* feature that came with C# 2005 was useful and easier to use than C++ templates. In the next sections, the differences between the two languages are discussed in detail.

1-3 The .NET Framework

The .NET Framework, introduced by Microsoft in 2002, is a programming platform and set of tools for building and running distributed applications in the Internet era. It also contains an object-oriented *class library* and a collection of reusable *types* (a type is a representation of data such as classes) that enable you to accomplish many common programming tasks such as file access, string manipulation, and database management. The class library is categorized into modules (referred to as *namespaces*) and includes types that support a variety of applications such as:

- Console applications
- Windows forms
- ASP.NET applications
- XML web services
- Windows services
- SQL Server applications
- Small device applications

In fact, C# is one of the .NET languages that Microsoft developed. The other languages that use .NET are Visual Basic .NET, J#, and Managed C++, in addition to languages developed by other companies. (See more details on the web site: http://www.dotnetpowered.com/languages.aspx). All these languages work under the .NET umbrella and use its libraries. Actually, you can write an application with modules written in different languages that support .NET.

In addition to the class library, the .NET Framework includes the *Common Language Runtime* (CLR), an integrated environment for executing applications using the .NET library.

There are other versions of the .NET Framework that work with operating systems other than Microsoft Windows, such as Mono. Mono can run on operating systems such as Mac OS X and Linux. There is also a subset of the .NET Framework called the Microsoft .NET Compact Framework that can be used with small devices and smart phones. There is even a Micro Framework for extremely low-power devices, such as watches.

1-3-1 CLR and Managed Code

The Common Language Runtime is responsible for executing applications and runtime services such as language integration, security enforcement, memory management, and thread execution. The CLR provides *metadata*, which is a consistent method for describing code.

The Common Language Specification (CLS) and the Common Type System (CTS), fundamental parts of the CLR, define the types and syntax that can be used with many .NET languages. The CTS is a standard that defines how CLR represents and manages types. The CLS is a subset of the features that programming languages must support in order to execute in the context of CLR.

The code that executes under control of CLR, such as C#, is called managed code, while the code that executes without requiring CLR, such as C++, is called unmanaged code. Prior to Visual Studio .NET 2002, all applications used unmanaged code. Applications such as MFC, ATL, and Win32 are unmanaged applications. When you are using managed code, the .NET Framework handles any interaction with the operating system, and you just concentrate on the application itself.

1-3-2 MSIL and JIT

When you compile a C# program, the compilation does not directly generate *native* (operating system-specific) code; it generates code written in *Microsoft Intermediate Language* (MSIL or IL). The MSIL code is translated to native code at run time. This compilation phase is called the *just-in-time* (JIT) compilation.

 Note Native code can also describe the output of the JIT compiler: the machine code that actually runs at run time.

1-3-3 Metadata

During compilation, the CLR creates information about your application. It includes class names, field names, method names, and method parameters. This information is called *metadata*, which means information on data. Metadata is used by the CLR and the Jitter (JIT compiler) for many purposes such as debugging and type checking. You can also use metadata to create instances of the classes and use class members regardless of the source code language.

1-3-4 Assemblies

The program compilation results in creating an *assembly*, which can be either an .exe file (executable) or a .dll file (library). An assembly contains:

- The *manifest* that contains the metadata, which provides the following information:

- Versioning information. The versioning information contains four parts: major version, minor version, build number, and revision number (for example, 1.0.32.72005)
- Security information
- External assembly references
- Exported types
- Culture information (the national language such as English, French, or Chinese)
- Custom attributes such as company name and product information
- One or more modules of MSIL code
- The resources used by the application

1-3-5 Garbage Collection

One of the most important benefits of using managed applications is the use of the *garbage collector (GC)*. The role of CLR does not end after compiling the IL code into native code. In fact, the CLR is responsible for managing memory during the code execution. It assures that the memory used by the program is totally freed up after the program exits. With unmanaged applications, programmers are responsible for managing the memory and resolving problems that might occur if a block of memory is left allocated after the program ends.

With a managed application, blocks of memory are allocated on the managed *heap*. (The heap is the part of memory that is used to store objects, as opposed to the *stack*, which is used to store references to objects — more on heap and stack later.) The GC keeps track of the referenced objects on the heap and automatically frees up the memory allocated to a specific object when it goes out of scope. Calling the GC programmatically is possible by invoking the method **System.GC.Collect**. However, this is not recommended because it is not guaranteed that it will destroy your objects. It is best to focus on the business logic and let the CLR determine the right time for garbage collection.

1-3-6 Putting Things Together

The .NET applications are handled according to the following procedure:

1. You start by coding your application using one of the .NET-compliant languages such as C#.

2. The C# code is compiled into MSIL and stored in an assembly. The C# code might be split across many source files, which are linked together during the compilation.
3. On executing the code, it is compiled into an operating system-specific (native) code by using the JIT compiler.
4. The application is executed under control of the CLR. When the program exits, the GC frees up the allocated memory.

1-3-7 ILASM and ILDASM

With Visual Studio, you have two programs for IL compilation:

- **ilasm.exe:** Used to compile programs written in IL and convert them to .exe or .dll files.
- **ildasm.exe:** Does the opposite process as it reads an .exe or .dll file and retrieves the IL file, which contains the manifest and the metadata.

In the next section, we use ildasm.exe to take a look at the contents of the assembly and get an idea about its properties.

1-4 A First Look at the C# Code

In the following sections we take a look at the C# code and the various ways to compile it and execute it without going into the details of the syntax.

1-4-1 The C# Code

The following code is an example of a C# class that can be compiled as a .dll file:

```csharp
// EmployeeDLL.cs

public class Employee
{
    // Fields:
    public string name;
    public string id;

    // Methods:
    public double CalculateSalary(int hoursWorked, double rate)
```

```
    {
        double salary;
        salary = rate * hoursWorked;
        return salary;
    }
}
```

This example contains the Employee class, which contains the following data fields of an employee:

- id
- name

The code also contains the method *CalculateSalary*. This method takes two parameters, *hoursWorked* (the number of hours worked) and *rate* (the payment per hour), and is used to calculate and return *salary* (the gross payment of the employee). The class can, of course, contain other details, but for the sake of the example this would be enough.

The file that contains this class (its name is written as a comment in the first line: EmployeeDLL.cs) can be compiled to a .dll. Then you can take a peek at this .dll file by using ildasm.exe. The output is shown in the following figure.

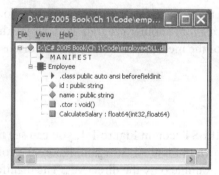

Figure 1-1: The IL and the manifest of the DLL.

In Figure 1-1, the contents of the **Employee** class (the fields and the method definition) are shown. Programmers who want to use this class would have enough information without seeing the source code.

1-4-2 **The IL Code**

If you click on any of the class members, such as the method **CalculateSalary**, you see its IL code, as shown in Figure 1-2.

```
Employee::CalculateSalary : float64(int32,float64)    _ □ X
Find  Find Next
.method public hidebysig instance Float64
          CalculateSalary(int32 hoursWorked,
                          Float64 rate) cil managed
{
  // Code size       12 (0xc)
  .maxstack  2
  .locals init (float64 V_0,
           Float64 V_1)
  IL_0000:  nop
  IL_0001:  ldarg.2
  IL_0002:  ldarg.1
  IL_0003:  conv.r8
  IL_0004:  mul
  IL_0005:  stloc.0
  IL_0006:  ldloc.0
  IL_0007:  stloc.1
  IL_0008:  br.s       IL_000a
  IL_000a:  ldloc.1
  IL_000b:  ret
} // end of method Employee::CalculateSalary
```

Figure 1-2: The IL file of the method CalculateSalary.

Ignore the text between the curly braces and examine the code preceded by a dot (this is called a directive). You will notice that the definition of the method **CalculateSalary** gives all the information you need to use this method:

```
CalculateSalary(int32 hoursWorked, float64 rate)
```

The beauty of the assembly is that it is self describing. Therefore, you can use this library file as a *component* in another program without looking at the source code. (The details of the method parameters will be discussed in the next chapters.)

1-4-3 The Manifest

By double-clicking the MANIFEST icon in Figure 1-1, you can see the content of the manifest, as shown in Figure 1-3. Again, ignore the code between the curly braces and examine only the directives. The manifest contains important information about the assembly, such as the external class library mscorlib, which is the core library that all .NET programs use:

```
.assembly extern mscorlib
```

It also contains the name of the file, the version, and other important information.

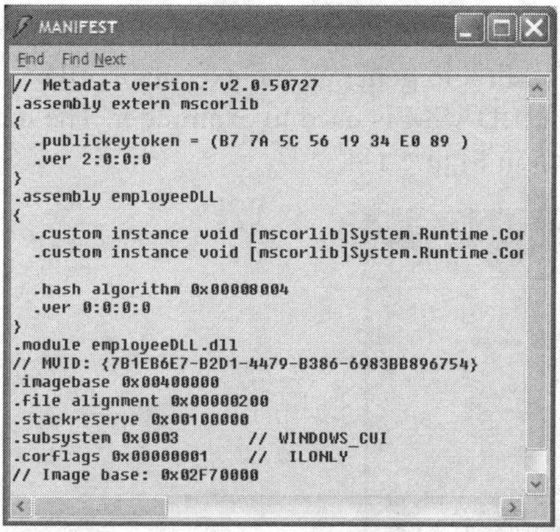

```
MANIFEST
Find  Find Next
// Metadata version: v2.0.50727
.assembly extern mscorlib
{
  .publickeytoken = (B7 7A 5C 56 19 34 E0 89 )
  .ver 2:0:0:0
}
.assembly employeeDLL
{
  .custom instance void [mscorlib]System.Runtime.Cor
  .custom instance void [mscorlib]System.Runtime.Cor

  .hash algorithm 0x00008004
  .ver 0:0:0:0
}
.module employeeDLL.dll
// MVID: {7B1EB6E7-B2D1-4479-B386-6983BB896754}
.imagebase 0x00400000
.file alignment 0x00000200
.stackreserve 0x00100000
.subsystem 0x0003       // WINDOWS_CUI
.corflags 0x00000001    //  ILONLY
// Image base: 0x02F70000
```

Figure 1-3: The manifest of the file EmployeeDLL.dll.

1-4-4 **Using the Library File**

To get the whole picture, let's write some code to use this library. The following C# program contains the source code needed to call the method **CalculateSalary** and display the result for one employee.

```
// MyProgram.cs

using System;

class MyClass
{
static void Main()
{
Employee emp = new Employee();
emp.name = "John Martin Smith";
emp.id = "ABC123";
double weeklyPayment = emp.CalculateSalary(40, 55);

Console.WriteLine("ID: {0}, Name: {1}", emp.id, emp.name);
Console.WriteLine("Payment= {0}", weeklyPayment);
}
}
```

When you compile this code you only need to link it to the .dll file. This way you are able to call the method **CalculateSalary** like this:

```
CalculateSalary(40, 55)
```

This method uses two parameters. The first is the number of worked hours (40) and the second is the rate of the employee (55). The details of the C#

code will be explained in detail later. Let us now examine the manifest of this file. The file is compiled first to generate the executable file (MyProgram.exe), and then ILDASM is used to examine it. The manifest of MyProgram.exe is shown in Figure 1-4.

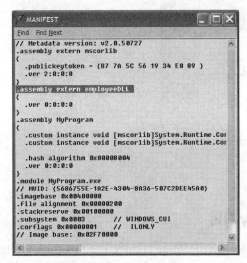

Figure 1-4: The manifest of the file MyProgram.exe.

Examine the directives in this file and pay attention to the highlighted one:

```
.assembly extern employeeDLL
```

This directive tells you that the .dll file (employeeDLL.dll) was linked to the source code during compilation.

1-5 How to Get a Free C# Compiler

When you buy Visual Studio 2005, you get the full-featured integrated development environment (IDE). You can also get a free C# compiler by using one of the following options:

- You can get the command-line compiler (csc.exe) from the site http://msdn.microsoft.com/netframework/downloads/updates/default.aspx.
  Download the redistributable package of the .NET Framework, which includes the compiler and the .NET Framework with C# 2005 syntax support.

- You can also get a smaller version of the IDE by downloading Visual C# Express from the web site http://lab.msdn.microsoft.com/express/vcsharp/default.aspx.
  This option enables you to build projects, and use the Code Editor and IntelliSense, which speeds up the development process (explained in Chapter 13).

1-5-1 Compiling Programs in the Command-Line Environment

There are two cases in which you can use the command-line environment:

- You only have the compiler that comes with the .NET Framework.
- You have the Visual Studio IDE that comes with C# Express.

1-5-1-1 If You Have the Compiler without the IDE

If you downloaded the C# command-line compiler only, you must include it in the path before using it. Do this by adding the location of the compiler to the PATH variable in the Windows environment. The compiler is located in the following directory:

%windir%\Microsoft.NET\Framework\<version>

where:

- %windir% is the environment variable that indicates the location of the Windows directory. If you are using Windows XP, this variable is replaced by "C:\WINDOWS."
- <version> is the version of the .NET Framework. The latest version is v2.0.50727, which makes the location "%windir%\Microsoft.NET\Framework\v2.0.50727."

To add the location of the compiler to the path, use the following steps:

1. Click the **Start** menu.
2. Select **All Programs**.
3. Select **Accessories**.
4. Click **Command Prompt**.
5. When the Command Prompt window opens, enter the following command:

   ```
   set path=%path%;%windir%\Microsoft.NET\Framework\v2.0.50727
   ```

Figure 1-5 shows the response to the **csc** command before and after setting the path, assuming that you are compiling a file called myProg.cs. Notice that before setting the path, the **csc** command was not recognized by the operating system. When the **set path** command was entered, the compilation completed.

```
Command Prompt                                                    _ □ ×
Microsoft Windows XP [Version 5.1.2600]
(C) Copyright 1985-2001 Microsoft Corp.

C:\Documents and Settings\Sam Abolrous>csc myProg.cs
'csc' is not recognized as an internal or external command,
operable program or batch file.

C:\Documents and Settings\Sam Abolrous>set path=%path%;%windir%\Microsoft.NET\Fr
amework\v2.0.50727

C:\Documents and Settings\Sam Abolrous>csc myProg.cs
Microsoft (R) Visual C# 2005 Compiler version 8.00.50727.42
for Microsoft (R) Windows (R) 2005 Framework version 2.0.50727
Copyright (C) Microsoft Corporation 2001-2005. All rights reserved.
```

Figure 1-5: Setting the path in the command prompt.

1-5-1-2 If You Have the Visual Studio IDE

If you downloaded the IDE, you don't need to set up the path. Just open the Visual Studio command prompt by using the following steps:

1. Click the **Start** menu.
2. Select **All Programs**.
3. Select **Microsoft Visual Studio**.
4. Select **Visual Studio Tools**.
5. Click **Visual Studio Command Prompt**.

This opens up the window shown in Figure 1-6. It also adds the location of the command-line compiler (csc.exe) to the path, in which case you can access the command-line compiler from any directory.

Figure 1-6 shows the response to the **csc** command in the Visual Studio 2005 Command Prompt window.

```
Visual Studio 2005 Command Prompt                                 _ □ ×
Setting environment for using Microsoft Visual Studio 2005 x86 tools.

C:\Program Files\Microsoft Visual Studio 8\VC>csc
Microsoft (R) Visual C# 2005 Compiler version 8.00.50727.42
for Microsoft (R) Windows (R) 2005 Framework version 2.0.50727
Copyright (C) Microsoft Corporation 2001-2005. All rights reserved.
```

Figure 1-6: The Visual Studio Command Prompt window.

1-6 **Comparison of C# and C++**

If you are coming from a C++ background, the following information will be useful for you as it contains a comparison of the two languages; otherwise, you can skip this section.

Table 1-1: Comparison of C# and C++

Feature	Comparison	See Chapter
Arrays	Array declaration in C# is different from that in C++.	4
Calling the members of the inherited class from the derived classes	In C# you can use the base keyword to do that.	6
Classes and structures	Unlike C++, you cannot declare a class in C# by using the keyword struct. The words class and struct are totally different in C#.	7
Constructors	Similar to constructors in C++. If you don't define a constructor, the compiler uses a default constructor to initialize objects with default values.	5 and 7
Default parameters	There are no default parameters in C#. Use method overloading instead.	6
Destructors	In C# you cannot control destructing objects as you do in C++. The destruction operations are done automatically by the garbage collector (GC).	5
Exception handling	In addition to throw, try, and catch, C# added the new keyword finally.	9
Function pointers	The delegate reference type in C# is similar to the function pointer in C++. The main difference is that a delegate is type safe.	10
Global variables and methods	Not permitted in C#. Variables and methods must be declared inside a class or struct.	2
Header files	There are no header files in C#. You can use preprocessor directives in conditional compilation. You can also use the using directives to reference types in namespaces to avoid using fully qualified names.	2 and 7
Inheritance	There is no multiple inheritance in C#. You can only inherit from one class.	5
Initialization list	Not in C#. Instead, use constructors to build the inherited class.	6
Initializing local variables	You cannot use a variable in C# before initializing it (assigning it a value).	2
Input/output	C# relies on the .NET class library in input and output operations.	2
Interface implementation	A class, a struct, or an interface can implement more than one interface at the same time.	8

Feature	Comparison	See Chapter
Keywords	C# changed the meaning of some keywords such as static and extern.	7
Long type	The long type in C# is 64 bits while it is 32 bits in C++.	3
The main method	The name and the declaration of the main method are different in C#.	2
Method overriding	You must use the keyword override to declare an override method in C#.	6
The new modifier	The new modifier is used to hide an inherited member in C#.	8
Operators	C# uses a new set of operators and adds new usage for some C++ operators.	4
Passing pointers to methods	Although C# doesn't support pointers (except inside an unsafe block), you can pass parameters as references by using the ref and out keywords.	6
Strings	Strings in C# are completely different from strings in C++.	3
The switch construct	Unlike C++, the C# switch does not allow fall through from one case to the next. You must use a branching statement.	4
Templates	The generics feature is similar to C++ templates, but is type safe.	12
Type conversion	It not possible to convert between some types in C#, such as bool and int. Unlike C++, the value false is not equivalent to zero and the value true is not equivalent to a non-zero value.	3

1-7 The Features of C# 2005

The following is a summary of the most important new features in C# 2005 covered in this book.

Table 1-2: New C# features covered in this book

Feature	Explanation	See Chapter
Anonymous methods	An anonymous method enables you to pass a code segment as a delegate parameter directly without declaring a separate method.	10
Contextual keywords	Contextual keywords are added to the C# keyword set. A contextual keyword is not a reserved word, but it provides a specific meaning in the code. Contextual keywords are: get, set, yield, value, partial, and where.	5, 11, and 12
Covariance and contravariance	With these two features there is more flexibility in matching the signatures of the delegate and the encapsulated method.	10

Feature	Explanation	See Chapter
Generics	This is the most important feature added to C# 2005. It facilitates code reuse and enhances the collection classes.	12
Iterators	An iterator is used to iterate through a collection and return an ordered sequence of values of the same type, thus providing a standard way to implement enumerators.	11
Namespace alias qualifier (::)	You can use this operator to search the global namespace for identifiers hidden by types or members in your code.	5
Nullable types	This feature enables you to assign the value null to a value-type variable.	3
Partial classes	This feature facilitates breaking a type (class, struct, or interface) into more than one section, each in a separate file.	5
Property accessor accessibility	With C# 2005 it is possible to define accessibility levels for the set and get accessors.	5
Static classes	A static class is a class whose members are all static and is declared using the modifier static. Static classes cannot be instantiated or inherited.	5

1-8 The New Features of C# 3.0

All the features of C# 3.0 that were introduced in the Community Technology Preview (CTP) of Microsoft Visual Studio Code Name "Orcas" are covered in detail in Chapter 14.

Summary

In this chapter:

- You saw an overview of object-oriented programming and how C# was built from the ground up as an OOP language.
- You learned about the .NET Framework and its elements: the class library and the Common Language Runtime (CLR).
- You also learned about the Common Language Specification (CLS) and Common Type System (CTS) and their role in creating .NET-supported languages.
- You learned about assemblies and how they are self described by using the manifest metadata.
- You also had an overview of the C# code, and examined the IL code and the manifest of a .dll and an executable file.

- You also have seen a comparison of C# and C++, from which C# evolved.
- Finally, you took a global look at the new features of C# 2005, which are explained throughout this book.

Chapter 2

Your First Go at C# Programming

Contents:
- Your first C# program
- Compilation
- Comments
- Displaying output
- Directives
- Local variables
- The C# program architecture
- Qualifying names
- Code conventions
- Code documentation

2-1 The "Hello, World!" C# Program

It is common to introduce a new language with an example that displays the phrase "Hello, World!" on the screen. Here is the C# version:

Example 2-1

```
// Example 2-1.cs
// The first program in C#

class HelloWorld
{
    static void Main()
```

```
    {
        System.Console.WriteLine("Hello, World!");
    }
}
```

Output:

```
Hello, World!
```

2-1-1 Compiling and Running the Program

Type the program text as a Notepad file, or use any other text editor, and save it with a name such as FirstProgram.cs. Some text editors force the filename to have a .txt extension. Although the C# compiler doesn't care about the file extension, the .cs extension is typically used for C# programs. Compile the program in the command environment by using the following command:

```
csc FirstProgram.cs
```

This compilation generates the executable file FirstProgram.exe. Run the program by typing its name (FirstProgram) and pressing Enter. This displays the phrase "Hello, World!" on your screen.

➔ **Note**   If you are using the Visual Studio IDE to build the program, you can use the console applications, as explained in Chapter 13.

In the following sections the main features of the "Hello, World!" program are explained.

2-1-2 Comments

The first two lines in the example contain comments:

```
// Example 2-1.cs
// The first program in C#
```

The two forward slash characters (//) at the beginning of the line convert the entire line into a comment, which is ignored by the compiler.

You can place the comment characters anywhere in the line, in which case they convert the text that follows into a comment. For example:

```
class HelloWorld      // This is a class declaration
```

You can also use the characters "/*" and "*/" to convert a group of lines into a single comment. For example:

```
/* This is a comment line.
This is another comment line.
This is a third comment line. */
```

2-1-3 Class Declaration

The main thing to remember about any C# program is that everything is included inside a class or a struct. The class used in the current example is called **HelloWorld**:

```
class HelloWorld
```

The class name goes after the keyword **class**, which is written, like all C# keywords, in lowercase letters. Like C++, the C# language is case sensitive.

The body of the entire class lies between braces ({ }). The class contains members such as fields and methods. In this example there is only one method, which is called **Main**. The **Main** method is necessary in all C# programs. The braces are used as delimiters for blocks of code, which can also contain other blocks. In fact, the class body might contain any number of nested classes.

2-1-4 The Main Method

As stated above, every C# program must have a method called **Main**. This method is similar to the C++ main function. Notice that the name of the **Main** method starts with an uppercase letter.

Note There is no difference between a function and a method; they both do the same job. In fact, some authors who come from a C++ background still use the word "function" to refer to a method. Throughout this book we use the word "method."

You cannot generate the executable file unless your program contains the **Main** method. Notice also the keyword **static** (explained later), which modifies the method. The type of the method can be **void**, which means the method does not return a value, like this:

```
static void Main()
{
}
```

It can also be **int**, which means it returns an integer:

```
static int Main()
{
    return 0;
}
```

There are other forms for the **Main** method that use arguments, such as:

```
static void Main(string[] args)
{
}
```

and

```
static int Main(string[] args)
{
    return 0;
}
```

The arguments of the **Main** method are explained in Chapter 4.

2-1-5 Using the .NET Methods for Displaying Results

As you can see in Example 2-1, its purpose is to display the string "Hello, World!" by using the method **WriteLine**, which is not part of the C# language. **WriteLine** is a .NET method. As mentioned in Chapter 1, the .NET class library is divided into namespaces, which contain classes. The **WriteLine** method is a member of the **Console** class in the **System** namespace. Therefore, when using such methods you have to use the full name, including the namespace and the class name, like this:

```
System.Console.WriteLine();
```

To display text, you enclose it in quotation marks inside the method's parentheses:

```
System.Console.WriteLine("Hello, World!");
```

A C# statement ends with a semicolon. This is the way the compiler recognizes the statements and separates them from each other.

You can also use the method **Write**, which belongs to the same .NET class and does the same job. The only difference between the two methods is that **WriteLine** includes a carriage return and a linefeed, which makes the cursor move to the next line. Successive **WriteLine** statements display each output on a separate line.

Drill 2-1

Add to Example 2-1 another printing statement to display a new string, such as "Hello, C# user!" The output of the program should be something like this:

```
Hello, World!
Hello, C# user!
```

Then replace the WriteLine methods with Write methods and make sure you get the following output:

```
Hello, World!Hello, C# user!
```

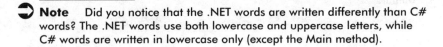

Note Did you notice that the .NET words are written differently than C# words? The .NET words use both lowercase and uppercase letters, while C# words are written in lowercase only (except the Main method).

2-2 Using Directives

You might be wondering, "Do I always have to write this long line of text in order to display one string?" The answer is no. A shorter way to display a string is by using directives. For example:

```
using System;
```

Add this directive to the beginning of your program outside any of the classes. Notice also that directives, like language statements, are followed by a semicolon.

This directive tells the compiler that you are going to use the namespace **System** in your program. You can then use the **WriteLine** statement without qualifying, like this:

```
Console.WriteLine("Hello, World!");
```

You still have to use the word Console, though, because it is the name of the class that contains the method. When you use other .NET statements that belong to other classes, though, the **using** directives can save you a lot of typing.

Example 2-2 shows the Hello, World! program after adding the directive.

Example 2-2

```
// Example 2-2.cs
// The second program in C#

using System;

class HelloWorld
{
   static void Main()
   {
      Console.WriteLine("Hello, World!");
   }
}
```

Output:

```
Hello, World!
```

2-3 Using Local Variables

Local variables are declared inside methods. You can use local variables to store data of various types. For example, in the previous program you could store the string "Hello, World!" in a variable of the type **string**, like this:

```
string myString = "Hello, World!";
```

Then you can display it by using the **WriteLine** method like this:

```
Console.WriteLine(myString);
```

You can also display a message with the same statement:

```
Console.WriteLine("The string is: " + myString);
```

Following is a program that uses a local variable and a text message.

Example 2-3

```
// Example 2-3.cs
// Local variables.

using System;

class MyClass
{
   static void Main()
   {
      string myString = "Hello, World!";
```

```
        Console.WriteLine("The string is: "+ myString);
    }
}
```

Output:

```
The string is: Hello, World!
```

The C# language contains many numeric data types, which are explained in the following chapters. For example, you can declare an integer variable like this:

```
int myInt;
```

You can also declare and initialize the variable in the same statement:

```
int myInt = 123;
```

As you can see in the example, to initialize a variable you actually assign it an initial value.

You can declare the variable anywhere inside the method. The only rule to follow in using variables is to declare and initialize the variable before using it. The C# language doesn't let you use uninitialized variables. If you try to use an uninitialized variable by displaying its value, for example, you get the following error message from the compiler:

```
"Use of unassigned local variable <variable-name>"
```

Like other languages, in C# you can add numeric variables by using the "+" operator like:

```
int sum = myInt + yourInt;
```

To display the value of a variable, use the **Console.WriteLine** or **Console.Write** method:

```
Console.WriteLine(myInt);
```

You can also display a numeric variable along with a message in one statement:

```
Console.WriteLine("My integer = " + myInt.ToString());
```

The method **ToString**, in this statement, is a .NET method that is used to convert a **numeric** data type to the **string** data type. In fact, you can drop the **ToString** method because it is embedded in the **WriteLine** method. For example:

```
Console.WriteLine("My integer = " + myInt);
```

You can also use another form of the **WriteLine** method like this:

```
Console.WriteLine("My integer = (0)", myInt);
```

In this form, (0) is replaced by the value of the variable myInt. If you would like to display several variables with one statement, you can use (0), (1), (2), and so forth.

```
Console.WriteLine("My integer = (0), Your integer = (1)", myInt,
yourInt);
```

In this statement, (0) is replaced by myInt, and (1) is replaced by yourInt.

Drill 2-2

Write a C# program to add the values of two integer variables, then display the result with an appropriate message.

2-4 The Program Architecture

A C# program may contain one or more files. Any file can contain any of the following elements (explained in the following chapters):

- Directives
- Namespaces (which can contain all other elements and namespaces)
- Classes
- Structs (structures)
- Interfaces
- Delegates
- Enums (enumerations)
- Function members (such as methods, properties, indexers, and so forth)

If the program consists of more than one file, only one **Main** method is required in one of the files.

In the following example, the program contains most of the elements mentioned above. Although the program does not produce any output, it compiles and runs.

Example 2-4

```
// Example 2-4.cs
using System;          // Directive

namespace Namespace1   // Namespace
{
   class Class1        // Class
   {
   }
```

```
struct Struct1              // Struct
{
}

interface Interface1        // Interface
{
}

delegate int Delegate1();   // Delegate

enum Enum1                  // Enumeration
{
}

namespace Namespace2        // Namespace
{
}

class Class2                // Class
{
    static void Main()      // The Main method
    {
    }
}
}
```

2-5 Qualifying Names

In real life, if you have two coworkers named John, it may be hard to distinguish between them unless you include the last name. At times, even using the last name is not enough. In programming, the complete name is referred to as the *fully qualified name*. When dealing with program elements, using the fully qualified name resolves any possible name conflicts. The fully qualified name includes the names of the containing namespace and the containing class. By using the fully qualified names you can use two methods that have the same name but belong to different classes in the same program and still be able to distinguish between them.

In the following example, there are two classes that have the same name (MyC2). If you use the fully qualified name for each, you can avoid any ambiguity. For example:

```
MyNS1.MyC1.MyC2
```

and

```
MyNS1.MyNS2.MyC2
```

The first name above represents the class MyC2 that is contained in the class MyC1 that is contained in the namespace MyNS1. The second name represents the same class, MyC2, that is contained inside the namespace MyNS2 that is contained inside the namespace MyNS1.

Example 2-5

```
// Example 2-5.cs
// Fully qualified names

namespace MyNS1                 // MyNS1
{
    class MyC1                  // MyNS1.MyC1
    {
        class MyC2              // MyNS1.MyC1.MyC2
        {
        }
    }
    namespace MyNS2             // MyNS1.MyNS2
    {
        class MyC2              // MyNS1.MyNS2.MyC2
        {
        }
    }
}
namespace MyNS3                 // MyNS3
{
    class MyC3                  // MyNS3.MyC3
    {
        static void Main()
        {
        }
    }
}
```

Notice in the above example that the qualified name is written as a comment beside each element. The elements in this example are described as follows:

- The namespaces MyNS1 and MyNS3 are contained in the global namespace that represents the root of the tree; therefore, their names are already fully qualified.
- The namespace MyNS2 is contained inside the namespace MyNS1; therefore, its fully qualified name is MyNS1.MyNS2.
- The class MyC1 is contained inside the namespace MyNS1; therefore, its fully qualified name is MyNS1.MyC1.

- The first instance of class MyC2 is contained inside the class MyC1; therefore, its fully qualified name is MyNS1.MyC1.MyC2.
- The second instance of class MyC2 is contained inside the namespace MyNS2; therefore, its fully qualified name is MyNS1.MyNS2.MyC2.

2-6 Common Conventions for Writing Code

Apart from the language rules, there are common conventions for writing code. Using these conventions makes your program consistent and easy to read by others. For the compiler, however, it doesn't matter how you write your code as long as you follow the rules.

- Type names for classes, structs, and methods using *Pascal* casing, which means that they start with a capital letter (for example, Class1 and Method1). If the name consists of words joined together, capitalize the beginning of each word (for example, MyFirstClass and CalculateYourBalance).
- Start interface names with the letter "I" (for example, IMyInterface and IInterface1).
- For local variables, use *camel* case, which means that the name starts with a lowercase letter and the first letter of each successive word is capitalized (for example, myVariable, yourInt, and myDoubleType-Variable). The uppercase bumps in the middle of the compound word make the name look like the humps of a camel.
- Use expressive names that convey the meaning or their use, such as myAccountNumber and yourSSN. Names like x, y, and z should be avoided unless they are used in the proper context, such as mathematical equations or coordinates.
- Start the left brace ({) on a separate line under the class or class member declaration. The right brace (}) is placed in the same column on a separate line. For example:

```
class HelloWorld
{
   // class body
}
```

Notice that the class body starts in the fourth column after the left brace (indented by three spaces).

- Leave a blank line after each distinct operation, such as after variable declarations, repetition loops, or conditional constructs.

2-7 Code Documentation

Three forward slash characters (///) are used to provide XML documentation comments in your code. These comments can precede types, members, and parameters. This information is especially useful if you work as part of a team. You can then describe your classes and how they are used as you type the code. If you are writing end user documentation such as an SDK or a programmer's reference, this information can also be useful. One of the important uses for this information is for generating the IntelliSense in the IDE environment (explained in Chapter 13).

The following is an example of documenting the Hello, World! program by using XML tags.

Example 2-6

```
// Example 2-6.cs
using System;

/// <summary>
/// A test project to show documentation comments.
/// </summary>
class MyClass
{
    /// <summary>
    /// The Main method of the program.
    /// </summary>
    /// <param name="args">Command-line arguments.</param>
    /// <returns>Does not return a value.</returns>
    static void Main(string[] args)
    {
        string myString = "Hello, World!";
        Console.WriteLine(myString);
    }
}
```

The C# compiler generates the documentation information and exports it to an XML file. To generate the documentation file, use the compiler option "/doc" as shown below. If you save this program with the name Ex2-6.cs, you can compile it using the following command:

```
csc /doc:Ex2-6.xml Ex2-6.cs
```

The following documentation file (Ex2-6.xml) will be generated:

```
<?xml version="1.0" ?>
- <doc>
 - <assembly>
  <name>Tester</name>
```

```
</assembly>
- <members>
 - <member name="T:MyClass">
 <summary>A test project to show documentation comments.</summary>
 </member>
 - <member name="M:MyClass.Main(System.String[])">
 <summary>The Main method of the program.</summary>
 <param name="args">Command-line arguments.</param>
 <returns>Does not return a value.</returns>
 </member>
 </members>
</doc>
```

For a complete list of XML tags, see "Compiler Options" in the help file.

Summary

In this chapter:

- You wrote your first program in C# and learned about its building blocks, including the declaration of a class, the **Main** method, and directives.

- You learned how to display the output by using the .NET methods **Write** and **WriteLine**. You also know how directives can save time and effort when using the .NET methods.

- You now know how to declare and initialize local variables inside a method. You also know that the C# language doesn't allow you to use a variable before initializing it.

- In the examples, you learned how to assign values to variables and perform some basic operations such as numeric variable addition.

- You know that the **ToString** method is used to convert other types to strings and that it is embedded in the **WriteLine** (or **Write**) method so you don't need to use it explicitly in displaying numeric output.

- You learned about the C# program architecture and how the building blocks work together to build the application.

- You were introduced to fully qualified names and their role in resolving name conflicts in the program.

- You learned about common conventions for writing your code that make it easy for others to read and understand.

- Finally, you learned how to create an XML documentation file for your code.

Chapter 3

C# Data Types

Contents:

- Data, value, and reference types
- Arithmetic operators and expressions
- Integral types
- The char type
- Formatting results
- The nullable types
- Using the "??" operator
- String operators and expressions
- Reading keyboard input
- Converting strings to numbers

3-1 Data Types

In C#, there are two types of data:

- **Value types:** Variables that store data values on the stack.

- **Reference types:** Variables that store memory addresses of the data stored on the heap.

There is also a third type of data, the pointer type, which is used in writing *unsafe code*. The pointer type is not covered in this book as it is added to the language for compatibility with C++. Although the C# language does not support pointers directly, it is possible for C++ programmers to write unsafe blocks of code and use pointers inside these blocks.

31

3-2 Built-in Data Types

The built-in data types are aliases of types originally defined in the .NET class library. These types and the corresponding .NET types are shown in the following table.

Table 3-1: C# built-in data types

C# Type	.NET Type
bool	System.Boolean
byte	System.Byte
sbyte	System.SByte
char	System.Char
decimal	System.Decimal
double	System.Double
float	System.Single
int	System.Int32
uint	System.UInt32
long	System.Int64
ulong	System.UInt64
object	System.Object
short	System.Int16
ushort	System.UInt16
string	System.String

Notice in the table that the word **Object** is a class in the .NET class library. It represents the root of all types. It is important to notice also that the C# object is lowercase. Needless to say, you can use either the C# type or the .NET type in your code. For example, the following two statements are equivalent; they both declare an integer variable and assign the value 25 to it:

```
int myInt = 25;
System.Int32 myInt = 25;
```

The following two statements are also equivalent; both declare a variable of the **object** type:

```
object myObject;
System.Object myObject;
```

In Table 3-1, all types except the **string** and **object** types are called *simple data types*.

3-3 Value Types

Value types include the numeric types (integers, floats, and so forth) and the Boolean type (**bool**). They also include user-defined types such as structs and enumerations. The following table shows the C# value types and a description of each type.

Table 3-2: Value types

C# Type	Description
bool	Boolean
byte	Unsigned integral
char	Unsigned integral
decimal	Signed numeric
double	Signed numeric
enum	Enumeration
float	Signed numeric
int	Signed integral
long	Signed integral
sbyte	Signed integral
short	Signed integral
struct	User-defined structure
uint	Unsigned integral
ulong	Unsigned integral
ushort	Unsigned integral

Value types are stored on the *stack*, which is the region in memory used to store local variables and their data. All value types are implicitly derived from the **Value Type** class in the **System** namespace. Value types, however, cannot be inherited.

3-3-1 Variable Initialization

To use a variable you must first initialize it with a value, as shown in the following examples:

```
int myValue = 123;
int myValue = 0;
int myValue = new int();
```

In the first example, we initialized the variable myValue with the value 123. In the second example, it is initialized with zero. In the third example, the variable is also initialized with zero by using the keyword **new**, which calls the default *constructor* (a constructor is a method that initializes an instance of a class) that initializes the variable with its default value — zero in this case. This means that the last two statements are equivalent.

3-3-2 Default Values

Each value type has a constructor that initializes it to its default value. The default value for each type is shown in the following table.

Table 3-3: The default values for each value type

Type	Default Value
bool	false
byte	0
char	'\0'
decimal	0.0M or 0.0m
double	0.0D or 0.0d
enum	The value resulting from evaluating the expression E(0), where E is the enumeration identifier.
float	0.0F or 0.0f
int	0
long	0L or 0l
sbyte	0
short	0
struct	The value resulting from initializing all value-type fields to their default values and reference-type fields to null.
uint	0
ulong	0
ushort	0

When using structs, you instantiate the struct by using the keyword **new**, which initializes the instance members with the default values. Following is an example of a struct that represents a point at the coordinates (x,y):

```
struct Point
{
int x;
int y;
}
```

In order to create an object of the type **Point**, use a statement like this:

```
Point myPoint = new Point();
```

This statement initializes all the members of the object (x and y in this case) with the value 0. This is called *definite assignment* of the struct. We'll talk more about structs later in this book.

3-4 **Reference Types**

A reference-type variable does not contain the data itself; it actually contains the memory address of the data. It is similar to pointers and references in C++, but much easier to use. The variable itself lives on the stack, like a value-type variable, but points to its data that lives on the heap.

➲ **Note**   The *heap* is the region in memory that stores the data pointed to by the reference-type variables.

3-4-1 **The C# Reference Types**

The following are the C# reference types:

- Class
- Interface
- Delegate
- Object
- String

It is possible to convert value types to reference types by using *boxing* and from reference types to value types by using *unboxing*.

3-4-2 **Boxing and Unboxing**

The boxing operation is accomplished by assigning the value-type variable to a variable of the type object:

```
int myInt = 123;
object myObj = myInt;   // boxing
```

This means moving the value 123 from the stack to the heap, as shown in the following figures.

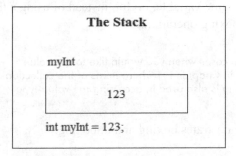

Figure 3-1: Memory before boxing.

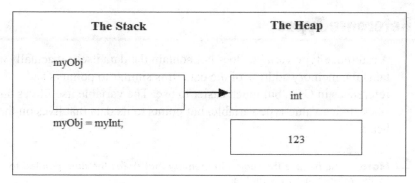

Figure 3-2: Memory after boxing.

In order to convert the variable back to a value type you use the unboxing operation, which is performed by casting the reference-type variable with (int). The following statement assigns the value pointed to by myObj to a new value-type variable, yourInt:

```
yourInt = (int) myObj;   // unboxing
```

This statement creates a new value-type variable that contains the same value, 123, as shown in Figure 3-3.

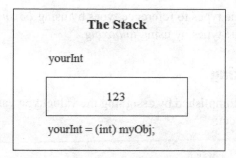

Figure 3-3: Memory after unboxing.

Notice that you can use the same variable, myInt, instead of using a third variable, yourInt, in the unboxing operation.

➲ **Note**   Boxing is necessary in cases when you would like to use value types in *collections* (explained in Chapter 11) where items of the collection are of the type object. Unboxing is also used in accessing the value-type contents of an object.

The following example demonstrates boxing and unboxing.

Example 3-1

```
// Example 3-1.cs
// Boxing and Unboxing

using System;

public class BoxingAndUnboxing
{
static void Main()
{
    // Declare a value type:
    int myInt = 123;
    // Boxing and changing the value:
    object myObj = myInt + 321;
    // Unboxing:
    int yourInt = (int) myObj;
    Console.WriteLine("myInt = {0}", myInt);
    Console.WriteLine("myObj = {0}", myObj);
    Console.WriteLine("yourInt = {0}", yourInt);
    }
}
```

In this example, we added the value 321 to the original value during the boxing operation. It is important to notice that this did not change the value of the original variable, myInt, which contained the same value after the unboxing operation. The variable yourInt, however, contains the value that was pointed to by the reference variable. You can see these values in the example output.

Output:

```
myInt = 123
myObj = 444
yourInt = 444
```

Although the concept of reference-type variables is the same as pointers in C++, reference types save you the trouble of handling pointer operations, especially deleting the memory that was allocated to pointers. These operations are done for you in the background.

3-5 Simple Data Types

The following table shows the C# simple data types along with the range and size in bytes for each type. Simple types include integral (**int**), floating point (**float**), Boolean (**bool**), and character (**char**). These types are called "simple" to distinguish them from user-defined types such as structs and enums. All simple types are, of course, value types.

Table 3-4: Simple data types

Type	Range	Size in Bytes
bool	true or false	1
byte	0 to 255 (unsigned)	1
char	U+0000 to U+ffff (Unicode character)	2
decimal	$\pm 1.0 \times 10^{-28}$ to $\pm 7.9 \times 10^{28}$	8
double	$\pm 5.0 \times 10^{-324}$ to $\pm 1.7 \times 10^{308}$	8
float	$\pm 1.5 \times 10^{-45}$ to $\pm 3.4 \times 10^{38}$	4
int	$-2,147,483,648$ to $2,147,483,647$	4
long	$-9,223,372,036,854,775,808$ to $9,223,372,036,854,775,807$	8
sbyte	-128 to 127	1
short	$-32,768$ to $32,767$	2
uint	0 to $4,294,967,295$ (unsigned)	4
ulong	0 to $18,446,744,073,709,551,615$ (unsigned)	8
ushort	0 to $65,535$ (unsigned)	2

Notice that there is no implicit conversion from the type **char** to any integral type as in C++. In other words, false does not equal zero and true is not a non-zero value.

The following are examples of using simple types in declarations:

```
int myInt;
char aChar;
long theLongNumber;
```

As mentioned before, you can also declare a variable and assign it a value at the same time:

```
byte myBite = 5;
short myShort = -223;
char myChar = 'A';
```

3-6 Creating and Manipulating Arithmetic Expressions

In the following sections, you will learn how to create and manipulate arithmetic expressions. You can build arithmetic expressions by using literals (data values), variables, and arithmetic operators. Expressions can be assigned to variables.

3-6-1 The Basic Arithmetic Operators (+, –, *, /)

Simple arithmetic expressions are built by using operators such as +, –, *, and /, which are used for addition, subtraction, multiplication, and division. In general, when an expression is evaluated, multiplication and division are evaluated before addition and subtraction because they have higher precedence. Consider the following expression:

```
6 + 4 * 5
```

In this expression, the part 4 * 5 is evaluated first, and then its value is added to 6. The result would be 26. You can use parentheses to change the precedence of operations:

```
(6 + 4) * 5
```

In this expression, the addition is evaluated first because the parentheses have higher precedence than the other operators. The addition evaluates to 10, which is multiplied by 5, giving the result 50.

It is possible to assign an expression to a variable, as in this example:

```
x = y * (2/3) – 1.0;
```

These operators are called *binary* operators because they operate on two *operands*.

3-6-2 The Modulus Operator (%)

The modulus operator (%) is used to get the remainder of division. For example, the following expression:

```
5 % 2
```

gives the result 1, while the expression:

```
4 % 2
```

gives the result 0.

➲ **Note** The modulus operator in C# can be applied to all numeric types. For example, the expression 5.2 % 5 evaluates to 0.2.

3-6-3 **The Assignment Operators**

The = assignment operator is used for assigning a value, expression, or variable to a variable. The following table shows the use of assignment operators combined with arithmetic operators.

Table 3-5: The assignment operators

Compound Assignment Operator	Example Statement	Equivalent Statement
*=	x *= y;	x = x * y;
/=	x /= y;	x = x / y;
%=	x %= y;	x = x % y;
+=	x += y;	x = x + y;
-=	x -= y;	x = x - y;

As you can see in the above table, each example in the Example Statement column is equivalent to a statement in the Equivalent Statement column. For example, the statement:

    x *= y;

means multiply x by y and store the result in x.

The statement:

    x %= y;

means divide x by y and store the remainder of the division in y.

3-6-4 **Increment and Decrement Operators (++, --)**

Increment and decrement operators are classified as *unary* or *primary* arithmetic operators because they have only one operand. Consider the following statements:

    x++;
    y--;

The first statement increments the value of x by 1, while the second decrements the value of y by 1. The value of the expression that contains this kind of operator changes according to whether the ++ or -- operator comes before (*prefix*) or after (*postfix*) the variable. For example, the expression:

    --y + x

means decrement y before adding its value to x. The expression:

    y-- + x

means decrement y after adding its value to x.

Example 3-2

```
// Example 3-2.cs
// Increment and Decrement

using System;

class ArithmeticOperators
{
    public static void Main()
    {
        int x = 10;
        int y = 100;
        int z = y-- + x;
        Console.WriteLine(z);    // result = 110
        Console.WriteLine(y);    // result = 99 – The value of y after
                                 // decrementing
        z = --z + x;
        Console.WriteLine(z);    // result = 119
    }
}
```

Output:

```
110
99
119
```

3-6-5 Operator Associativity

Associativity is the direction in which an expression is evaluated. Consider an expression that contains two operators of the same precedence, like the following:

```
80 / 4 * 2
```

How can the compiler decide which operator to apply first? If you apply the division first (left-to-right associativity), the result would be evaluated as follows:

```
(80 / 4) * 2 = 40
```

But if you apply the multiplication first (right-to-left associativity), the result would be evaluated as follows:

```
80 / (4 * 2) = 10
```

It is clear that the direction of evaluation changes the result. As you can see in this example, using parentheses changes the order in which expressions are evaluated. But if you leave out the parentheses, the rule for the compiler is to evaluate operators by using left-to-right associativity. In this case, the expression 80 / 4 * 2 is evaluated as 40.

In general, binary arithmetic operators use left-to-right associativity, while *primary* and *unary* arithmetic operators use right-to-left associativity.

The following table shows the C# arithmetic operators along with their precedence and associativity. In this table, the operators are divided into four categories. The operators in each category have the same precedence. The operators in the first row have the highest precedence, while those in the last row have the lowest precedence.

Table 3-6: Arithmetic operators

Precedence	Category	Operator Symbol and Name	Associativity
Highest	Primary	() (Parentheses) ++ (Postfix increment) -- (Postfix decrement)	Right to left
	Unary	+ (Positive sign) - (Negative sign) ++ (Prefix increment) -- (Prefix decrement)	Right to left
	Binary	* (Multiplication) / (Division) % (Modulus)	Left to right
Lowest	Binary	+ (Addition) - (Subtraction)	Left to right

Drill 3-1

Start with the following assignments:

```
int x = 10;
int y = 100;
int z = y;
```

Then write a C# program to compute and display the values of the variables y and z after executing these expressions:

```
y = y++ + x;
z = ++z + x;
```

Notice that the expression:

```
y+++x
```

is equivalent to the expression:

```
y++ +x
```

This is because the associativity for the increment and decrement operators is from right to left, which is not the case with the binary operators. It is preferred, however, to use a blank space or parentheses to make the code easier to read.

3-6-6 How to Get the Type Name

By using the .NET method **GetType**, you can get the type name of any local variable or object. This is how to use it:

```
Console.WriteLine(myVariable.GetType());
```

In this statement, myVariable is the local variable, expression, or object for which you would like to get the type name.

Drill 3-2

Try these statements in a program:

```
Console.WriteLine(123.GetType());
Console.WriteLine(3.14.GetType());
```

Your output should be:

```
System.Int32
System.Double
```

3-6-7 Evaluating Expressions with Mixed Types

If you write an expression that contains different real (floating-point) types and integral types, it is evaluated as follows:

- If the expression contains a double value, the result would be double.
- If the expression doesn't contain a double value, the result would be float.
- If the expression contains any integral type and a real type, the integral type would be converted to the real type and the result would be of the real type.

In the following example, an expression that contains integral types and floating-point types is evaluated as double.

Example 3-3

```
// Example 3-3.cs
// Expressions with mixed types

using System;

class NumbersClass
{
    static void Main()
    {
        int x = 128;
        short y = 34;
        double z = 3.14;

        // Print the result and the type of result:
        Console.WriteLine("Sum: {0}", x + y + z);
        Console.WriteLine("Type: {0}", (x + y + z).GetType());
    }
}
```

Output:

```
Sum: 165.14
Type: System.Double
```

3-6-8 Adding a Suffix to Numeric Data

It is necessary with some data types to add a suffix to the numeric literals to distinguish them from other types. This is explained further in the following sections.

3-6-8-1 Real Types

The compiler treats a real number as a double type unless you add a suffix to define its type explicitly as follows:

- Use M or m with the **decimal** type. For example, 23.4M.
- Use F or f with the **float** type. For example, 23.4F.

When you declare a real type variable you must use the proper suffix; otherwise, the compiler issues an error message. For example, the following declarations generate error messages:

```
decimal myAmount = 23.4;  // error
float myRealNumber = 23.4 // error
```

➲ **Note**   Although you can use either lowercase or uppercase letters in suffixes, we use uppercase letters in the programs in this book.

Example 3-4

```
// Example 3-4.cs
// Suffixing real types

using System;

class MyPoint
{
    static void Main()
    {
        decimal myDecimal = 23.4M;
        float myFloat = 23.4F;
        double myDouble = 23.4;

        Console.Write("myDecimal = {0}\nmyFloat = {1}\nmyDouble = {2}",
            myDecimal, myFloat, myDouble);
    }
}
```

Output:

```
myDecimal = 23.4
myFloat = 23.4
myDouble = 23.4
```

→ **Note** The new line character (\n) inside the quotation marks allows the string literal to print on more than one line, as shown in the above example.

Drill 3-3

Test the variable types in Example 3-4 and make sure you get the following result:

```
System.Decimal
System.Single
System.Double
```

3-6-8-2 Integral Types

With integral types, you don't have to suffix data values because the appropriate storage is automatically chosen for you when the expression is evaluated.

You can, however, use the suffixes L, U, or UL to determine the type of numeric value and the proper storage for it. Follow these rules when using the suffixes:

- When you use the suffix L, the number is considered of the **long** or **ulong** type according to its value. For example, the following number is treated as a **long** because it is less than the limits of **ulong**:

  ```
  4294967296L
  ```

- When you use the suffix U, the number is treated as either **long** or **uint** according to its value. For example, the following number is treated as a **uint** because it is less than the limits of the type **long**.

  ```
  4294967290U
  ```

- When you use the letters U and L together, in any order, the number is treated as a **ulong**.

Drill 3-4

Try the following statements in a C# program and check the results:

```
Console.WriteLine(9223372036854775808L.GetType());
Console.WriteLine(123UL.GetType());
Console.WriteLine(4294967296L.GetType());
Console.WriteLine(4294967290U.GetType());
```

These are the expected results:

```
System.UInt64
System.UInt64
System.Int64
System.UInt32
```

3-6-9 Conversion between Types

In C# there are two methods of type conversion: *implicit* and *explicit*. For example, you can write the following statements to declare real variables:

```
double myVar = 4;
float myVar = 33;
```

These declarations include implicit conversions from the integer type to **float** and **double**. Such conversions are performed in the background for you. You cannot, however, type the following statement:

```
float myVar = 3.3;   // compilation error
```

This statement means that you want to store the value 3.3, a **double** value (as mentioned in the previous section), into a smaller storage type, which is of type **float**. The compiler doesn't accept this statement and sends you an error message. Of course, you can use the suffix F to specify that the number is a **float**; this results in converting the literal itself to the **float** type.

The general rule for type conversion is that you can store the smaller size storage type into the larger size, but not the opposite. Consider the following declarations:

```
int x = 4;
double y = 3.0;
```

With these declarations the following statements are not allowed:

```
short z1 = x;    // compilation error
short z2 = y;    // compilation error
```

The reason is that there is no implicit conversion from **int** or **double** to **short** — they are both larger than the size of the storage. To complete this conversion, you must use a *cast*, as shown in the following statements:

```
short z1 = (short)x;
short z2 = (short)y;
```

This kind of conversion is called explicit conversion.

With integral types, it is important to check the destination storage before performing an assignment. For example, the following statement shows an incorrect attempt to store an **int** into a **short** storage.

```
short x = 32768;  // compilation error
```

You cannot use a cast in this case because this value exceeds the size of the **short** type (32767).

3-7 **The char Type**

C# characters are stored as 16-bit Unicode characters. With the Unicode system, it is possible to represent characters of any language including Chinese, Japanese, Hebrew, and Arabic. You can write characters in multiple ways. The following examples represent the letter "A".

You can write it as a literal character:

```
char myChar = 'A';
```

as hexadecimal code:

```
char myChar = '\x0041';
```

as a Unicode character:

```
char myChar = '\u0041';
```

or by casting the ASCII code:

```
char myChar = (char)65;
```

The character code is enclosed in single quotes in all instances except when you use the cast. The following example introduces two methods for coding the letter "A" and displaying the results, once as a character and once in ASCII code.

Example 3-5

```
// Example 3-5.cs
// char conversion

using System;

class CharClass
{
    static void Main()
    {
        char myChar = (char)65;
        int yourChar= 'A';

        // Print the result:
        Console.WriteLine("The character is: {0}", myChar);
        Console.WriteLine("The code of the character is: {0}", yourChar);
    }
}
```

Output:

```
The character is: A
The code of the character is: 65
```

Notice that it was possible in the example above to write the statement for declaring the **char** as:

```
int yourChar= 'A';
```

This means that there exists an implicit conversion from the type **char** to the type **int**, but the opposite is not allowed. Thus, the following statement is incorrect:

```
char myChar = 65;   // compilation error
```

You can, however, use explicit conversion (casting) like this:

```
char myChar = (char)65;
```

3-8 Formatting Results

In most applications you would want to display the results in the appropriate format. For example, in some applications you need to show two decimal places, and in other applications you need to display the dollar sign or the pound sign. This is all done through the **Write** or **WriteLine** methods, as explained in the following sections.

3-8-1 The Currency Format

To display a number with its associated currency symbol and the appropriate number of decimal places, use the currency character "C" or "c", as in the following example:

```
Console.WriteLine ("{0:C}", 1.2);
```

The number 1.2 appears in the output like this: $1.20.

If the number 1.2 is negative, like this:

```
Console.WriteLine ("{0:C}", -1.2);
```

it appears inside parentheses like this: ($1.20).

➔ **Note**   The currency symbol depends on the Regional Options setting of your machine. For example, if this option is set to English (United Kingdom), you get the English pound symbol (£) instead of the dollar symbol.

3-8-2 The Decimal Format

To display a number preceded by a specified number of zeroes, use the format character "D" or "d", like this example:

```
Console.WriteLine ("{0:D5}", 123);
```

The result of this statement is 00123. The number following the letter "D" determines the number of decimal places in the output.

3-8-3 The Fixed-point Format

To display a number followed by a specified number of decimal places, use "F" or "f", like these examples. The output of each statement is written next to it as a comment.

```
Console.WriteLine("{0:F2}", 12);    // 12.00 - two decimal places
Console.WriteLine("{0:F0}", 12);    // 12 - no decimal places
```

```
Console.WriteLine("{0:F0}", 12.3);    // 12 - omitting fractions
Console.WriteLine("{0:F2}", 12.3);    // 12.30 - two decimal places
```

3-8-4 The General Format

To display a number in the default format, use the letter "G" or "g" like this:

```
Console.WriteLine("{0:G}", 1.2);    // 1.2
Console.WriteLine("{0:G}", 1.23);   // 1.23
```

As you can see in the comments that follow the statements, this is the same output produced by no formatting at all. The statements are then equivalent to these statements:

```
Console.WriteLine("{0}", 1.2);
Console.WriteLine("{0}", 1.23);
```

3-8-5 The Numeric Format

To display a number with decimal points and commas, use the letter "N" or "n", like this example:

```
Console.WriteLine("{0:N}", 1230000000);
```

This statement gives the following output:

```
1,230,000,000.00
```

3-8-6 The Scientific Format

To display a number in the exponential form, use the letter "E" or "e", like this example:

```
Console.WriteLine("{0:E}", 12300000);
```

The resulting number is:

```
1.230000E+007
```

3-8-7 The Hexadecimal Format

To display a number in hexadecimal form, use the letter "X" or "x", like these examples:

```
Console.WriteLine ("{0:X}", 123);    // 7B
Console.WriteLine ("{0:X}", 65535);  // FFFF
```

The hexadecimal output of each statement is shown in the comment following it.

The following example demonstrates all of the above formats in one program.

Example 3-6

```
// Example 3-6.cs
// Formatting Results

using System;
class Format
{
   static void Main()
   {
      string s;

      // Currency:
      s ="Currency";
      Console.WriteLine("{0} Format:", s);
      Console.WriteLine("{0:C}", 1.2);
      Console.WriteLine("{0:C}", -1.2);

      // Decimal:
      s = "Decimal";
      Console.WriteLine("\n{0} Format:", s);
      Console.WriteLine("{0:D5}", 123);

      // Fixed-point:
      s = "Fixed-point";
      Console.WriteLine("\n{0} Format:", s);
      Console.WriteLine("{0:F2}", 12);
      Console.WriteLine("{0:F0}", 12);
      Console.WriteLine("{0:F0}", 12.3);
      Console.WriteLine("{0:F2}", 12.3);

      // General:
      s = "General";
      Console.WriteLine("\n{0} Format:", s);
      Console.WriteLine("{0:G}", 1.2);
      Console.WriteLine("{0}", 1.23);

      // Numeric:
      s = "Numeric";
      Console.WriteLine("\n{0} Format:", s);
      Console.WriteLine("{0:N}", 1230000000);

      // Scientific:
      s = "Scientific";
      Console.WriteLine("\n{0} Format:", s);
```

```
        Console.WriteLine("{0:E}", 12300000);

        // Hexadecimal:
        s = "Hexadecimal";
        Console.WriteLine("\n{0} Format:", s);
        Console.WriteLine ("{0:X}", 123);
        Console.WriteLine ("{0:X}", 65535);
    }
}
```

Output:

```
Currency Format:
$1.20
($1.20)

Decimal Format:
00123

Fixed-point Format:
12.00
12
12
12.30

General Format:
1.2
1.23

Numeric Format:
1,230,000,000.00

Scientific Format:
1.230000E+007

Hexadecimal Format:
7B
FFFF
```

3-9 **The Nullable Types**

The nullable types were added to value types with C# 2005. This feature enables you to assign the value null to a value-type variable. You need this with databases where a variable can assume any value including null. The nullable variable is declared by using the ? symbol next to the type name, like this:

```
myType? myVariable;
```

where myType is one of the value types including the **struct** type. It is called the underlying type of the nullable type. For example, consider the following statement:

```
int myInt? = null;
```

In this statement, the underlying type is **int**. This means that the variable myInt can accept all the values that can be assigned to **int** in addition to null, which means "not used" or "empty." In the following example,

```
bool myBool?;
```

myBool can assume one of the values true, false, or null. In databases, this feature is important because a database field may contain null to indicate that the variable is not defined. This is the same concept used with reference types where the value null has been used to indicate that a variable is not initialized.

In the following example, you declare some nullable-type variables, assign them various values, and display the result. Notice that the values of the variables that were assigned null are displayed as blanks.

Example 3-7

```
// Example 3-7.cs
// Nullable types

using System;

class MyPoint
{
    static void Main()
    {
        int? myInt = null;
        bool? myBool = null;
        float? myFloat = 1.23F;
        char? myChar = 'C';
```

```
        Console.WriteLine("myInt = {0}\n"+
        "myBool = {1}\n" +
        "myFloat = {2}\n" +
        "myChar = {3}\n",
        myInt, myBool, myFloat, myChar);
    }
}
```

Output:

```
myInt =
myBool =
myFloat = 1.23
myChar = C
```

3-9-1 Using the Nullable Structure Properties

The C# nullable type is an instance of the **System.Nullable** structure. The two essential properties of the Nullable structure are **HasValue** and **Value**. The **HasValue** property is a Boolean value. If the **HasValue** property of a nullable variable is true, the value of this variable can be accessed with the **Value** property. The **Value** property represents the underlying type of the nullable variable. For example:

```
if (myInt.HasValue) yourInt = myInt.Value;
```

In this statement the **HasValue** property of myInt is checked to determine whether it is true or false. If it is true, the value of myInt is assigned to the variable yourInt.

If the **HasValue** property is false, the value of the variable is undefined and an attempt to use the **Value** property throws an exception. More details on properties and conditional statements are explained in the next chapters.

3-9-2 Using the ?? Operator

As you can see in the preceding example, all of the variables that contain null are displayed as blanks. You can change this by assigning a default value to the nullable variable. Use the **??** operator to assign a default value that will be applied when a variable with the value null is assigned to another variable. For example:

```
int? myInt = null;
int yourInt = myInt ?? -5;
```

The first statement assigns null to myInt, and the second statement assigns the default value (−5) to myInt, and then assigns it to yourInt. Now when you display yourInt you get −5.

The following example demonstrates using the nullable-type properties and the ?? operator.

Example 3-8

```
// Example 3-8.cs
// The operator ??

using System;

class MyPoint
{
   static void Main()
   {
      // Using the operator ??:
      double? myDouble = null;
      double myDouble1 = myDouble ?? -1.0;
      Console.WriteLine("myDouble1 = {0}", myDouble1);

      // Using HasValue:
      int? myInt = 123;
      int? yourInt = null;
      if (myInt.HasValue)     // true
      {
         yourInt = myInt.Value;
         Console.WriteLine("myInt = {0}", yourInt);
      }

      int? theirInt = null;
      if (theirInt.HasValue)    // false
         yourInt = 0;
      else
         Console.WriteLine("The variable theirInt does not
            have a value.");
   }
}
```

Output:

```
myDouble1 = -1
myInt = 123
The variable theirInt does not have a value.
```

3-10 The string Type

If you are familiar with C or C++, you might be aware of the difficulty of creating and manipulating strings. The C language does not contain the string keyword; instead a string is declared as a character pointer or a character array. This can cause some confusion for beginners as well as the possibility of memory leakage, which takes some time to resolve. C# has solved this problem once and for all. You declare a string variable by using the keyword **string** and use it in the same way you use any other variable. In the background, the compiler does the complicated chores C and C++ require you to do with pointers.

3-10-1 String Expressions

To declare a string variable, use the **string** keyword in a declaration like this:

```
string myString;
```

You can, of course, initialize the string in the same statement:

```
string myString = "Welcome to the string world!";
```

The string literal (data value) is placed between the quotation marks. You can also include any of the escape sequence characters, such as the new line character, in the string. For example:

```
string myString = "My friend,\nWelcome to the string world!";
```

This statement displays the following:

```
My friend,
Welcome to the string world!
```

In order to include any special characters in the string, such as a backslash or a quotation mark, you must precede the special character with a backslash. For example:

```
string myString = "To go to the next line use the new line character:
\"\\n\"";
```

This statement displays the following:

```
To go to the next line use the new line character: "\n"
```

As in C++, the double backslash is used in folder names (directories). For example:

```
string myDir = "C:\\Documents\\Letters\\friends.doc";
```

A summary of the commonly used escape sequence characters is shown in the following table.

Table 3-7: The escape sequence characters

Description	Escape Sequence Character
Single quotation mark	\'
Double quotation mark	\"
Backslash	\\
Backspace	\b
Form feed	\f
New line	\n
Carriage return	\r
Horizontal tab	\t
Vertical tab	\v
Null	\0

3-10-2 String Operators

To manipulate strings, you use the string operators, which are explained in the following sections.

3-10-2-1 String Concatenation (+, +=)

To concatenate two strings, use the + operator as in this example:

```
string myString = "Hello" + ", " + "World!";
```

With this statement the string myString would contain the phrase "Hello, World!"

You can also concatenate string variables. First declare and initialize the variables:

```
string hello = "Hello";
string commaAndSpace = ", ";
string world = "World!";
```

Then concatenate the variables in an ordered manner:

```
string myString = hello + commaAndSpace + world;
```

You can also use the addition assignment operator (+=):

```
hello += commaAndSpace + world;
```

The above statement concatenates the three strings and then assigns them to the variable on the left-hand side. That is, this statement says: Concate-nate "hello" to "commaAndSpace" and "world", and put the result in the variable "hello". Notice that the order of the concatenated variables (or literals) matters.

In practice, you would rarely use this method to concatenate strings; you would use the **StringBuilder** class (explained in the next section) and its methods instead.

3-10-2-2 Using the StringBuilder Class

The C# string type is an alias of the **System.String** class. A **String** object is immutable, which means you cannot change its value once you have created it. When you make a change to a string you are actually creating a new string with new contents. If you would like to modify the contents of the actual string, you use the **StringBuilder** class (a member of the **System.Text** namespace). For example, you can create a string that contains "Hello," like this:

```
StringBuilder myString = new StringBuilder("Hello,");
```

You can then append it with the string "World!" by using the method **Append**:

```
myString.Append("World!");
```

You can also insert a space in the sixth place by using the method **Insert**:

```
myString.Insert(6, " ");
```

Now, when you display myString it will contain the string "Hello, World!"

Note Refer to the Visual Studio help for more information on the StringBuilder class and its members.

3-10-2-3 The Equality Operator (= =)

The equality operator is used to determine if two strings are identical. For example, the following statement checks to see if the strings stored in myString and yourString are equivalent.

```
Console.WriteLine(yourString == myString);
```

The result of this statement is true if they are equal or false otherwise.

3-10-2-4 The [] Operator

This operator is used to access the individual characters of a string—which is the same concept as a character array in C++. You can, for example, display the letter "W" in the string "Hello, World!" by accessing the seventh character (notice that the starting index is 0), as shown in the following statement:

```
Console.WriteLine("Hello, World!"[7]);
```

If the string is stored in a variable, such as myString, you can access the character like this:

```
Console.WriteLine(myString[7]);
```

3-10-2-5 The @ Symbol

With the @ symbol you can display any string without using the escape characters inside the string. For example, instead of writing the following statement:

```
string myDoc = "C:\\Documents\\Letters\\friends.doc";
```

you can precede the string with the @ symbol, like this:

```
string myDoc = @"C:\Documents\Letters\friends.doc";
```

Both methods declare a string that contains the string "C:\Documents\Letters\friends.doc."

In fact, anything inside the quotation marks is displayed as is. For example:

```
string myString = @"Dear Sir,
I have read your manuscript 'Learn C# in Three Days', and I would like
to inform you that we are interested in publishing the book.

Yours,
Dylan A. Combel";
```

If you display this string you get the following:

```
Dear Sir,
I have read your manuscript 'Learn C# in Three Days', and I would like
to inform you that we are interested in publishing the book.

Yours,
Dylan A. Combel
```

In order to display a quotation mark inside the text, use two quotation marks instead of one. For example:

```
@"He said, ""You should stop by when you can,"" OK?"
```

This string is displayed like this:

```
He said, "You should stop by when you can," OK?
```

The last use of the @ symbol is to prefix C# keywords in order to use them as variables. Although you cannot use keywords such as **bool** and **int** as variables, the words @bool and @int are allowed.

Example 3-9

```
// Example 3-9.cs
// Strings

using System;

class MyClass
{
    static void Main()
    {
        bool isEqual;
        string a = "\u0048ello my friend.\n";
        string b = @"You can compose Unicode letters using the escape
            characters.
However, you cannot use the @ symbol with that.";

        // Print both a and b:
        Console.WriteLine(a + b);

        // Check for equality:
        isEqual = (a == b);
        Console.WriteLine("BTW, the equality is: {0}.", isEqual );
    }
}
```

Output:

```
Hello my friend.
You can compose Unicode letters using the escape characters.
However, you cannot use the @ symbol with that.
BTW, the equality is: False.
```

Drill 3-5

Write a C# program that uses Unicode characters to compose the three letters A, B, and C in the following sentence:

```
A, B, and C are the first three letters.
```

3-11 Reading the Keyboard Input

To read input from the keyboard, use the .NET method **ReadLine**. It reads anything you type in the command line before you press the Enter key. Therefore, you would expect that this method reads strings. For example, the following statement:

```
string myString = Console.ReadLine();
```

reads the data value from the command line and stores it in the variable myString. In the following example, you type a number from the keyboard and the program reads it and stores it into the variable theNumber, and then displays it with the proper message.

Example 3-10

```
// Example 3-10.cs
// Reading from the keyboard

using System;

public class Keyboard
{
    public static void Main()
    {
        Console.Write("Please enter a number: ");
        string theNumber = Console.ReadLine();
        Console.WriteLine("Your number is: {0}", theNumber );
    }
}
```

Sample Run:

```
Please enter a number: 33
Your number is: 33
```

Although the program displays the same number you entered from the keyboard, it is in fact a string. If you try to add it to another integer, the compiler will issue the error message:

```
Cannot implicitly convert type 'string' to 'int'.
```

3-12 Converting Strings to Numbers

A string read from the keyboard can be converted to any type of data by using the conversion methods explained in the following sections.

3-12-1 Using the Convert Class

The class **Convert** belongs to the **System** namespace. You can use it to convert a string to another type, such as an integer, like this example:

```
int myInt = Convert.ToInt32(myString);   // convert to int
```

In this statement, myString is converted to the type Int32, which is equivalent to the C# type **int**. Similar conversions to various types are shown in the examples below:

```
long myLong = Convert.ToInt64(myString);        // convert to long
float myFloat = Convert.ToSingle(myString);     // convert to float
double myDouble = Convert.ToDouble(myString);   // convert to double
decimal myDecimal = Convert.ToDecimal(myString); // convert to decimal
```

It is also possible to add another value to the number in the same statement:

```
int myInt = Convert.ToInt32(theNumber) + 20;
```

In Example 3-11, conversions to various numeric types are performed.

Example 3-11

```
// Example 3-11.cs
// Converting strings to numbers

using System;

public class Keyboard
{
    public static void Main()
    {
        Console.Write("Please enter a number: ");
        string theNumber = Console.ReadLine();
        Console.WriteLine("Your string number is: {0}", theNumber);

        double d = Convert.ToDouble(theNumber);
        float f = Convert.ToSingle(theNumber);
        decimal c = Convert.ToDecimal(theNumber);

        Console.WriteLine("Your decimal number is: {0}", c);
        Console.WriteLine("Your double number is: {0}", d);
```

```
        Console.WriteLine("Your float number is: {0}", f);
    }
}
```

Sample Run:

```
Please enter a number: 3.14    → Input from the keyboard
Your string number is: 3.14
Your decimal number is: 3.14
Your double number is: 3.14
Your float number is: 3.14
```

3-12-2 Using the Parse Method

The second way to convert strings to numbers is by using the **Parse** method, one of the .NET methods. It can be used like this:

```
int myInt = Int32.Parse(myString);
```

In this example, the string myString is converted to the integer myInt. You can, of course, convert to other types:

```
Int64.Parse(myString)      // convert to long
Single.Parse(myString)     // convert to float
Decimal.Parse(myString)    // convert to decimal
Double.Parse(myString)     // convert to double
```

Example 3-12

```
// Example 3-12.cs
// Parsing input

using System;

public class ParseClass
{
    static void Main()
    {
        Console.Write("Please enter an integer: ");
        string str = Console.ReadLine();

        long myLong = Int64.Parse(str);
        int myInt = Int32.Parse(str);
        double myDouble = Double.Parse(str);

        Console.WriteLine("Your long number is: {0}", myLong);
        Console.WriteLine("Your int number is: {0}", myInt);
        Console.WriteLine("Your double number is: {0}", myDouble);
    }
}
```

Sample Run:

```
Please enter an integer: 12  → Input from the keyboard
Your long number is: 12
Your int number is: 12
Your double number is: 12
```

Needless to say, you cannot enter a number that contains a decimal point in this program because the conversion to the **int** and **long** types would generate exceptions.

 Note In Chapter 14, you are going to learn an easy way to declare variables and arrays without specifying their types, like these examples:

```
var myVariable = 1.23;
var yourVariable = "Hello, World!";
var myArray = new int{} { 1, 2, 4, 8, 64 };
```

In such cases the compiler (C# 3.0) will figure out the types from the values used in the initialization.

Summary

In this chapter:

- You took a look at different data types. You learned about the two main types: value types and reference types. You also learned how to convert between these two types by using boxing and unboxing.
- You now know how to build expressions using variables, literals, and operators.
- You dealt with the numeric and string expressions and operators.
- You learned about formatting results using the general, decimal, numeric, scientific, currency, and hexadecimal formats.
- You were introduced to the nullable type, a new type that was added to the language in C# 2005.
- You learned how to use the character type in C# and how to access individual characters in a string.
- Finally, you learned how to convert the strings read from the keyboard to numbers by using the **Convert** class and the **Parse** method.

Chapter 4

Building the Program Logic

Contents:

- *Relational and logical expressions*
- *Conditional statements*
- *The conditional expression*
- *Building and using DLLs*
- *Loops*
- *Arrays*
- *Program arguments*
- *Using .NET methods with arrays*

4-1 Using Conditions

In this section, you will learn how to build conditions in your program by using selection statements such as **if** and **switch**. Selection statements are used to determine which and when a statement or group of statements should be executed in your program. Selection statements rely on relational or logical expressions and operators.

4-1-1 Relational Operators

The relational operators (or comparison operators) are used in building relational (or Boolean) expressions to compare literals, variables, or expressions. The following are some examples of relational expressions:

```
x > y              // x is greater than y
y < 255            // y is less than 255
myInt == x + y     // myInt is equal to x + y
```

The following table lists the relational operators in C#.

Table 4-1: The C# relational operators

Operator	Description
>	Greater than
>=	Greater than or equal to
<	Less than
<=	Less than or equal to
==	Equal
!=	Not equal

Relational expressions are evaluated as either true or false. This means that the result is a Boolean value. As mentioned in Chapter 3, unlike C++, in C# the value false doesn't equal zero and the value true doesn't mean a non-zero value.

The following example demonstrates the use of some relational expressions.

Example 4-1

```
// Example 4-1.cs
// Relational Operators

using System;

class OperatorClass
{
    static void Main()
    {
        char myChar = 'A';
        int myInt = 55;
        int yourInt = 44;

        Console.WriteLine(myChar == 'A');      // true
        Console.WriteLine(myInt >= yourInt);   // true
        Console.WriteLine(100 > 100.2);        // false
    }
}
```

Output:

```
True
True
False
```

4-1-2 Logical Operators

Logical operators are used to combine relational expressions to build a logical (or Boolean) expression. A logical expression is also evaluated as either true or false. Some operators operate on two operands (binary), while others operate on one operand (unary). The following table contains a list of the commonly used C# logical operators and their descriptions.

Table 4-2: The commonly used C# logical operators

Operator	Description
&&	AND (Short-circuit evaluation)
||	OR (Short-circuit evaluation)
&	AND
|	OR
!	NOT

The following are some examples of logical expressions assuming that x equals 5 and y equals 10:

$(x > 5)$ && $(y == 10)$ // false — The second operand is not evaluated
$(x > 5)$ & $(y == 10)$ // false
$(x == 5)$ || $(y == 12)$ // true — The second operand is not evaluated
$(x == 5)$ | $(y == 12)$ // true
$! (x == 7)$ // true

These examples are discussed in detail in the following sections.

4-1-2-1 The Logical AND Operators (&&, &)

Notice in the first example that there is no need to evaluate the second operand as long as the first one is evaluated false. This is because in an AND operation, if one of the operands is false the whole expression becomes false. This is called short-circuit evaluation.

In the second example, however, both operands are evaluated in order to evaluate the whole expression. The result is false because the first operand is false and the second is true. The result can be true only if both operands are true.

4-1-2-2 The Logical OR Operators (||, |)

Notice in the third example that there is no need to evaluate the second operand as long as the first operand is evaluated true. This is because in the || operation, if one of the operands is true the whole expression becomes true. This is also called short-circuit evaluation.

In the | example, however, both operands are evaluated in order to evaluate the whole expression. The first operand is true; therefore, the whole expression is evaluated true. The result can be true if one operand is true.

4-1-2-3 **The Logical NOT Operator (!)**

In the fifth example the NOT operator operates on one operand:

```
!(x == 7)
```

Because the operand is an expression that is evaluated false (remember that x equals 5), the result of the operation is true. In other words, "!true" is evaluated false and "!false" is evaluated true.

This expression can also be written like this:

```
(x != 7)
```

4-1-2-4 **The Bitwise Operators**

The logical operators && and || can be used with integral operands, in which case they compute the bitwise AND and the bitwise OR of their operands. The following examples perform bitwise AND and OR operations on two integers (21 and 4) and display the results in several formats:

```
// Hexadecimal:
Console.WriteLine("0x{0:x}",0x15 | 0x4);   // 0x15
Console.WriteLine("0x{0:x}",0x15 & 0x4);   // 0x4
// Decimal:
Console.WriteLine(21 | 4);   // 21
Console.WriteLine(21 & 4);   // 4
```

4-2 **The if-else Construct**

The **if-else** construct is used to build a conditional statement. It takes the form:

```
if (condition)
    statement(s)_1          // The original result
[else
    statement(s)_2]         // The alternative result
```

where:

condition is a relational or logical expression.

statement(s)_1 is a statement (or a block of statements) that is executed if the condition is true.

statement(s)_2 is a statement (or a block of statements) that is executed if the condition is false.

Notice that what goes inside the brackets ([]) is always optional.

As you can see in the **if-else** construct, you can use the **if** keyword and the original result to build the conditional statement, like this example:

```
if (salary > 2000)
    Console.Write("Salary is greater than 2k");
```

You can also add to it the optional part to represent the alternative result:

```
if (salary > 2000)
    Console.Write("Salary is greater than 2k");   // The original result
else
    Console.Write("Salary is less than or equal to 2k");   // The
                    alternative result
```

If you use more than one statement to express either one of the results, include the statements inside block braces ({}). For example, when the following condition becomes true, all the statements in the following block are executed:

```
if (salary > 2000)
{
    Console.WriteLine("Original result_1");
    Console.WriteLine("Original result_2");
    Console.WriteLine("Original result_3");
}
```

It is possible for the original result or the alternative result to be another **if-else** construct. For example, you can test the case of the character entered from the keyboard by using the following algorithm:

- If the character is a letter, check to see whether it is:
  - Lowercase: display the appropriate message.
  - Uppercase: display the appropriate message.
- If the character is not a letter, display the appropriate message.

This algorithm is illustrated in the following C# example.

Example 4-2

```
// Example 4-2.cs
// Character Tester

using System;

public class CharacterTester
{
    public static void Main()
```

```
    {
        Console.Write("Please enter a character: ");
        char yourChar = (char) Console.Read();
        if (Char.IsLetter(yourChar))
            if (Char.IsLower(yourChar))
                Console.WriteLine("The letter {0} is lowercase.", yourChar);
            else
                Console.WriteLine("The letter {0} is uppercase.", yourChar);
        else
            Console.WriteLine("The character {0} is not alphabetic.",
                    yourChar);
    }
}
```

Sample Runs:

```
Please enter a character: A
The letter A is uppercase.

Please enter a character: a
The letter a is lowercase.

Please enter a character: 33
The character 3 is not alphabetic.
```

Notice also that the program ignores anything that follows the first character; therefore, the number 33 is read as 3.

4-2-1 Manipulating Characters

As you can see in the last example, you have to cast the **Read** method with the cast "(char)" in order to explicitly convert the data entered from the keyboard to the type **char**. Without the cast, the **Read** method returns an integer that is the ASCII code of the input character.

The example also demonstrated some .NET methods for manipulating characters such as **Char.IsLetter** to check if a character is a letter. Similarly, if you would like to check to see if the character is a digit, you can use the method **Char.IsDigit**.

In the example, the method **IsLower** is used to check if a letter is a lowercase. Similarly, you can use the method **IsUpper** to check if the letter is an uppercase letter.

4-2-2 Nested if-else Statements

Although the **if-else** statement is intended for binary choice, it can be
expanded to handle more complex choices. It is possible to build a whole
ladder of nested **if-else** statements as shown in the following form:

```
if (condition_1)
    statement_1;
else if (condition_2)
    statement_2;
else if (condition_3)
    statement_3;
...
else
    statement_n;
```

The conditions in the ladder are evaluated from the top down, and whenever a condition is evaluated as true, the corresponding statement is
executed and the rest of the construct is skipped. If no condition has been
satisfied, the last **else** will be brought into action.

Drill 4-1

Rewrite Example 4-2 using a nested if-else statement.

4-3 The switch Construct

The **switch** construct is used to select from multiple choices, such as
selecting a floor in an elevator, an item from a vending machine, or a
choice from a menu. In these cases, you select only one of the available
choices. The **switch** construct takes the following form:

```
switch (expression)
{
    case constant-1:
        statement(s)
        jump-statement
    case constant-2:
        statement(s)
        jump-statement
    case constant-3:
    ...
    ...
```

```
[default:
    statement(s)
    jump-statement]
}
```

where:

expression represents a value that corresponds to the associated switch choice.

statement(s) is a statement or block of statements that is executed if the corresponding condition is evaluated true.

jump-statement is a branching statement to transfer control outside the specific case, such as **break** or **goto** (explained later in the chapter).

default deals with all the other cases.

According to the value of the expression, the control of the program is transferred to one of the **case** labels and the corresponding statement is executed. The cases actually represent the different possible values of the expression. Take a look at the example below, which simulates a menu for selecting sandwiches (beef, fish, or chicken). When you select an item, the program gives you the cost. If you enter a number that does not exist in the menu, you get a message asking you to select 1, 2, or 3. In both cases, the program gives you a thank-you message for using the machine.

Example 4-3

```
// Example 4-3.cs
// switch example

using System;

class FastFoodClass
{
    public static void Main()
    {
        Console.WriteLine("Sandwiches: 1=Beef 2=Fish 3=Chicken");
        Console.Write("Please enter your selection: ");
        string s = Console.ReadLine();
        double totalCost = 0;
        switch(s)
        {
            case "1":
                totalCost = 4.5;
                break;
```

```
        case "2":
            totalCost = 5.25;
            break;
        case "3":
            totalCost = 4.2;
            break;
        default:
        Console.WriteLine("Invalid selection. Please select 1, 2,
                           or 3.");
            break;
        }
        if (totalCost != 0)
            Console.WriteLine("Please pay {0:C}.", totalCost);
        Console.WriteLine("Thank you for your business.");
    }
}
```

Sample Run 1:

```
Sandwiches: 1=Beef 2=Fish 3=Chicken          // the first run
Please enter your selection: 3               // the entered number
Please pay $4.20.                            // the result
Thank you for your business.
```

Sample Run 2:

```
Sandwiches: 1=Beef 2=Fish 3=Chicken          // the second run
Please enter your selection: 0               // the entered number
Invalid selection. Please select 1, 2, or 3. // the result
Thank you for your business.
```

In the second trial, the user incorrectly selected 0, which is not a valid choice; therefore, he or she received the message, "Invalid selection. Please select 1, 2, or 3."

Note The use of the default case is very similar to the use of the last else in a nested if-else statement. It is recommended to use the default case for detecting and catching errors.

When you deal with multiple choices, you can write your conditions either in the form of nested **if** statement or as a **switch** construct. In cases like that of the example above, the **switch** is easier to write than a nested **if**. It is also more efficient in most cases, which means it runs faster.

Note for C++ programmers: There is a difference between the C# switch and the C++ switch. In C++, if you don't have a branching statement, control is transferred directly to the next case. But in C#, the compiler will complain about the missing statement. You can compensate for this by using some empty cases so control can fall through until it reaches a valid case. For example:

```
switch(n)
{
    case 1:   // fall through to case 3
    case 2:   // fall through to case 3
    case 3:
        Console.WriteLine("cases 1 & 2 come here!");
        break;
        // ...
}
```

The C# switch was designed without the fall through feature in order to avoid problems that might occur in the program if you mistakenly omit a break statement. In that case, one or more switch cases might be executed unintentionally, causing bugs in the program.

4-4 The Conditional Expression

The conditional expression is used to build a simple conditional statement. It takes the form:

```
condition ? expression_1 : expression_2
```

where:

condition is the Boolean expression to test.
expression_1 is the expression evaluation if the condition is true.
expression_2 is the expression evaluation if the condition is false.

Of course, you can assign the entire expression to a variable, as in this example:

```
result = (x != 0.0) ? Math.Tan(x) : 1.0;
```

(Notice that the parentheses around the condition are optional. They are used for better readability.)

This statement says, "if x is not equal to zero, assign the value Math.Tan(x) to result; otherwise, assign the value 1.0 to result." This statement is equivalent to the following code segment:

```
if (x != 0.0)
    result = Math.Tan(x);
else
    result = 1.0;
```

Tan, a method from the **Math** class, is used to calculate the tangent of an angle.

In the following example, the conditional expression is demonstrated.

Example 4-4

```
// Example 4-4.cs
// Conditional expression example

using System;

class Conditional
{
    public static void Main()
    {
        double x = Math.PI/3, result = 0;
        result = (x != 0.0) ? Math.Tan(x) : 1.0;
        Console.WriteLine("Exact value = {0}", result );
        Console.WriteLine("Approximate value = {0}",
                Math.Round(result ));
    }
}
```

Output:

```
Exact value = 1.73205080756888
Approximate value = 2
```

In the preceding example, notice the way we declared and initialized two variables with one statement:

```
double x = Math.PI/3, result = 0;
```

This statement is equivalent to the following statements:

```
double x = Math.PI/3;
double result = 0;
```

Notice also that we used some other members of the **Math** class. The **Round** method is used to round a value to the nearest integer or specified number of decimal places according to the specified format (refer to the section titled "Formatting Results" in Chapter 3). The public field **PI** represents the ratio of the circumference of a circle to its diameter.

You can find the rest of the mathematical constants and trigonometric and logarithmic methods on the web site http://www.msdn.microsoft.com.

4-5 Using Libraries

When you call a method in a Dynamic Linking Library (DLL), the method is linked to the application at run time. The following example contains a method for computing the factorial. It can be compiled as a DLL to be used by another program:

Example 4-5

```
// Example 4-5a.cs
// Compile as DLL.

public class Class1
{
    public static long Factorial(long i)
    {
        return ((i <= 1) ? 1 : (i * Factorial(i-1)));
    }
}
```

To compile this code, use the following command line (assuming the filename is Ex4-5a.cs):

```
csc/t:library Ex4-5a.cs
```

This will generate the library file Ex4-5a.dll.

The following code file is calling the **Factorial** method, which resides in the DLL. Notice in this code that the method name is qualified by the class name **Class1**.

```
// Example 4-5b.cs
// Compile as DLL.

using System;

public class MyClass
{
    static void Main()
    {
        Console.Write("Please enter an integer: ");
        long n = Convert.ToInt64(Console.ReadLine());
        Console.WriteLine(Class1.Factorial(n));   // calling the method
    }
}
```

To compile this code, use the following command line (assuming the filename is Ex4-5b.cs):

```
csc/r:Ex4-5a.dll Ex4-5b.cs
```

You can now run the application Ex4-5b, which reads a number and displays the factorial.

Sample Run:

```
Please enter an integer: 4
24
```

4-6 Repetition Loops

Repetition loops are used to repeat one or more statements. The repetition might continue for a specified number of times, until a specific condition is satisfied, or indefinitely. There is more than one statement you can use to create a loop, as explained in the following sections.

4-6-1 The for Loop

The **for** loop repeats an operation as long as a specified condition is satisfied. It takes the form:

```
for ([initialization]; [control_expression]; [counter_update])
    statement(s)
```

where:

initialization is the counter initialization statement.
control_expression is a condition to be satisfied during the loop execution.
counter_update is the counter increment or decrement statement.
statement(s) is the statement or block of statements to be repeated.

The following example shows a **for** loop that displays the numbers from 1 to 5, each on a separate line:

```
for (int counter = 1; counter <= 5; counter++)
{
    Console.WriteLine(counter);
}
```

Notice in this example that the counter variable is declared and initialized inside the loop's parentheses. Notice also that the statement to be repeated is placed inside block braces. Using a block is not necessary in this case because there is only one statement to execute. If you need to execute more than one statement, you must use a block.

The following example demonstrates a simple loop to print odd numbers from 1 to 10.

Example 4-6

```
// Example 4-6.cs
// for loop example

using System;

class ForLoop
{
    static void Main()
    {
        for (int counter = 1; counter <= 10; counter=counter +2)
        {
            Console.WriteLine(counter);
        }
    }
}
```

Output:

```
1
3
5
7
9
```

4-6-1-1 Using continue and break

It is possible to skip a specific counter value by using the **continue** statement. For example, the statement:

```
if (counter == 3) continue;
```

causes the loop to skip the counter value 3 and jump to the next counter value.

It is also possible to abort the loop completely by using the **break** statement, as in the following statement:

```
if (counter == 7) break;
```

This will cause the loop to end when the counter value is equal to 7. When the loop is terminated, control is transferred to the next statement immediately following the loop.

4-6-1-2 Available Options in the for Loop

Notice that all the **for** loop control elements are optional, which means that the following **for** loop runs indefinitely:

```
for ( ; ; )
{
   Console.WriteLine("Hello again!");
}
```

This loop will continue to display the phrase "Hello again!" until you break the execution of the program by pressing Ctrl+C. The previous state-ment is equivalent to the following statement:

```
for ( ; true; )
{
   Console.WriteLine("Hello again!");
}
```

It is also possible to use more than one counter to control the loop; just separate them with commas like this:

```
for (i  =  0,  j = 10;  i<= j,  i++;  j = j-1)
{
   // do something
}
```

4-6-1-3 Nesting Loops

The **for** loops can be nested inside each other as in the following example, which displays the prime numbers from 2 to 10. The prime numbers are those numbers that can only be divided either by 1 or by themselves, such as 3, 7, 43, and so forth. In this program, there are two loops, one using the counter i (the i-loop) and one using the counter j (the j-loop). Nesting the j-loop inside the i-loop means that for each value of i, the entire range of j values is tested.

Example 4-7

```
// Example 4-7.cs
// Prime Numbers

using System;

class Prime
{
   static void Main()
   {
      for (int i = 2; i <= 10; i++)
      {
         bool x = false;
         for (int j = 2; j <= i - 1; j++)
```

```
            {
                if (i % j == 0) x = true;
            }
            if (x == false) Console.WriteLine(i);
        }
    }
}
```

Output:

```
2
3
5
7
```

Notice also the use of the operator % to test the remainder of the division by using the following statement:

```
if (i % j == 0) x = true;
```

This statement says, "if i is divided by j without remainder, set x to true." When the j-loop exits and x is still false, the value of i will contain a prime number.

When the i-loop is done, all the prime numbers within the range of 2 to 10 are displayed. You can increase the maximum value of the counter i to see more prime numbers.

4-6-2 The while Loop

The **while** loop is used to execute a block of statements as long as a specific condition is satisfied. The **while** loop statement takes the form:

```
while (control_expression)
    statement(s);
```

where:

control_expression is a condition be satisfied during the loop execution.
statement(s) is a statement (or the block of statements) to be executed.

Because the **while** loop starts with testing the condition, the statement block might not execute at all if the condition fails.

The following code segment displays the numbers from 1 to 5, each on a separate line. Notice that you must initialize the counter before the loop starts.

```
while (counter < 6)
{
    Console.WriteLine(counter);
    counter++;
}
```

The following example also displays the counter numbers, but by using a different logic. The control expression says, "if counter is not equal to zero." This condition is always true because the counter is initialized to the value 1. Inside the loop, the **break** statement is used to terminate the loop when a specified condition is satisfied.

Example 4-8

```
// Example 4-8.cs
// while loop example

using System;

class WhileClass
{
    public static void Main()
    {
        int counter = 1;
        while (counter != 0)
        {
            counter++;
            if (counter == 2) continue;     // Skip the value 2
            if (counter > 5) break;         // Terminate the loop
            Console.WriteLine(counter);
        }
    }
}
```

Output:

```
3
4
5
```

In the example above, notice that the **continue** statement is used to resume the loop execution after skipping the value 2 according to the condition:

```
if (counter == 2) continue;
```

The **break** statement causes the loop to terminate when the counter exceeds the value 5:

```
if (counter > 5) break;
```

4-6-3 The do-while Loop

The **do-while** loop is used to repeatedly execute a block of statements as long as some condition is satisfied. This loop takes the following form:

```
do statement(s)
while (control_expression);
```

where:

control_expression is a condition to be satisfied during the loop execution.
statement(s) is a statement (or the block of statements) to be executed.

The **do-while** loop is distinguished by being executed at least once regardless of the condition. This is because the condition is tested after executing the statement(s).

The following example displays the even numbers from 1 to 10 using a **do-while** loop. Notice the use of the **continue** statement to skip the odd numbers and the use of the **return** statement to terminate the loop early.

Example 4-9

```
// Example 4-9.cs
// do-while example

using System;

public class DoWhileClass
{
    static void Main ()
    {
        int x = 0;
        do
        {
            x++;
            if (x%2 != 0)            //   if the number is odd
                continue;
            if (x == 8)
                return;              //   terminate the loop and return
            Console.WriteLine(x);
        }
            while(x < 100);
    }
}
```

Output:

```
2
4
6
```

In this example, the **return** statement is doing the same job that the **break** statement does. Although both statements terminate the loop, there is a difference between them. The **break** statement transfers control to the statement that follows the loop, if one exists. The **return** statement transfers control to the calling method. Suppose that the loop exists inside a method named MyMethod, which is invoked from another method named YourMethod. When the **return** statement is encountered in MyMethod, the program control will be transferred to YourMethod. In this example, **return** ends the execution of the **Main** method; therefore, if you add any statement immediately after the loop, it will not be executed.

Try this code snippet:

```
static void Main ()
{
    int x = 0;
    do
    {
        x++;
        if (x == 4)
            return;
        Console.WriteLine(x);
    }
    while(x < 100);
    Console.WriteLine("The loop is done!");
}
```

When you run this code, you will notice that the last statement that displays "The loop is done!" is not executed.

➔ **Note** If you have to choose between using a while loop and a do-while loop, in most cases the while loop is a better choice. However, in some applications where the user has to input some data before processing it in a loop, the do-while is the appropriate choice.

Drill 4-2

Write a C# program to compute the value of a number raised to the power of a second number. Read the two numbers from the keyboard.

4-6-4 Branching Statements

The following statements are used to exit repetition loops:

- break
- goto
- return
- throw

You have seen already some examples of **return** and **break** in the preceding sections. In many languages, including C#, the statement **goto** is not recommended because it corrupts the program structure. However, it can be used in some cases to exit from deeply nested loops. It is also used in the **switch** construct to jump from one case to another. For example:

```
case 1:
    // do something
    goto case 3;
```

In general, the **goto** statement takes the following forms:

```
goto label;
goto case expression;
goto default;
```

where:

label is a label name.

The label is an identifier followed by a colon, as in the following example that contains the label "Finish."

```
goto Finish;
    ...
Finish:
    Console.WriteLine("You are done here!");
```

The **throw** statement is used in catching *exceptions* that may occur during the program execution. Exceptions are explained in depth in Chapter 9.

4-7 Arrays

An array represents a group of elements of the same type. The array can be of one or more dimensions. The *single-dimensional* array can represent a group of people lining up in a queue. The *two-dimensional* array can represent students in a classroom whose positions are organized in rows and columns. The array elements might be arrays themselves, in which case the array is called a *jagged array* or an *array of arrays*.

Arrays descend from the **System.Array** class, which serves as the base class for all arrays in the Common Language Runtime. The use of some methods of this class will be demonstrated in the following sections.

4-7-1 **One-Dimensional Arrays**

You can declare a one-dimensional array like this example:

```
int[] myIntArray = new int [10];
```

This declaration allocates memory for ten integers under the name myIntArray. The array elements start from the element myIntArray[0] up to the element myIntArray[9]. The **new** operator is used here to initialize the array elements to their default values — zero in this case.

It is possible to declare an array of any type (reference or value type), as in this example, which declares an array of strings:

```
string[] myStringArray = new string [10];
```

The only difference between value-type elements and reference-type elements is that value-type elements are initialized to their default values, while those of reference type are initialized with the value null. (The default values were discussed in Chapter 3, Section 3-3-2.)

4-7-2 **Declaring and Initializing Arrays**

Like any other variable, you can initialize the array when you declare it:

```
int[] myIntArray = new int [] { 1, 2, 3, 4, 5 };
```

In this case, there is no need to specify the number of elements of the array because it is obvious.

The following example declares and initializes an array for days of the week:

```
string[] myDay = new string []
{ "Sat", "Sun", "Mon", "Tue", "Wed", "Thu", "Fri" };
```

In the following kind of declaration, you can omit the **new** operator because the type of element is obvious to the compiler:

```
int[] myIntArray = { 1, 2, 3, 4, 5 };
string[] myDay = { "Sat", "Sun", "Mon", "Tue", "Wed", "Thu", "Fri" };
```

It is also possible to declare an array without initializing it, in which case you must initialize it before using it in the program. Here is an example:

```
int[] myIntArray;                    // Declaration
myIntArray = new int[] { 1, 3, 5, 7, 9 };  // Initialization
```

4-7-3 Multi-Dimensional Arrays

You can declare and initialize a two-dimensional array by using a state-ment like this:

```
int[,] myTwoDimArray = new int[3, 2] { {1, 2}, {3, 4}, {5, 6} };
```

This declares an array with dimensions [3, 2] named myTwoDimArray. You can visualize the two-dimensional array as a table that contains rows and columns. In this example, it has three rows and two columns.

In the following example, you declare a **string** array named grades with dimensions [2, 4].

```
string[,] grades = new string[2, 4] { {"Pass"," Good", "VeryGood",
"Distinct"}, {"55%", "65%", "75%", "85%"} };
```

This array stores the grade names and corresponding percentages.

As with one-dimensional arrays, you can omit the dimensions as long as you initialize the array:

```
int[,] myTwoDimArray = new int[,] { {1, 2}, {3, 4}, {5, 6} };
string[,] grades = new string[,] { {"Pass", "Good", "VeryGood",
"Distinct"}, {"55%", "65%", "75%", "85%"} };
```

You can also omit the **new** operator:

```
int[,] myTwoDimArray = { {1, 2}, {3, 4}, {5, 6} };
string [,] grades = { {"Pass", "Good", "VeryGood", "Distinct"},
{"55%", "65%", "75%", "85%"} };
```

4-7-4 Jagged Arrays

To declare a jagged array with the name myJaggedArray, use a statement like this:

```
int[][] myJaggedArray =
    new int[2][] { new int[] {2, 3, 4}, new int[] {5, 6, 7, 8, 9} };
```

This array is a one-dimensional array that contains two elements. Each ele-ment is a one-dimensional array with a different number of elements; in this case, three and five.

It is possible to omit the dimensions of the first array, like this:

```
int[][] myJaggedArray =
    new int[][] { new int[] {2, 3, 4}, new int[] {5, 6, 7, 8, 9} };
```

You can also omit the first **new** operator:

```
int[][] myJaggedArray =
    { new int[] {2, 3, 4}, new int[] {5, 6, 7, 8, 9} };
```

4-7-5 Accessing Array Elements

By accessing the array elements, you can manipulate and display them. For example, you can change the contents of the element [2] of the one-dimensional array myIntArray by using the following statement:

```
myIntArray[2] = 45;
```

In the same way, you can change the element [0,0] of the two-dimensional array myTwoDimArray by using the statement:

```
myTwoDimArray[0,0] = 133;
```

The following statements access the elements of myJaggedArray and assign the value 11 to the first element of the first array and the value 22 to the third element of the second array:

```
myJaggedArray[0][0] = 11;
myJaggedArray[1][2] = 22;
```

The easiest way to read from or assign to array elements is to use loops. For example, to print the contents of the array myIntArray, use the following loop:

```
for (int i = 0; i <= 4; i++)
    Console.WriteLine(myIntArray[i]);
```

Always remember that the index of an array starts at 0.

In the case of two-dimensional arrays, you need two nested loops, one for each dimension:

```
for (int i = 0; i <= 2; i++)
    for (int j = 0; j <= 1; j++)
        Console.WriteLine(myTwoDimArray[i,j]);
```

In order to display this array in the form of a table with three rows and two columns, insert a new line after each row:

```
for (int i=0; i<= 2; i++)
{
    for (int j=0; j<= 1; j++)
    {
        Console.Write(myTwoDimArray[i,j] + " ");
    }
    Console.WriteLine();   // Blank line
}
```

This loop displays the array as follows:

```
1 2
3 4
5 6
```

The following example demonstrates how to declare a jagged array, change the values of its elements, and display them.

Example 4-10

```
// Example 4-10.cs
// Jagged array example

using System;

class JaggedClass
{
   static void Main ()
   {
      int[][] myJaggedArray =
         { new int[] {2, 3, 4}, new int[] {5, 6, 7, 8, 9} };
      myJaggedArray[0][0] = 11;   // Change the first element of the
                                  //                      first array
      myJaggedArray[1][2] = 22;   // Change the third element in the
                                  //                     second array

      // Display the first array:
      Console.WriteLine("First array:");
      for (int j = 0; j <= 2; j++)
      {
         Console.WriteLine(myJaggedArray[0][j]);
      }
      // Display the second array:
      Console.WriteLine("Second array:");
      for (int j = 0; j <= 4; j++)
      {
         Console.WriteLine(myJaggedArray[1][j]);
      }
      Console.WriteLine("The job is done!");
   }
}
```

Notice that we used some extra braces to make the program easier to read.

Output:

```
First array:
11      // new element
3
4
Second array:
5
6
22      // new element
```

```
8
9
The job is done!
```

Drill 4-3

Display the contents of the two-dimensional array called "grades" that was discussed in this section. Make sure you get the following result:

```
Grade=Pass        Score=55%
Grade=Good        Score=65%
Grade=VeryGood    Score=75%
Grade=Distinct    Score=85%
```

4-8 Using Program Arguments

One possible form of the Main method is:

```
static void Main(string[] args)
```

Using this form allows the C# program to accept as arguments a sequence of strings. The arguments are received as **string** array elements named args[0], args[1], and so forth. The **string** arguments can also be converted to other data types, as explained in Chapter 3.

In the following example, the program receives two arguments at run time. The program converts the first one to a **long** number and the second to a **double** number, and then displays them and their product.

Example 4-11

```
// Example 4-11.cs
// Parsing arguments

using System;

public class ParseClass
{
    static void Main(string[] args)
    {
        long myLong = Convert.ToInt64(args[0]);
        double myDouble = Convert.ToDouble(args[1]);
        double result = myLong * myDouble;
```

```
        Console.WriteLine("Your long number is: {0}", myLong);
        Console.WriteLine("Your double number is: {0}", myDouble);
        Console.WriteLine("The result of multiplication is: {0}",
                        result);
    }
}
```

Sample Run:

Assuming that the program is called "example," enter the following at the command line:

```
> example 2 1.1
```

The output should be:

```
Your long number is: 2
Your double number is: 1.1
The result of multiplication is: 2.2
```

Drill 4-4

Rewrite the program created for Drill 4-2 to read the number and the power as program arguments. For example, if the program is called "power," you can invoke it as shown in these sample runs:

Sample Run 1:
```
>power 4 2
The number 4 raised to the power 2 = 16
```

Sample Run 2:
```
>power 4 3
The number 4 raised to the power 3 = 64
```

4-9 Using .NET Properties and Methods with Arrays

As mentioned earlier, arrays are inherited from the class **System.Array**, which contains several methods and properties for manipulating arrays. In the following sections, some of these properties and methods are introduced.

4-9-1 Array's Length (Length)

The **Length** property is the number of elements in an array. Consider the following array:

```
int[,] myArray= new int[10,4];        // Array declaration
```

The following statement displays the number 40, which represents the number of elements:

```
Console.WriteLine(myArray.Length);   // Get and display the length
```

4-9-2 Array's Rank (Rank)

The **Rank** property is the number of dimensions of an array. Consider the following declarations:

```
int[,] myArray= new int[1, 3];         // Two dimensions
int[,,] yourArray= new int[10, 4, 5]; // Three dimensions
```

The following statements display the numbers 2 and 3, which represent the rank of myArray and yourArray, respectively:

```
// Display the rank:
Console.WriteLine(myArray.Rank);      // 2
Console.WriteLine(yourArray.Rank);    // 3
```

4-9-3 Sorting an Array (Array.Sort)

The **Array.Sort** method is used to sort an array. Consider the following declaration:

```
int[] myArray = { 3, 4, 56, 8 };
```

In order to sort this array, use the statement:

```
Array.Sort(myArray);
```

The result is the sorted array: 3, 4, 8, 56.

4-9-4 Reversing an Array (Array.Reverse)

The **Array.Reverse** method is used to reverse an array. Consider the following declaration:

```
int[] myArray = { 3, 4, 8, 56 };
```

In order to reverse this array, use the statement:

```
Array.Reverse(myArray);
```

The result is the reversed array: 56, 8, 4, 3.

In the following example, you create a one-dimensional array and display it. Then you apply the **Array.Sort** and **Array.Reverse** methods and display the array after each change.

Example 4-12

```
// Example 4-12.cs
// Array methods

using System;

class MyClass
{
    static void Main()
    {
        int[] myArray = { 1, 4, 25, 3 };

        // Display the array:
        for (int i=0; i<=3; i++)
            Console.Write("{0} ", myArray[i]);
        Console.WriteLine("Original");

        // Sort, then display:
        Array.Sort(myArray);
        for (int i=0; i<=3; i++)
            Console.Write("{0} ", myArray[i]);
        Console.WriteLine("Sorted");

        // Reverse, then display:
        Array.Reverse(myArray);
        for (int i=0; i<=3; i++)
            Console.Write("{0} ", myArray[i]);
        Console.WriteLine("Reversed");
    }
}
```

Output:

```
1 4 25 3 Original
1 3 4 25 Sorted
25 4 3 1 Reversed
```

4-9-5 **Resizing an Array (Array.Resize)**

One of the biggest problems beginners struggle with involves setting the size of an array. Does the program need to use a fixed size right at the start? What happens if it needs to be made larger? The .NET Framework version 2.0 introduced a solution to this problem by adding the **Array.Resize** method, which is used to change the size of an array. Because the array size is immutable (the size cannot be changed at run time), this method actually copies the elements of the array to another array and then renames the new array and discards the old one. This is a generic method, which means it can work with any array type. (Generics are explained in detail in Chapter 12.)

For example, if you have an array named myArray initialized with three elements, you can extend its size to six elements by using the following statement:

```
Array.Resize<int>(ref myArray, 6);
```

In this statement, <int> is the type argument. (The type argument is explained in Chapter 12, Section 12-1.) You can also use the following statement to extend the size to six:

```
Array.Resize (ref myArray, 6);
```

In the following example, the sizes of two arrays — an **int** array and a **string** array — are increased from three to six. When the newly sized arrays are displayed, the null elements of the **string** array are filled with the string "empty." This is done by using the ?? operator.

```
yourArray[i] = yourArray[i] ?? "empty";
```

Example 4-13

```
// Ex4-13.cs
// Resizing an array

using System;

public class MyClass
{
    public static void Main()
    {
        int [] myArray = { 1, 2, 3 };
        string[] yourArray = { "Tom", "Dick", "Harry" };

        // Resize the int array:
        Array.Resize(ref myArray, 6);
```

```
            // Display it:
            for(int i = 0; i < myArray.Length; i++)
            {
                Console.Write(myArray[i] + " ");
            }
            Console.WriteLine();

            // Resize the string array:
            Array.Resize(ref yourArray, 6);

            // Display it:
            for(int i = 0; i < yourArray.Length; i++)
            {
                // Use the ?? operator to assign "empty" to null elements:
                yourArray[i] = yourArray[i] ?? "empty";

                Console.Write(yourArray[i]+ " ");
            }
        }
    }
}
```

Output:

```
1 2 3 0 0 0
Tom Dick Harry empty empty empty
```

4-10 The foreach Loop

The **foreach** loop is used with arrays and collections. The topic will be revisited after we discuss collections in Chapter 11. The **foreach** loop accesses arrays in a unique way without using counters. The **foreach** statement takes the form:

```
    foreach (type identifier in expression) statement(s);
```

where:

type is the data type, such as **int** or **string**.
identifier is the variable name.
expression is the name of the array (or collection).
statement(s) is the statement or block of statements to be executed.

Consider, for example, the following array:

```
    int[,] myIntArray = { {1, 3, 5},{2, 4, 6} };
```

You can display the elements of this array by using the following statement:

```
foreach(int i in myIntArray)
Console.Write("{0} ", i);
```

The result should be:

```
1 3 5 2 4 6
```

It is important to notice that the number of dimensions doesn't matter because **foreach** accesses all the elements sequentially. If the array is a one-dimensional array like this:

```
int[] myIntArray = {1, 3, 5, 2, 4, 6};
```

you can still display it by using the same statement. If the array is a **string** array, you need only to change the type from **int** to **string**:

```
foreach(string i in myIntArray)
    Console.Write("{0} ", i);
```

➔ **Note** The foreach loop can be applied to your custom data structures to do more advanced data processing. This will be covered in Chapter 11.

In the following example, you create a **string** array and display it along with the rank and number of elements using **foreach**.

Example 4-14

```
// Example 4-14.cs
// foreach example

using System;

class foreachClass
{
    static void Main ()
    {
        string [,] nameArray =
            { {"Hazem","Pille"}, {"Isabella","Angelina"} };
        foreach(string n in nameArray )
            Console.Write("{0} ", n);

    // Blank line:
        Console.WriteLine();
    // Number of elements
        Console.WriteLine("Number of array elements = {0}",
                            nameArray.Length);
```

```
        // The rank of the array:
        Console.WriteLine("Dimensions of the array = {0}",
                            nameArray.Rank);
    }
}
```

Output:

```
Hazem Pille Isabella Angelina
Number of array elements = 4
Dimensions of the array = 2
```

Drill 4-5

Rewrite Example 4-12 using the foreach statement to display the arrays.

Summary

In this chapter:

- You had a tour of the **if-else** constructs and learned how to use them to express conditions and to nest them to build more complex conditions.
- You also learned the **switch** construct and used it to express multiple choices.
- You now know that a condition can be expressed in a simple form by using the *conditional expression*, which uses two operators.
- You learned how to compile and use libraries in your programs.
- You had a complete tour of loops and you are now familiar with many kinds of loops, such as **for**, **while**, and **do-while**. You also learned about the **foreach** loop, which combines power and simplicity in handling arrays.
- You learned some branching statements that you can use in controlling the flow of the program such as **goto**, **break**, and **return**.
- Finally, you used arrays in different dimensions and learned how to declare and initialize them, and how to access and display their elements. You also learned about some useful .NET properties and methods that are used to process arrays.

Chapter 5

Using Classes

Contents:
- *Declaring and using classes*
- *Using namespaces*
- *Accessibility and access levels*
- *Using properties*
- *Accessor accessibility*
- *Static members and classes*
- *Constants*
- *Constructors*
- *Read-only fields*
- *Inheritance*
- *Destructors*
- *Partial classes*

5-1 Classes

The class is the most important element in C# because everything must be included inside a class (or a struct). Unlike other languages, the C# compiler doesn't allow you to declare any variables or methods outside a class. As we mentioned before, global variables are not permitted in the language. In fact, object-oriented programming is based on the concept of classes. Structs are similar to classes in some aspects and can be used instead of classes in some applications. The main difference between a class and a struct is that the class is a reference type, while the struct is a value type. (Refer to Chapter 3, Sections 3-3 and 3-4 for more information on value types and reference types.)

5-1-1 **Class Declaration**

You declare a class by using the keyword **class** as follows:

```
class MyClass
{
    // Class implementation
}
```

The class implementation (or class body) goes between the braces ({}).
You can declare a struct in the same way by using the keyword **struct**:

```
struct MyStruct
{
    // Struct implementation
}
```

Structs are discussed in detail in Chapter 7.

5-1-2 **Field Initialization**

In the following example, you declare the class **Point**, which contains two
fields — x and y:

```
class Point
{
    int x;
    int y;
}
```

You can initialize the fields with values like this example:

```
class Point
{
    int x = 0;
    int y = 0;
}
```

This declaration initializes the fields x and y to their default values. Of
course, you can use any other values to initialize the fields.

5-1-3 **Class Instantiation**

To create objects from the **Point** class, use the following statement:

```
Point myPoint;    // create the object
```

You can also create the object and initialize the fields in the same
statement:

```
Point myPoint = new Point();
```

Notice, however, that you cannot use an uninitialized object — this is the same rule that applies to uninitialized variables. In the second statement, when the object is created the default constructor is invoked to initialize fields to their default values.

You can, of course, create more than one instance from the class:

```
Point p1 = new Point();
Point p2 = new Point();
```

Then you can assign each object its own coordinates:

```
p1.x = 15;
p1.y = 22;
p2.x = 10;
p2.y = 12;
```

As you can see from these statements, the fields x and y are associated with the objects p1 and p2. In the following example, you see the complete picture of the class and the object created from it. In this example, the object is created in the **Main** method, but you can create objects inside any other method. You cannot, however, create an object inside the class itself.

Example 5-1

```
// Example 5-1.cs
// Class instantiation

using System;

class Point
{
    int x;
    int y;

    static void Main()
    {
        // Create a Point object:
        Point p1 = new Point();
        // Assign values to fields:
        p1.x = 22;
        p1.y = 25;
        // Display the fields
        Console.Write("x = {0}, y = {1}", p1.x, p1.y);
    }
}
```

Output:

```
x = 22, y = 25
```

5-2 Namespaces

A *namespace* is a container that includes classes and other types. You can place the class inside a namespace. The benefit of using namespaces is being able to fully qualify members included in the same namespace. If two classes in two different namespaces have the same name, you can refer to each one by using the fully qualified name, for example:

```
MyNameSpace.Class1
YourNameSpace.Class1
```

5-2-1 Nesting Namespaces

It is also possible to nest namespaces inside other namespaces. In that case, you need to use the fully qualified names to distinguish between similar class names:

```
MyParentNameSpace.MyNestedNamespace.MyClass1
MyParentNameSpace.MyClass1
```

In the following example, you declare two classes that have the same name, MyClass. One class is contained in a namespace called MyNameSpace, and the other is contained in a namespace called YourNameSpace. In the **Main** method, which lies in MyNameSpace, you instantiate both classes and create the objects mc1 and mc2. In order to instantiate the class in YourNameSpace you have to use the fully qualified name of the class.

Example 5-2

```
// Example 5-2.cs
// Namespace example

namespace MyNameSpace
{
    using System;

    class MyClass
    {
        int field1 = 1;
        int field2 = 2;
        public void MyMethod()
        {
            Console.WriteLine("MyNameSpace.MyClass fields:");
            Console.WriteLine("Value of field1 = {0}", field1);
            Console.WriteLine("Value of field2 = {0}", field2);
        }
```

```csharp
    static void Main()
    {
        // Create an object of MyClassNameSpace.MyClass:
        MyClass mc1 = new MyClass();

        // Invoke MyMethod on the mc1 object:
        mc1.MyMethod();

        // Create an object of YourNameSpace.MyClass:
        // Notice the use of the fully qualified name:
        YourNameSpace.MyClass mc2 = new YourNameSpace.MyClass();

        // Invoke MyMethod on the mc2 object:
        mc2.MyMethod();
    }
  }
}

namespace YourNameSpace
{
   using System;

   class MyClass
   {
      int field1 = 3;
      int field2 = 4;
      public void MyMethod()
      {
         Console.WriteLine("YourNameSpace.MyClass fields:");
         Console.WriteLine("Value of field1 = {0}", field1);
         Console.WriteLine("Value of field2 = {0}", field2);
      }
   }
}
```

Output:

```
MyNameSpace.MyClass fields:
Value of field1 = 1
Value of field2 = 2
YourNameSpace.MyClass fields:
Value of field1 = 3
Value of field2 = 4
```

5-2-2 The Namespace Alias Qualifier

There may be times when you want to use special names for your classes, such as System or Console. It is obvious that these names will cause conflicts with the .NET classes that have similar names. For example, a class named **System** would hide the **System** class of the .NET library. Although this is not a common case, C# 2005 allowed for this possibility by adding the namespace alias qualifier operator (::). You can use this operator to search the global namespace for identifiers hidden by types or members in your code.

The :: operator goes between two identifiers, like this:

```
global::System.Console.WriteLine("Hello, World!");
```

The left-hand identifier that precedes the :: operator is where the search starts. The right-hand identifier is the identifier to look for. When the left-hand identifier is the word "global," the search starts at the global namespace.

Consider the following example in which a class named **System** is used. This class name causes a problem that is solved only by using the namespace alias qualifier, like this:

```
global::System.Console.WriteLine(mc.myClassNumber);
global::System.Console.WriteLine(ms.mySystemNumber);
```

If you try to use the following statements instead, you get a compiler error:

```
System.Console.WriteLine(mc.myNumber);    // error
System.Console.WriteLine(ms.myNumber);    // error
```

Example 5-3

```
// Example 5-3.cs
// The namespace alias qualifier

class MyClass
{
    int myClassNumber = 123;

    public class System
    {
        public int mySystemNumber = 555;
    }


    static void Main()
    {
        // Instantiate classes:
        MyClass mc = new MyClass();
```

```
            System ms = new System();

            // Display fields:
            global::System.Console.WriteLine(mc.myClassNumber);   // 123
            global::System.Console.WriteLine(ms.mySystemNumber);  // 555
    }
}
```

Output:

```
123
555
```

5-3 Access Levels

It is a common practice that one programmer creates a class, and then other programmers use that class in their code. This code is usually called the *client*. One important feature of OOP is encapsulation, which enables you, as a class creator, to protect your class fields by restricting access to them. The clients in this case can access those fields only through public methods. You probably noticed that the keyword **public** was used in most class declarations in the previous chapters. In this section you learn about **public** and other keywords used for protecting types and members. The following keywords can be used to restrict or permit access to types and members:

- public
- private
- protected
- internal

These keywords are referred to as *access modifiers* because they are used to modify the declarations. For example:

```
public int MyMethod()
```

 Note   The set of access modifiers is a subset of the C# modifiers, which are used for different purposes.

Access modifiers are used to create five access levels, which are explained in the following table.

Table 5-1: Access levels

Access Level	Description
public	Used with types and members. Access is not restricted.
private	Used with members. Access is permitted only through member methods of the same class.
protected	Used with members. Access is permitted through member methods of the same class or a derived class.
internal	Used with types and members. Access is permitted through methods in the same assembly.
protected internal	Used with members. Access is permitted through member methods of the class or a derived class, in addition to the methods in the same assembly.

The following table shows the default access levels and the allowed access levels to use with different type members. (More on types in Chapters 7 and 8.)

Table 5-2: Access levels of type members

Member Of	Default Access Level	Allowed Access Levels
enum	public	n/a
class	private	public
		protected
		internal
		private
		protected internal
interface	public	n/a
struct	private	public
		internal
		private

 Notes:
- There are no access levels for namespaces.
- For classes nested inside other classes, the default access level is internal. The allowed access levels are public or internal.

In the following example, the **Point** class is used to demonstrate access levels.

Example 5-4

```
// Example 5-4.cs
// Access Levels

using System;

class OuterClass
```

```
{
    // The private access level is permitted only for
    // classes inside other classes:
    private class Point
    {
        // The public access level on the fields
        // makes them accessible from other classes:
        public int x;
        public int y;
    }

    class MainClass
    {
        static void Main()
        {
            Point p1 = new Point();
            p1.x = 33;
            p1.y = 22;
            Console.WriteLine("x = {0}, y = {1}", p1.x, p1.y);
        }
    }
}
```

Output:

```
x = 33, y = 22
```

There are several parts of this example worth discussing:

- The example contains three classes: **Point**, **MainClass**, and the containing class, **OuterClass**. The **Main** method is placed inside a class other than the **Point** class in order to test the effect of the access levels. Note that you could not access the fields of the **Point** class if they did not have the **public** modifier. To test that, change the **public** modifier to **private** or **protected** and see the error message from the compiler.

- The containing class, **OuterClass**, is used as a container to the other classes so that we can give the **Point** class the **private** access level (see Table 5-2). If you remove the outer class, the compiler will complain about using the word **private**. The access level of the outer class has no effect on the program though.

Drill 5-1

Try changing the access level of the classes and members in Example 5-4 and check the results.

5-4 Properties

The easiest way to protect the fields of a class is to use properties. The properties are in fact methods like other member functions, but they facilitate the access of the private fields by the client. The client can use the properties in the same way it uses fields. The traditional method that is used in C++ is to dedicate some functions for accessing the private fields. For example:

```
set_MyPoint_x();    // C++
get_MyPoint_x();    // C++
```

The job of the first function is to assign a value to the field x, and the job of the second function is to read the value of that field. The C# properties are used like the following example:

```
private string item;
public string Item
{
    get
    {
        return item;
    }
    set
    {
        item = value;
    }
}
```

The field "item" is declared private, and the property "Item" is declared public. (This naming system is not mandatory but is a common convention.) A property contains the method **get** to read the field and the method **set** to assign a value to the field. The methods **get** and **set** are called *accessors*. They are classified as *contextual keywords*, which are words that have special meaning when used with properties or indexers.

Notice the use of the **return** keyword in the get accessor. Notice also the use of another contextual keyword, **value**, which is used to change the value of the field. The following example shows how to use the property to read or write a field name:

```
Item = "C# book";          // using the set method
Console.Write(Item);       // using the get method
```

As you can see in the first example, using the set accessor means assigning a value to the property. (The contextual keyword **value** is never used explicitly.). In the second example, the get accessor is also used implicitly for retrieving the property value (reading it).

Note Although keywords are reserved words, contextual keywords are not. You cannot use a keyword as an identifier without prefixing it with the @ symbol, but contextual keywords can be used as identifiers.

Unless you need to write additional code in the set accessor, you can deviate from the common coding convention by writing the property like this:

```
public string Item
{
    get { return item; }
    set { item = value; }
}
```

5-4-1 Using Properties

Properties expose a convenient public way for reading and setting field values instead of dealing directly with the fields. One advantage of using properties as opposed to using fields directly is that you can validate the data before changing the value of the field. For example, if the field contains a specific date, you can check to see if the value to be assigned to the field is within a specific range.

In the following example, the valid value for the field called number should be within the range 100 to 1000. If you try to assign a value less than 100 or greater than 1000, it won't be accepted and you will get a message from the set accessor telling you about the error. Regardless of whether or not the entered value is accepted, the program displays the current value of the field.

Example 5-5

```
// Example 5-5.cs
// Using properties

using System;

class MyClass
{
    private int number = 144;
    public int Number
    {
        get { return number; }
        set
        {
            if ((value >= 100) && (value <= 1000))
                number = value;
```

```
            else
                Console.WriteLine(
                    "The value is not within the permitted range");
        }
    }

    static void Main()
    {
        // Create an object:
        MyClass mc = new MyClass();

        // Read a value from the keyboard:
        Console.Write("Please enter the new value: ");
        int myInt = Int32.Parse(Console.ReadLine());

        // Assign the value to the property:
        mc.Number = myInt;

        // Display the value:
        Console.WriteLine("The current value is: {0}", mc.Number);
    }
}
```

Sample Run 1:

```
Please enter the new value: 10
The value is not within the permitted range
The current value is: 144
```

Sample Run 2:

```
Please enter the new value: 199
The current value is: 199
```

5-4-2 Read-only Properties

Sometimes you need to protect the fields from any change by the user. For example, a field containing the company name should not be changed. In such cases, you omit the set accessor and keep the get accessor to read the field. This kind of property is called a *read-only property*, while the regular property is called a *read-write property*.

In the following example, both property kinds are used. The person's name is a read-write property, while the company name is a read-only property.

Example 5-6

```csharp
// Example 5-6.cs
// Read-only properties

using System;

public class Employee
{
   // Private fields:
   private string companyName = "Microsoft";
   private string employeeName;

   // EmployeeName - read-write property:
   public string EmployeeName
   {
      get { return employeeName; }
      set { employeeName = value; }
   }

   // CompanyName - read-only property:
   public string CompanyName
   {
      get { return companyName; }
   }
}

public class MainClass
{
   public static void Main()
   {
      Employee emp = new Employee();
      // Assign to the read-write property:
      emp.EmployeeName = "Hazem Abolrous";

      // Read both properties:
      Console.WriteLine("Company Name: {0}", emp.CompanyName);
      Console.WriteLine("Employee name: {0}", emp.EmployeeName);
   }
}
```

Output:

```
Company Name: Microsoft
Employee name: Hazem Abolrous
```

5-4-3 Accessor Accessibility

In C# 2002, the two accessors, set and get, have the same accessibility as the property they act upon. In C# 2005, each accessor can have its own access level. This way, you can restrict the accessibility of the set accessor while keeping the get accessor public. In this case, the value of the property can only be changed by the class designer.

The following example shows a property with public get and protected set.

```
public string EmployeeName
{
    get { return employeeName; }
    protected set { employeeName = value; }
}
```

There are, however, some restrictions when using this feature:

- Access modifiers are allowed only on one of the accessors — usually it is the set accessor.
- If you use one accessor only (as in the read-only property), you cannot use an access modifier on the accessor. Of course in this case, the accessor accessibility is the same as that of the property.
- On interfaces (explained in Chapter 8), no access modifiers are allowed on accessors.
- The accessibility of the accessor must be more restrictive than the accessibility of the property itself.

5-5 Static Members and Static Classes

Assume you are building a class that represents a group of employees working for a company as shown in Example 5-6. The employees' names change with each instance of the class, while the company name stays the same. In other words, the employee name belongs to the corresponding employee object, while the company name belongs to the class. In this case you can modify the declaration of the company name with the modifier **static**, which qualifies it to belong to the class rather than a specific object. Here is the new declaration:

```
private static string companyName = "Microsoft";
private string name;
```

When you use a static field, you associate it with the class name rather than a particular object:

```
Console.WriteLine("Company Name: {0}", Employee.CompanyName);
```

This leads to classifying the class members into two categories:

- Instance members
- Static members

This classification applies to methods and fields.

In the following example, the class **Employee** is modified to include the company name and the property associated with it as static members.

Example 5-7

```
// Example 5-7.cs
// Static properties example.

using System;

public class Employee
{
    // Declare the private fields:
    private static string companyName = "T-Mobile";
    private string name;

    // The Name property--read-write:
    public string Name
    {
        get {return name;}
        set {name = value;}
    }

    // The company name property--read-only:
    public static string CompanyName
    {
        get {return companyName;}
        private set
        {
            companyName = value;
        }
    }
}

public class MainClass
{
    public static void Main()
```

```
    {
        Employee emp = new Employee();
        emp.Name = "Sally Abolrous";
        Console.WriteLine("Company Name: {0}", Employee.CompanyName);
        Console.WriteLine("Employee name: {0}", emp.Name);
    }
}
```

Output:

```
Company Name: T-Mobile
Employee name: Sally Abolrous
```

Examples of static members that we used earlier in this book are the methods of the **Math** class, such as **Math.Tan** and **Math.Round**. We also used static fields such as Math.PI. These members are always associated with the class name. All the members of the **Math** class are static members. In fact, the **Math** class itself is a *static class*. A static class is a class whose members are all static and is declared using the modifier **static**. Static classes cannot be instantiated or inherited.

5-6 Constants

A constant is a name that represents a constant value. The modifier **const** is used to declare a constant field or local variable whose value cannot be changed after declaration. For example, the value of the PI constant we used earlier cannot be changed and we never need to change it. Here is an example of a class that uses constant fields:

```
class MyClass
{
    public const int field1 = 3, field2 = 10;
}
```

Notice that the constant fields in this declaration are initialized as declared. This is a requirement for declaring constants. The same applies for the constant local variables. If you used constants as in the following examples:

```
const double myDoubleConst = 3.1;
const int myIntConst = 25;
```

you cannot later change their value with other statements such as:

```
int x = ++myIntConst;    // error
myIntConst = 26;         // error
```

You can use a constant to build other constants, like this example:

```
const string language = "C#";
const string productName =  language + " "+ "2005";
```

Here the value of the productName constant is "C# 2005."

When you declare variables that represent conversion ratios in your programs, it is best to declare them using the modifier **const**. In the following program, the conversion ratio convRatio is used to convert kilometers to miles.

Example 5-8

```
// Example 5-8.cs
// const example

using System;

public class TestClass
{
    public static void Main()
    {
        const double convRatio = 0.6211;  // Kilos to miles
        double miles = 10;
        double kilos = miles/convRatio;

        Console.WriteLine("{0} Mile(s) = {1:F2} Km", miles, kilos);
    }
}
```

Output:

```
10 Mile(s) = 16.10 Km
```

5-7 Constructors

A class can contain one or more methods to build and initialize objects. These methods are called *constructors*. Constructors are divided into three categories:

- Instance constructors
- Private constructors
- Static constructors

These constructors are explained in the following sections.

5-7-1 Instance Constructors

Instance constructors are the most common and sometimes referred to as just constructors. A constructor is named the same as the class. It is invoked when you create a new object. For example:

```
Point myPoint = new Point();
```

The class might also contain a constructor with parameters, such as:

```
Point myPoint = new Point(int x, int y);
```

As you might have noticed in the previous examples, if the class doesn't contain a constructor, the default constructor is invoked. The default constructor is a parameterless constructor such as **Point()**. This constructor initializes the created object with default parameters — zero in case of integer fields.

Example 5-9

```
// Example 5-9.cs
// Constructor example

using System;

class Point
{
    public int x, y;

    // Default constructor:
    public Point()
    {
        x = 0;
        y = 0;
    }

    // A constructor with parameters
    public Point(int x1, int y1)
    {
        x = x1;
        y = y1;
    }
}

class MyClass
{
    static void Main()
```

```
    {
        Point p1 = new Point();
        Point p2 = new Point(2, 10);

        Console.WriteLine("First Point at: ({0}, {1})", p1.x, p1.y);
        Console.WriteLine("Second Point at: ({0}, {1})", p2.x, p2.y);
    }
}
```

Output:

```
First Point at: (0, 0)
Second Point at: (2, 10)
```

5-7-1-1 Declaring Constructors

Although the default parameterless constructor is automatically created by the compiler, you cannot declare one constructor with parameters without declaring the parameterless constructor. The compiler provides the default constructor only if the class does not have any constructors. In other words, in order to use the statement:

```
Point p1 = new Point();
```

you must declare a parameterless constructor.

5-7-1-2 Using this

As in C++, in C# the **this** keyword is used to access data members in instance constructors (methods or accessors). For example, you can declare the constructor in the preceding example like this:

```
public Point(int x, int y)
{
    this.x = x;
    this.y = y;
}
```

In this case, you can use the same names for both fields and parameters (x and y). This is because the expression "this.x" represents the field "x" of the current object, while "x" is the method parameter. It is obvious that the keyword **this** cannot be used with static constructors or fields.

Note   In C++, the this keyword is classified as a pointer, but in C#, it is called "this-access." The word "pointer" is used only in unsafe code.

5-7-2 Private Constructors

Private constructors are used with classes that contain only static members. Other classes, except those nested in the same class, are not allowed to create instances of that class. Consider the following example:

```
public class MyClass
{
    private MyClass() {}    // private constructor
    public string companyName;
    public string employmentDate;
}
```

In this example, the private constructor is an empty constructor whose job is to prevent the generation of a default constructor for the class. Notice that the private constructor uses the access modifier **private**, which is a common convention but not necessary because the default access level is private. It is recommended to declare the class as a static class when its members are all static.

Drill 5-2

Use the preceding code segment in a program and try the following statement, then observe the compilation result:

```
MyClass mc = new MyClass();
```

5-7-3 Static Constructors

A static constructor is used to initialize a class. It is called before any objects are created and before any call to any static member of the class.

In the following example, the static constructor MyClass contains two printing statements. There is also a method, MyMethod, that contains another printing statement. Notice that when MyMethod is called, the static constructor is automatically invoked.

Example 5-10

```
// Example 5-10.cs
// Static constructor example

using System;

class MyClass
{
    // Static constructor:
```

```
   static MyClass()
   {
      Console.WriteLine("Hey, I am the static constructor! " +
                        "I am called automatically!");
   }

   public void MyMethod()
   {
      Console.WriteLine("Hi, I am MyMethod. I was called after " +
                        "the static constructor had been invoked!");
   }
}

class MainClass
{
   static void Main()
   {
      MyClass myObject = new MyClass();
      myObject.MyMethod();
   }
}
```

Output:

```
Hey, I am the static constructor! I am called automatically!
Hi, I am MyMethod. I was called after the static constructor had
been invoked!
```

➲ **Note** In Chapter 14, you are going to learn about object initializers that let you save the time and effort of writing redundant code to declare constructors that do the same job. For example, if you have a class called Point with two properties, X and Y, that are used to set the coordinates x and y, you can declare and initialize its objects like these examples:

```
Point p = new Point { X = 10, Y = 20 };
```

OR

```
var p = new Point { X = 10, Y = 20 };
```

5-8 Read-only Fields

The **readonly** keyword is used to declare read-only fields. There are only two ways to assign values to read-only fields. The first way is to assign the value in the declaration statement, as in this example:

```
public readonly int readOnlyInt1 = 55;
```

The second is to use a constructor, as in this example:

```
public MyClass()
{
    readOnlyInt1 = 66;
}
```

The following example demonstrates the read-only fields.

Example 5-11

```
// Example 5-11.cs
// readonly example

using System;

class MyClass
{
    public int myRegularInt;
    public readonly int readOnlyInt1 = 55;
    public readonly int readOnlyInt2;

    public MyClass()
    {
        readOnlyInt2 = 66;
    }

    public MyClass(int l, int m, int n)
    {
        myRegularInt = l;
        readOnlyInt1 = m;
        readOnlyInt2 = n;
    }
}
class MainClass
{
    static void Main()
    {
        MyClass obj1 = new MyClass(11, 22, 33);   // OK
        Console.WriteLine("obj1 fields are: {0}, {1}, {2}" ,
        obj1.myRegularInt, obj1.readOnlyInt1, obj1.readOnlyInt2);

        MyClass obj2 = new MyClass();
        obj2.myRegularInt = 44;   // OK
        Console.WriteLine("obj2 fields are: {0}, {1}, {2}" ,
        obj2.myRegularInt, obj2.readOnlyInt1, obj2.readOnlyInt2);
    }
}
```

Output:

```
obj1 fields are: 11, 22, 33
obj2 fields are: 44, 55, 66
```

Notice in this example that you cannot change the value of the read-only field in the **Main** method by using a statement like this:

```
obj1.readOnlyInt1 = 55;    // error
```

 Note The difference between a read-only field and a constant field is that you can change the value of the first by using the allowed ways mentioned above. The constant fields, however, cannot be changed after declaration.

5-9 **Inheritance**

It is possible for a class to inherit another class as in the following example:

```
class MyDerivedClass: MyBaseClass
{
    // ...
}
```

In this example, you declared the class MyDerivedClass, which inherits the class MyBaseClass. In the declaration, the colon (:) is used between the name of the *derived* class and the name of the *base* class. Inheritance means that the derived class contains all the members of the base class. You can also add new members to the inherited members. For example, the **Employee** class inherits all the characteristics of the **Person** class and adds to them the characteristics of an Employee.

The following rules control inheritance:

1. All members of the base class are inherited (except instance constructors, destructors, and static constructors).

2. If you declare a member in the derived class with the same name as that in the base class, it hides the member in the base class. In that case, the member of the base class is not accessible through the derived class.

3. Function members in the base class can be overridden by those in the derived class, making it possible to exhibit polymorphism. (Polymorphism is explained in Chapter 6.)

4. In C#, unlike C++, a class can inherit from *one class only*. However, it can implement more than one interface. When a class implements

an interface, it "inherits" its members. (Interfaces are explained in Chapter 8.)

5. Structs cannot inherit from classes or other structs, but they can implement interfaces. They also cannot be inherited.

Note Sometimes the expressions *specialization* and *generalization* are used to express inheritance. For example, the Cow class specializes the Mammal class, and the Mammal class generalizes the Cow class. The base class is also referred to as the *superclass* or *parent* class, and the derived class is referred to as the *subclass* or *child* class.

In the following example, the class Employee, which inherits from the class Citizen, is demonstrated.

Example 5-12

```
// Example 5-12.cs
// Inheritance example

using System;

class Citizen
{
    string idNumber = "111-2345-H";
    string name = "Pille Mandla";

    public void GetPersonalInfo()
    {
        Console.WriteLine("Name: {0}", name);
        Console.WriteLine("ID Card Number: {0}", idNumber);
    }
}
class Employee: Citizen
{
    string companyName = "Technology Group Inc.";
    string companyID = "ENG-RES-101-C";

    public void GetInfo()
    {
        // Calling the base class GetPersonalInfo method:
        Console.WriteLine("Citizen's Information:");

        GetPersonalInfo();

        Console.WriteLine("\nJob Information:");
        Console.WriteLine("Company Name: {0}", companyName);
        Console.WriteLine("Company ID: {0}", companyID);
    }
```

```
    }

class MainClass {
   public static void Main()
   {
      Employee E = new Employee();
      E.GetInfo();
   }
}
```

Output:

```
Citizen's Information:
Name: Pille Mandla
ID Card Number: 111-2345-H

Job Information:
Company Name: Technology Group Inc.
Company ID: ENG-RES-101-C
```

Notice in this example that all the member methods have the access level public. This is necessary for accessing the class fields.

5-10 Destructors

Destructors are used to destruct objects. A destructor is declared as shown in this example:

```
~MyClass()
{
   // Destruction statements.
}
```

The destructor of a class uses the same name as the class but is preceded with the tilde (~) character. You cannot, however, call a destructor as it is called automatically when the object finishes its work and goes out of scope. In case of inheritance, the destruction starts with the children and goes up in the inheritance tree.

The following example shows how destructors are called to destruct objects in the order of their position in the inheritance hierarchy.

Example 5-13

```
// Example 5-13.cs
// Destructor example

using System;
```

```
class Parent            // parents
{
   ~Parent()
   {
      Console.WriteLine("Calling the Parent destructor.");
   }
}

class Kid: Parent       // kids
{
   ~Kid()
   {
      Console.WriteLine("Calling the Kid destructor.");
   }
}

class GrandKid: Kid     // grandkids
{
   ~GrandKid()
   {
      Console.WriteLine("Calling the Grandkid destructor.");
   }
}

public class MyClass
{
   public static void Main()
   {
      GrandKid myObject = new GrandKid();
   }
}
```

Output:

```
Calling the Grandkid destructor.
Calling the Kid destructor.
Calling the Parent destructor.
```

Notice in this example that the grandkid was destructed first, then the kid, and finally the parent.

Although destructors play an important role in C++ (as you use them to deallocate memory that was allocated for the pointers), in C# you don't need to use them because the garbage collector does that task for you automatically when the objects finish their work and are no longer in use.

In C#, you can still use destructors to clear unmanaged resources such as files and network connections. This topic, however, will not be discussed here as it is beyond the level of this book. For more information on that, read about the **Dispose** method on the Microsoft web site: http://msdn.microsoft.com.

 Note You can force the garbage collector to start the cleaning process by using the .NET GC.Collect method, but this is not recommended as it might cause undesirable results.

5-11 Partial Classes

Partial classes were added to C# 2005 to facilitate breaking a type (class, struct, or interface) into more than one section and each in a separate file. This is useful when writing large projects or using machine-generated code. This feature also helps developer teams to collaborate on the same application.

To declare a partial class, all sections of the class must use the modifier **partial** right before the word **class**. Other modifiers can precede the keyword **partial**. The following example declares a class called **TimeSheet** divided into two files:

```
// File1.cs
public partial class TimeSheet
{
    public void AddWorkingHours()
    {
        // ...
    }
    public void CalculateSalary()
    {
        // ...
    }
}

// File2.cs
public partial class TimeSheet
{
    public void SubtractVacationTime()
    {
        // ...
    }
}
```

On compilation, all sections of the class are put together to create the class. All the sections of course must be included in the same namespace, but cannot span assemblies.

The following rules and restrictions control the use of partial classes:

1. All partial classes that constitute one class must use the same accessibility level.
2. If one part of the class is declared using the modifiers **abstract** or **sealed**, the modifier will apply to the whole class.
3. If one partial class is derived from a base class, all the other partial classes will inherit this base class even if it is not mentioned in their declarations. This means that if you have two partial classes, as in this example:

```
partial class  Employee: Person
{
   // ...
}
partial class Employee: Citizen
{
   // ...
}
```

the class Employee would effectively be:

```
class Employee: Person, Citizen
{
   // ...
}
```

4. What applies to inheritance from classes applies to implementing interfaces.

The following example consists of two files — file1.cs and file2.cs — that contain a definition of the Employee class. Each file contains part of the class declared as partial. To compile the program, use the following command:

```
csc/out:Ex5-14.exe file1.cs file2.cs
```

This combines the two files, file1.cs and file2.cs, and generates an executable file named Ex5-14.exe.

Example 5-14, file1.cs

```
// Example 5-14.cs
// file1.cs

public partial class Employee
{
   private string name;
   private string id;
```

```
   public string Name
   {
      get { return name; }
      set { name = value; }
   }

   public string Id
   {
      get { return id; }
      set { id = value; }
   }
}
```

Example 5-14, file2.cs

```
// Example 5-14.cs
// file2.cs

using System;

public partial class Employee
{
   public void DisplayInfo()
   {
      Console.WriteLine("Employee's name: {0}", name);
      Console.WriteLine("Employee's id: {0}", id);
   }
}

class MyClass
{
   static void Main(string[] args)
   {
      // Create object:
      Employee emp = new Employee();

      // Read name and id:
      Console.Write("Please enter the employee's name: ");
      emp.Name = Console.ReadLine();
      Console.Write("Please enter the employee's id: ");
      emp.Id = Console.ReadLine();
      // Display information:
      emp.DisplayInfo();
   }
}
```

Sample Run:

```
Please enter the employee's name: Craig Combel
Please enter the employee's id: XYZ-cTQ
Employee's name: Craig Combel
Employee's id: XYZ-cTQ
```

Drill 5-3

Make the necessary changes to Example 5-14 to make the Employee class a subclass of the Citizen class. Display some properties from the Citizen class, such as the SSN and Age. The output should look something like:

```
Citizen's Information:
SSN: 555-55-5555
Age: 36

Job Information:
Company Name: Pille Mandla
Company ID: 123-WxYz
```

Summary

In this chapter:

- You were introduced to the details of classes. You learned how to initialize a class and how to instantiate it.
- You also learned about namespaces and their role in fully qualifying the names of the classes and their members.
- You saw how to use access modifiers and learned about the accessibility levels that can be used with types and members to provide the necessary protection to them.
- You used properties and learned about the read-only properties. You also learned about the new feature of accessor accessibility, and how to use it to control the accessibility of each successor separately.
- You learned about static members and static classes. You know now when to declare a member static and when to declare a class static.
- You now know the constant fields and local variables and the difference between the modifiers **const** and **readonly** and their use.
- You learned about constructors and that there are three types of constructors.

Summary

- You also learned about destructors and garbage collection in C#. You know now that you don't need to invoke destructors because the garbage collector does the cleaning up for you.
- You took a tour of inheritance and learned about its important role in reusing code and polymorphism.
- Finally, you had a tour of partial classes and you learned that you can split the code of a class into sections, with each section in a separate file.

Chapter 6

Function Members

Contents:
- *Defining function members*
- *Polymorphism*
- *Using abstract classes and methods*
- *Method overloading*
- *Passing parameters to methods*
- *Declaring and using indexers*
- *User-defined operators*
- *Overriding ToString()*

6-1 Function Members

All members of a class or a struct (except fields and constants) are classified as *function members*. If you are a C++ programmer you might compare this to member functions, which use the same concept.

Function members are:

- Methods
- Properties
- Events
- Indexers
- User-defined operators
- Constructors
- Destructors

You learned about some of these members earlier, in Chapters 1 through 5. The rest will be explained in the following chapters of this book.

6-2 Polymorphism

One important benefit of inheritance is code reusability. For example, if another programmer already created a class called **Person**, there is no need for you to rewrite the same class in order to create the **Employee** class or the **PoliceMan** class. Many characteristics of these classes are already included in the **Person** class. All you need to do is inherit the **Person** class and add to it the characteristics of **Employee** or **PoliceMan**. This will save you the effort of reinventing the wheel.

The second benefit of inheritance is polymorphism. In programming, you deal with many kinds of user interface windows in the Microsoft Windows environment, such as message boxes that convey a message or a warning and windows for painting or writing. If you wrote, for example, a method called **DrawWindow**, you can associate this method with various objects that represent different kinds of windows. Based on the object associated with the method, the result would be different. Consider these examples:

```
myButton.DrawWindow();        // draws a button
myMsg.DrawWindow();           // draws a message box
myPaintSurface.DrawWindow();  // draws a painting window
```

The three objects — myButton, myMsg, and myPaintSurface — are not instances of the same class, but instances of other classes derived from the base class that contains the original **DrawWindow** method. Each object is used to invoke a new definition of the method **DrawWindow**.

6-2-1 Virtual and Override Methods

To use the polymorphic methods introduced in the preceding section, declare the DrawWindow method with the keyword **virtual** in the base class:

```
public virtual void DrawWindow()
{
    // The method definition in the base class.
}
```

Then, in each of the classes that inherit the base class, declare a DrawWindow method using the keyword **override**:

```
public override void DrawWindow()
{
    // The method definition in one of the derived classes.
}
```

The method declared with the keyword **override** is called an override method. It can override another method that has the same name, signature, and accessibility in the base class. When you override a method, you can change its original behavior in the derived class. An override method can override any of the methods declared with the following modifiers:

- virtual
- abstract
- override

When a virtual method in a derived class has the same name, accessibility, and signature as that of another method in the base class but is not qualified with the **override** modifier, it simply *hides* the method of the base class. (More on hiding members of the base class in Chapter 8.) To make the method override the one in the base class, you must modify its declaration with the keyword **override**. An abstract method is implicitly a virtual method, and therefore, it can be overridden without using the **virtual** modifier (since it can't use the **virtual** modifier anyway).

 Note You cannot use the virtual modifier with the following modifiers: static, abstract, or override.

You cannot combine the override modifier with the following modifiers: static, abstract, virtual, or new.

6-2-2 Calling Members of the Base Class

Sometimes when you inherit a class, the methods in the derived class can override methods in the base class. What if you wanted to call one of the overridden methods from within the derived class? The keyword **base** is the solution to this problem. To call an overridden method, such as GetInformation, you can call it by using this statement:

```
base.GetInformation();
```

This statement calls the original GetInformation method, which was overridden by a method with a similar name in the derived class.

 Note You cannot use the keyword base inside a static method.

In other cases, you need to build the object of the base class before you build the object of the derived class. You can also do that using the **base** keyword like the following example:

```
public MyDerived(int x) : base(x)
{
    // ...
}
```

This is the constructor of the class MyDerived, which builds the base class object on the fly. You need to do this in cases when constructing the base class is necessary to construct the derived class. For example, let's say the base class represents the area of a circle, and the derived class represents an area of a sphere (which uses the area of a circle). In this case, you must instantiate the area of the circle before you can instantiate the area of the sphere (see Example 6-1).

Note for C++ programmers: Notice that this way of building the base class is equivalent to the initialization list in C++.

6-2-3 Overriding Virtual Methods on the Base Class

In this section, we will use an example that demonstrates calculating the areas of different shapes. The example includes inheritance and overriding the virtual methods on the base class. The class contains two dimensions, x and y, and a virtual method to calculate the area:

```
public virtual double Area()
{
    return 0;
}
```

The returned value (zero) doesn't mean much now because other methods will override this method and change its behavior.

Several classes will inherit this class, such as the **Point**, **Circle**, **Sphere**, and **Cylinder** classes. The common factor among all these classes is the x and y dimensions. The dimension x might represent a side of a square or a radius of a circle or a sphere. The dimension y could be the length of a rectangle or the height of a cylinder. Inheriting these dimensions will certainly facilitate creating the derived classes. Each of the derived classes contains a method that has the same name: **Area**.

This is the **Area** method of the **Circle** class:

```
public override double Area()
{
    return Math.PI * x * x;
}
```

This is the **Area** method of the **Sphere** class:

```
public override double Area()
{
    return 4 * Math.PI * x * x;
}
```

This is the **Area** method of the **Cylinder** class:

```
public override double Area()
{
    return 2 * Math.PI * x * x + 2 * Math.PI * x * y;
}
```

All these methods use the modifier **override**, which enables them to override the **Area** method in the base class. The area of the point is, of course, zero. It will use the value returned by the base class.

When you create these classes, it is important to build the base class when you build the derived class. For example:

```
public Cylinder(double r, double h): base(r, h)
{
}
```

In this constructor, the **base** keyword is used to call the base class constructor before building the cylinder object. The reason for that is to pass the parameters h and r to the corresponding fields in the base class. Here is the complete example:

Example 6-1

```
// Example 6-1.cs
// virtual Example

using System;

// The base class:
public class AreasClass
{
    // Fields:
    protected double x, y;

    // Constructors:
    public AreasClass()
    {
    }
    public AreasClass(double x, double y)
    {
        this.x = x;
        this.y = y;
```

```
   }

   // Methods:
   public virtual double Area()
   {
      return 0;
   }
}

// The Point class uses a parameterless constructor:
class Point: AreasClass
{
   public Point(): base()
   {
   }
}

// The Circle class:
class Circle: AreasClass
{
   public Circle(double r): base(r, 0)
   {
   }
   public override double Area()
   {
      // The area of a circle.
      // The radius is represented by x:
      return Math.PI * x * x;
   }
}

// The Sphere class:
class Sphere: AreasClass
{
   public Sphere(double r): base(r, 0)
   {
   }
   public override double Area()
   {
      // The radius is represented by x:
      return 4 * Math.PI * x * x;
   }
}

// The Cylinder class:
class Cylinder: AreasClass
{
   public Cylinder(double r, double h): base(r, h)
   {
```

```
        }
    public override double Area()
    {
        // The radius is represented by x and
        // the height is represented by y:
        return 2 * Math.PI * x * x + 2 * Math.PI * x * y;
    }
}

class MyClass
{
    public static void Main()
    {
        // Receive numbers from the keyboard:
        Console.Write("Please enter the radius: ");
        double radius = Convert.ToDouble(Console.ReadLine());
        Console.Write("Please enter the height: ");
        double height = Convert.ToDouble(Console.ReadLine());

        // Create objects:
        Point myPoint = new Point();
        Circle myCircle = new Circle(radius);
        Sphere myShpere = new Sphere(radius);
        Cylinder myCylinder = new Cylinder(radius,height);

        // Display results:
        Console.WriteLine("Area of your point    = {0:F2}",
                    myPoint.Area());
        Console.WriteLine("Area of your circle   = {0:F2}",
                    myCircle.Area());
        Console.WriteLine("Area of your sphere   = {0:F2}",
                    myShpere.Area());
        Console.WriteLine("Area of your cylinder = {0:F2}",
                    myCylinder.Area());
    }
}
```

When you run this program you will be asked to enter two numbers that represent the radius and the height. It will then display the corresponding areas of the circle, sphere, and cylinder.

Sample Run:

```
Please enter the radius: 4      → input
Please enter the height: 6      → input
Area of your point    = 0.00
Area of your circle   = 50.27
Area of your sphere   = 201.06
Area of your cylinder = 251.33
```

Drill 6-1

Modify Example 5-12 to make use of the virtual and override methods. Instead of using two methods, GetPersonalInfo and GetInfo, use only one virtual method, GetInformation, to display the same output.

6-3 Abstract Classes and Methods

The purpose of an abstract class is to be inherited by other classes. It cannot be instantiated. The abstract method is, by default, a virtual method. It can exist only inside an abstract class.

Declare abstract classes or abstract methods using the **abstract** keyword as in this example:

```
abstract class MyBaseClass          // abstract class
{
    public abstract void MyMethod();  // abstract method
    ...
}
```

The abstract class might contain abstract methods and properties. When an abstract class is inherited, the derived class must implement all of its methods and properties. As you can see in the code segment above, the abstract method doesn't contain any implementation. The implementation goes inside the overriding methods of the derived classes.

The following keywords are not allowed in the abstract method declaration:

- static
- virtual

➲ **Note for C++ programmers:** The abstract method is equivalent to the pure virtual function in C++.

Abstract properties are similar to abstract methods except in the way they are declared. The following example demonstrates abstract classes, methods, and properties.

Example 6-2

```
// Example 6-2.cs
// Abstract classes, methods, and properties

using System;

// Abstract class:
abstract class MyBaseClass
{
  // Fields:
  protected int number = 100;
  protected string name = "Dale Sanders";

  // Abstract method:
  public abstract void MyMethod();

  // Abstract properties:
  public abstract int Number
  { get; }
  public abstract string Name
  { get; }
}

// Inheriting the class:
class MyDerivedClass: MyBaseClass
{
  // Overriding properties:
  public override int Number
  {
    get { return number; }
  }
  public override string Name
  {
    get { return name; }
  }

  // Overriding the method:
  public override void MyMethod()
  {
    Console.WriteLine("Number = {0}", Number);
    Console.WriteLine("Name = {0}", Name);
  }
}

class MainClass
```

```
{
    public static void Main()
    {
        MyDerivedClass myObject = new MyDerivedClass();
        myObject.MyMethod();
    }
}
```

Output:

```
Number = 100
Name = Dale Sanders
```

Drill 6-2

You now know that the override methods can override other override methods. That means that you can add another override method named MyMethod to a new class derived from MyDerivedClass. For example:

```
class MySecondDerivedClass: MyDerivedClass
{
    public override void MyMethod()
    {
        // Method implementation.
    }
}
```

Add this method to the preceding example with an appropriate implementation and then call it from within the Main class.

6-4 Method Overloading

Overloading methods means that you can give the same name to more than one method and let the compiler load the appropriate method according to the number and type of parameters. It might be suitable to use method overloading if the purposes of the methods are similar. For example, if you would like to create one method to return the square root of an integer and another to return the square root of a real number, you would use the same name for both methods:

```
int SquareIt(int x)
double SquareIt(double f)
```

Then if you use the following call:

```
SquareIt(3.25);
```

the compiler will invoke the method **SquareIt(double f)**, which uses a real parameter.

When you use the following call:

```
SquareIt(44);
```

the compiler will invoke the method **SquareIt(int x)**, which uses an integer parameter.

The return type does not have any effect on overloading. That means that methods might have similar names and return types, but the compiler can still differentiate between them as in the following example:

```
void SquareIt(int x)
void SquareIt(double f)
```

 Note The binding between the specific method and the call is done at compile time, before the program runs. This is called static or early binding, as opposed to dynamic or late binding used with virtual methods.

It is also possible to overload methods that use the same type but a different number of parameters. For example:

```
void MyMethod(int m1) { }
void MyMethod(int m2, int m3) { }
```

One important use of overloading is operator overloading to invent new uses for operators, as explained in Section 6-8.

In the following example, three methods use the name MyMethod, but each uses different parameters. The three methods are called from within the **Main** method and generate three different results.

Example 6-3

```
// Example 6-3.cs
// Overloading methods

using System;

class MyClass
{
    // Using a string parameter:
    static void MyMethod(string s1)
    {
        Console.WriteLine(s1);
    }
```

```
// Using an integer parameter:
static void MyMethod(int m1)
{
    Console.WriteLine(m1);
}

// Using a double parameter:
static void MyMethod(double d1)
{
    Console.WriteLine(d1);
}

static void Main()
{
    string s = "This is my string";
    int m = 134;
    double d = 122.67;

    MyMethod(s);
    MyMethod(m);
    MyMethod(d);
}
}
```

Output:

```
This is my string
134
122.67
```

Drill 6-3

Write a program to test the overloading of two methods that use different numbers of parameters of the same type.

6-5 Passing Parameters to Methods

When you pass a parameter to a method, it is important to know what is going on in the background in order to avoid unexpected results. For example, you may create a method to change the value of a variable, and then find out in the end that the change affected only the local variable and not the original value. One common example of this problem is swapping the values of two variables.

In C#, there are two ways to pass a parameter to a method: by value (which is the default) or by reference. Passing parameters by reference makes the changes to the variable values persist. To pass a parameter by reference, modify the parameter with the **ref** keyword.

The following example demonstrates swapping the values of two variables.

Example 6-4

```
// Example 6-4.cs
// Swap method example - successful trial

using System;

class MyClass
{

    static void Swap(ref int x, ref int y)
    {
        int temp = x;
        x = y;
        y = temp;
    }
    static void Main()
    {
        int x = 25;
        int y = 33;
        Console.WriteLine ("Before swapping: x={0}, y={1}", x, y);
        Swap(ref x, ref y);
        Console.WriteLine ("After swapping: x={0}, y={1}", x, y);
    }
}
```

Output:

```
Before swapping: x=25, y=33
After swapping: x=33, y=25
```

As you can see in the preceding example, the **Swap** method is using the **ref** keyword to modify the parameters in both the method header and the method call. This method did swap the two variables, as indicated in the output.

In the following example, take a look at how this function will behave if you pass the parameters by value — without the keyword **ref**.

Example 6-5

```
// Example 6-5.cs
// Swap method example - unsuccessful trial

using System;

class MyClass
{

    static void Swap(int x, int y)
    {
      int temp = x;
      x = y;
      y = temp;
      Console.WriteLine ("Values inside the method: x={0}, y={1}", x, y);
    }
    static void Main()
    {
      int x = 25;
      int y = 33;
      Console.WriteLine ("Before swapping: x={0}, y={1}", x, y);
      Swap(x, y);
      Console.WriteLine ("After swapping:  x={0}, y={1}", x, y);
    }
}
```

Output:

```
Before swapping: x=25, y=33
Value inside the method: x=33, y=25
After swapping:  x=25, y=33
```

As you can see in the output, the values of x and y did not change after invoking the **Swap** method. The change took place only inside the method, but when the method returned to the caller, the values were the same. Recall that in Example 6-4 we passed the memory addresses that contain the variables. That is why the **Swap** method succeeded.

Drill 6-4

Write a method to swap the values of two string variables, such as:

```
string s1 = "John";
string s2 = "Smith";
```

Then call the method from within the Main method. Compare the output you get with the following:

```
Before swapping: s1 = John, s2 = Smith
Inside the swap method: s1 = Smith, s2 = John
After swapping: s1 = Smith, s2 = John
```

6-6 Various Ways to Pass Parameters to Methods

There is more than one way to pass parameters to a method by reference. There are three parameter modifiers, each of which results in saving the changes of the variable values after the method returns to the caller. The three modifiers are:

- ref
- out
- params

The three modifiers, however, have different uses, as explained in the following sections.

6-6-1 Using ref

As you have seen in the preceding examples, the **ref** keyword is used to pass variables to a method and reflect back the changes that occurred on the original variables. When you use **ref** to pass a variable to a method, the variable must be initialized first; otherwise, you will get a compiler error. For example:

```
string myVariable = "This my string";    // initialize the variable
MyMethod(ref myVariable);                // invoke the method
```

When the method returns the variable, myVariable will retain the changes that occurred to it in MyMethod.

6-6-2 Using out

The **out** keyword does the same work as the **ref** keyword when used as a parameter modifier. It does not require initializing the variable before passing it to the method, but it does require initializing the variable in the method itself. For example, the method might look something like this:

```
void MyMethod(out string myVariable)
{
    myVariable = "This is my string";
}
```

In order to call this method, use the **out** keyword:

```
MyMethod(out myVariable);
```

The variable myVariable might not be initialized at all. It will be assigned the value "This is my string" when the method returns to the caller. Notice that the **out** keyword is used in both the method header and the call.

It is possible to use more than one parameter, as in this example:

```
void YourMethod(out int x, out int y, out int z)
{
    ...
}
```

This method is called in the same way:

```
YourMethod(out m, out n, out l);
```

 Note   It is not enough to have different parameter modifiers in order to overload a method. Methods must also be different in the type of parameters they use.

In the following example, the **out** keyword is used to pass an uninitialized array to the method MyMethod. When the method returns to **Main**, its elements are initialized.

Example 6-6

```
// Example 6-6.cs
// out Example

using System;

public class MyClass
{
    public static void MyMethod(out int[] myList)
```

```
    {
        myList = new int[] {1945, 1966, 1987, 1997};   // initialize the
                                                        //    array
    }

    public static void Main()
    {
        int[] myarray;              // declare an uninitialized array
        MyMethod(out myarray);      // pass it as a parameter

        // Display the array:
        for (int i = 0 ; i < myarray.Length ; i++)
        Console.Write("{0} ", myarray[i]);
    }
}
```

Output:

```
1945 1966 1987 1997
```

Notice in the example above that MyMethod was declared **static** in order to be called directly without the need to create an object.

Drill 6-5

Modify the preceding example to do the following:

- Use MyMethod without the static modifier.
- Use more than one integer parameter instead of the array.
- Add another method with the same name and the same number and type of parameters, but that uses the keyword ref instead of out. Test the method overloading after making this change — you might change the number of parameters if necessary.

6-6-3 **Using params**

The keyword **params** is used with arrays. It lets you pass any number of parameters to a method without the need to declare them in an array. This keyword is required only in the method declaration. For example, the method:

```
static void MyMethod(params object[] myObjArray)
```

can be called like this:

```
MyMethod(123, 'A', "My original string");
```

The parameters passed in this call are all of the type object, which means they can include any types descended from the object class.

Consider also the following method:

```
static void MyMethod(params int[] myIntArray)
```

This method can be called by passing a group of integers that constitute an integer array regardless of its length, for example:

```
MyMethod(2, 4, 7);
```

Any method that uses the **params** keyword cannot use more than one parameter.

In the following example, the use of the **params** keyword in the declaration of the method is demonstrated. It also demonstrates the overloading of two methods with the same name and different parameters. One method uses an object array and the second method uses an integer array. Both methods change the content of the array passed to it. The content of each array is displayed before and after the change takes place inside the method.

Example 6-7

```csharp
// Example 6-7.cs
// params and overloading example

using System;

public class MyClass
{
    // Declare MyMethod that uses integer parameters:
    public void MyMethod(params int[] myIntArray)
    {
        // Display the integer array before the change:
        Console.WriteLine("My original integer list:");
        for (int i = 0 ; i < myIntArray.Length; i++)
            Console.WriteLine(myIntArray[i]);
        Console.WriteLine();

        // Changing the second array element:
        myIntArray[1] = 555;

        // Display the integer array after the change:
        Console.WriteLine("My integer list after the change:");
        for (int i = 0 ; i < myIntArray.Length; i++)
            Console.WriteLine(myIntArray[i]);
        Console.WriteLine();
    }
```

```
        // Declare MyMethod that uses object parameters:
        public void MyMethod(params object[] myObjArray)
        {
            // Display the object array before the change:
            Console.WriteLine("My original object list:");
            for (int i = 0 ; i < myObjArray.Length; i++)
                Console.WriteLine(myObjArray[i]);
            Console.WriteLine();

            // Changing the third array element:
            myObjArray[2] = "My new string";

            // Display the results after the change:
            Console.WriteLine("My object list after the change:");
            for (int i = 0 ; i < myObjArray.Length; i++)
                Console.WriteLine(myObjArray[i]);
            Console.WriteLine();
        }
    }

    class MainClass
    {
        static void Main()
        {
            // Declare an object array:
            object[] myObjList = new object[] {123, 'A', "My old string"};

            MyClass mc = new MyClass();

            // Pass four integers to the "first" MyMethod:
            mc.MyMethod(11, 22, 33, 44);          // using numeric parameters

            // Pass an object array to "second" MyMethod:
            mc.MyMethod(myObjList);               // using an object array

        }
    }
```

Output:

```
My original integer list:
11
22
33
44
```

```
My integer list after the change:
11
555
33
44

My original object list:
123
A
My old string

My object list after the change:
123
A
My new string
```

Drill 6-6

Write a method that can receive parameters by using any of the following calls:

```
mc.MyMethod(11, 22, 33);
mc.MyMethod(45.33, 'A', "My string");
```

6-7 Indexers

Using indexers, you can treat classes as if they were arrays or *collections*; that is, you can access the indexer's elements by using square brackets ([]). An indexer is similar to properties in that it also uses the accessors get and set to express its characteristics.

The declaration of the indexer takes the form:

```
indexer-type this [parameter-type parameter]
{
    get {};
    set {};
}
```

where:

indexer-type is the type of the indexer.

parameter-type is the type of the parameter.

parameter is a parameter or a parameter list.

The keyword **this** points to the object to which the indexer belongs. Although the indexer doesn't have a name, it is recognized by its signature (types and number of parameters). It is possible to modify the indexer declaration with the keyword **new** or one of the access modifiers.

In the following example, you declare an array and an indexer of the type **string**. Then the indexer is used to access the elements of the object as if they were array elements.

Example 6-8

```
// Example 6-8.cs
// Indexer example

using System;

class MyClass
{
    private string[] myArray = new string[10];

    // Indexer declaration:
    public string this[int index]
    {
        get
        {
            return myArray[index];
        }
        set
        {
            myArray[index] = value;
        }
    }
}

public class MainClass
{
    public static void Main()
    {
        MyClass s = new MyClass();

        // Using the indexer to initialize the elements #1 and #2:
        s[1] = "Tom";
        s[2] = "Edison";

        for (int i=0; i<5; i++)
        {
            Console.WriteLine("Element #{0}={1}", i, s[i]);
        }
    }
}
```

Output:

```
Element #0=
Element #1=Tom
Element #2=Edison
Element #3=
Element #4=
```

Notes on using indexers:

- It is common to use the accessors set and get in inspecting the limits of the indexer to avoid errors. For example:

  ```
  if (!(index < 0 || index >= 10))
  // ...
  ```

- It is possible for interfaces to have indexers. They are declared in the same way with the following exceptions:

  - Interface indexers don't use modifiers.

  - There is no implementation of accessors in interfaces.

The following is an example of an interface indexer:

```
string this[int index]
{
    get;
    set;
}
```

6-8 User-defined Operators

By using overloading, you can invent new roles for some operators. The need for this feature arises when you deal with objects. In some cases, you might want to test the equality between two objects using the equality operator (==). In this case, you redefine the equality operator in your program to make it work with objects.

Operator overloading is accomplished by using the keyword **operator**, as shown in the following example:

```
public static Point operator+(Point p1, Point p2)
{
    // Implementation of the + operator:
}
```

This example overloads the + operator in order to use it in adding two objects of the type Point.

Adding two points means adding the x and y coordinates of each point. If the coordinates of the first point are (x1, y1) and the coordinates of the second point are (x2, y2), the result is a new point at the location (x1+x2, y1+y2). These details should be included in the implementation of overloading the operator +.

Notice in the syntax that the redefined + operator follows the keyword **operator**. Other examples are:

```
operator+
operator-
operator==
```

The method used for operator overloading is always static.

The following table lists the operators that can be overloaded. The operators that are classified as binary operate on two operands, such as + and *. The operators that are classified as unary operate on one operand, such as ++ and --.

Table 6-1: Overloadable C# operators

Operator	Note on Overloading
+, -, !, ~, ++, --, true, false	Unary operators
+, -, *, /, %, &, |, ^, <<, >>	Binary operators
==, !=, <, >, <=, >=	Must be overloaded in pairs, that is, to overload == you must overload !=. The same is true for (<, >) and (<=, >=).
&&, ||	Cannot be overloaded directly. They can be redefined by overloading & and |.
+=, -=, *=, /=, %=, &=, |=, ^=, <<=, >>=	The operator = cannot be overloaded. It can be redefined by overloading +=.

The following example overloads the + operator to add two points, p1 and p2, and displays the coordinates of the resulting point.

Example 6-9

```
// Example 6-9.cs
// Overloading operators

using System;

public class Point
{
    public int x;
    public int y;

    // Constructor:
    public Point(int x, int y)
    {
        this.x = x;
        this.y = y;
    }
```

```
// Overloading the + operator:
public static Point operator+(Point p1, Point p2)
{
    // Return the sum as a point:
    return new Point(p1.x + p2.x, p1.y + p2.y);
}

static void Main()
{
    Point p1 = new Point(15, 33);
    Point p2 = new Point(10, 12);

    // Add the two Point objects using the overloaded + operator:
    Point sum = p1 + p2;

    // Display the objects:
    Console.WriteLine("Point #1: ({0}, {1})", p1.x, p1.y);
    Console.WriteLine("Point #2: ({0}, {1})", p2.x, p2.y);
    Console.WriteLine("Sum of the two points: ({0}, {1})",
                      sum.x, sum.y);
}
}
```

Output:

```
Point #1: (15, 33)
Point #2: (10, 12)
Sum of the two points: (25, 45)
```

6-9 **Overriding the ToString Method**

The **ToString** method is one of the most important methods in the .NET
library as it always works in the background with the methods **Console.Write** or **Console.WriteLine**. It is used to convert an expression to a
string. As you know, you can use it explicitly like this:

```
Console.WriteLine(myVariable.ToString());
```

but if you omit the **ToString** method, which is always the case since it is
embedded, you still get the same result.

This method is an override method defined in the class **System.AppDomain** as follows:

```
public override string ToString();
```

In some cases you might need to override it to change its behavior, such as when you would like to display an object as if it were a regular variable. Instead of displaying a Point object like this (as in the example above):

```
Console.WriteLine("Point #1: ({0},{1})", p1.x, p1.y);
```

you can display it like this:

```
Console.WriteLine("Point #1: {0}", p1);
```

To do that, you must override the method **ToString** to be able to display objects of the type Point. Here is an example of the code to do this:

```
// Overriding the ToString method:
public override string ToString()
{
    return (String.Format("({0}, {1})", x, y));
}
```

In this code segment, the **String.Format** method replaces the format items, {0} and {1}, with the text equivalent to the value of the specified objects, x and y. Thus, the output of this method would be the values of the point (x, y). You can add this method to the preceding example and display the Point objects directly as single variables.

Drill 6-7

A complex number contains two parts, a real part and an imaginary part, such as 34 + 21i. When you add two complex numbers, you add the real parts and the imaginary parts separately. For example, adding 3+4i and 4+5i gives the result 7+9i.

The following method overloads the + operator to use it in adding complex numbers:

```
public static CompNum operator+(CompNum n1+CompNum n2)
{
    // Implementation of the operator
}
```

Write a complete program to implement this method and display the sum of two complex numbers in the proper format by overloading the ToString method.

Summary

In this chapter:

- You learned about function members of a class and learned more details about methods and properties.

- You also learned about polymorphism and how to accomplish it either by overriding the virtual methods in the base class or by overloading methods.

- You now understand the abstract classes, whose only role is to be inherited. You also understand the abstract methods, which exist only in the abstract classes.

- You had a complete tour of method parameters and learned how to pass them by using the keywords **ref**, **out**, and **params**.

- Using indexers, you learned how to treat classes as if they were arrays or collections.

- You also had a tour of user-defined operators and learned how to declare and implement methods to overload operators and redefine a new role for them.

- Finally, you learned how to override the **ToString** method to change its behavior.

Chapter 7

Structs, Enums, and Attributes

Contents:

- Declaring and using structs
- Passing structs and classes as parameters
- Declaring and using enums
- Using attributes
- Combining attributes
- Calling native functions
- Emulating unions

7-1 Structs vs. Classes

The word "struct," originally an abbreviation of structure, has become a part of the programming terminology. In C#, the **struct** is a user-defined value type. It might, however, contain members of both reference types and value types.

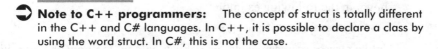

Note to C++ programmers: The concept of struct is totally different in the C++ and C# languages. In C++, it is possible to declare a class by using the word struct. In C#, this is not the case.

The struct is used to represent lightweight objects such as a point, which contains two fields (x and y). It can also represent a color, which contains three fields (red, blue, and green). Although we use the **Point** class in the examples, the struct is a more suitable type for such objects as it consumes a small amount of memory. You can see the difference if you create a large array of points represented as classes. In this case, the required memory would be huge because each point is using a reference that points to it.

7-2 Declaring and Using Structs

To declare a struct, use the **struct** keyword like this example:

```
struct MyStruct
{
    // The struct members
}
```

You can modify the declaration with any valid combination of access modifiers or the **new** keyword. When you use a struct, keep in mind the following points:

- Unlike classes, the fields of a struct *cannot be initialized*. That means that the following statements will generate error messages:

```
struct MyStruct
{
    int x = 0;   // error
    int y = 0;   // error
}
```

- A struct can use one or more constructors, but you cannot declare a default constructor (parameterless constructor) for a struct. Thus, the following constructor is invalid:

```
struct MyStruct
{
    MyStruct()     // error
    {
        //...
    }
}
```

The compiler always provides a default constructor to initialize the members of a struct to their default values.

- Like classes, you can use the **new** operator to create struct objects as shown in the following example:

```
MyStruct ms = new MyStruct();
```

Unlike classes, you can declare an object without the **new** operator, like this:

```
MyStruct ms;
```

In the latter case, you must initialize the struct fields before using it.

- As mentioned in the preceding chapters, a struct cannot be inherited or inherit from another type, but it can implement one or more interfaces. For example:

```
struct MyStruct: IMyInterface
{
    // ...
}
```

Although structs cannot inherit other types, the **struct** type itself descends from the **Object** class.

The following example demonstrates the **Color** struct, which contains three fields (r, g, and b) representing the three basic colors (red, green, and blue). The program uses a constructor to create two objects with different colors.

Example 7-1

```
// Example 7-1.cs
// struct example

using System;

public struct Color
{
    // Fields:
    private int r;
    private int g;
    private int b;

    // Constructor:
    public Color(int r, int g, int b)
    {
        this.r = r;
        this.g = g;
        this.b = b;
    }

    // Override the method ToString():
    public override string ToString()
    {
        return (String.Format("Red = {0}, Green = {1}, Blue = {2}",
                            r, g, b));
    }
}

class MyClass
{
    static void Main()
    {
        // Declare objects:
```

```
Color c1 = new Color();   // uses the default values
Color c2 = new Color(100, 100, 0);

// Display objects:
Console.WriteLine("The first object:");
Console.WriteLine("The colors are: {0}", c1);
Console.WriteLine("The second object:");
Console.WriteLine("The colors are: {0}", c2);
    }
}
```

Output:

```
The first object:
The colors are: Red = 0, Green = 0, Blue = 0
The second object:
The colors are: Red = 100, Green = 100, Blue = 0
```

In the above example, two struct instances, c1 and c2, were used. The first one uses a default constructor; therefore, all of its fields contain the value zero. The second instance is constructed using the parameters 100, 100, and 0. These values are assigned to the fields r, g, and b.

The objects are displayed directly by using the statement:

```
Console.WriteLine("The colors are: {0}", c1);
```

This requires overriding the **ToString** method to display objects in the appropriate format.

In the following example, the three properties **R**, **G**, and **B** are used to access the private fields r, g, and b. This makes it possible to access the fields directly through the properties, which is an alternative to using constructors.

Example 7-2

```
// Example 7-2.cs
// Using properties with structs

using System;

public struct Color
{
    // Fields:
    private int r;
    private int g;
    private int b;
```

```
    // Properties:
    public int R
    {
        get { return r; }

        set { r = value; }
    }

    public int G
    {
        get { return g; }

        set { g = value; }
    }

    public int B
    {
        get { return b; }

        set { b = value; }
    }

    // Override ToString():
    public override string ToString()
    {
        return (String.Format("Red = {0}, Green = {1}, Blue = {2}",
                              R, G, B));
    }
}

class MyClass
{
    static void Main()
    {
        Color c1 = new Color();
        Console.WriteLine("The colors are: {0}", c1);
        c1.R = 100;
        c1.G = 100;
        c1.B = 0;
        Console.WriteLine("The colors are: {0}", c1);
    }
}
```

Output:

```
The colors are: Red = 0, Green = 0, Blue = 0
The colors are: Red = 100, Green = 100, Blue = 0
```

Notice in the above example that we used one object created with the default constructor. Then we used the color properties to assign color values to the corresponding fields:

```
c1.R = 100;
c1.G = 100;
c1.B = 0;
```

The object was displayed twice — once with the default values and once after assigning the values to the properties. You can, of course, use a constructor with three parameters to achieve the same result.

Drill 7-1

It is obvious that you can include the entire program inside the struct container, as you did with classes. In that case, the members' accessibility will differ from the case when there is a container for the members and another for the Main method. Try to rewrite the previous example and put everything inside the struct. Also try to mix Examples 7-1 and 7-2 to include both the properties and the constructors in the struct.

7-3 Passing Structs and Classes to Methods

You learned in Chapter 6 that you can pass variables to methods either by value or by reference. You also learned that passing variables by reference reflects any changes that occur to them on their original values, while passing them by value results in modification of only their copies in the method, and the original variables stay the same. Structs, being value types, are created on the stack. When passed to methods, they are passed by value. Since classes are reference types, they are created on the heap. When passed to methods, they are passed by reference.

The following example demonstrates this concept. In the example, you declare a class called MyClass and a struct called MyStruct. Then you instantiate the class and the struct and initialize the field in each with the value 555. You pass both objects to the methods MyMethod1 and MyMethod2 to change their fields to 100. The output, however, indicates that the field of the class has changed but not that of the struct.

Example 7-3

```
// Example 7-3.cs
// Passing struct & class objects to methods

using System;

class MyClass
{
    public int classField;
}

struct MyStruct
{
    public int structField;
}

class MainClass
{
    public static void MyMethod1(MyStruct s)
    {
        s.structField = 100;
    }
    public static void MyMethod2(MyClass c)
    {
        c.classField = 100;
    }

    static void Main()
    {
        // Create class and struct objects:
        MyStruct sObj = new MyStruct();
        MyClass cObj = new MyClass();

        // Initialize the values of struct and class objects:
        sObj.structField = 555;
        cObj.classField = 555;

        // Display results:
        Console.WriteLine("Results before calling methods:");
        Console.WriteLine("Struct member = {0}", sObj.structField);
        Console.WriteLine("Class member = {0}\n", cObj.classField);

        // Change the values through methods:
        MyMethod1(sObj);
        MyMethod2(cObj);
```

```
    // Display results:
    Console.WriteLine("Results after calling methods:");
    Console.WriteLine("Struct member = {0}", sObj.structField);
    Console.WriteLine("Class member = {0}", cObj.classField);
  }
}
```

Output:

```
Results before calling methods:
Struct member = 555
Class member = 555

Results after calling methods:
Struct member = 555    → the same value
Class member = 100     → the value has changed
```

Drill 7-2

In the preceding example, change the field type in both the class and the struct to string and verify that the type of the field doesn't affect the result.

7-4 Enumerations

The *enumeration* type is a value type used to store a set of named constants such as days of the week, months of the year, and so forth. Each enumeration has an underlying type (also called the base type), which can be any one of the integral types (**byte**, **sbyte**, **short**, **ushort**, **int**, **uint**, **long**, or **ulong**). The default underlying type is **int**. The enumeration is usually referred to as enum.

7-4-1 Declaring Enumerations

You can declare the enumeration by using the **enum** keyword, as shown in the following example that enumerates the seasons of the year:

```
enum Seasons { Summer, Fall, Winter, Spring };
```

Each enumeration element (enumerator) has a value. The value of the first enumerator is 0 by default. The value of each successive element is incremented by 1. Thus the values of the elements in this enum are:

```
enum Seasons
{
    Summer,   // 0
    Fall,     // 1
    Winter,   // 2
    Spring    // 3
};
```

You can force the elements to start at 1 as in this example:

```
enum Seasons { Summer = 1, Fall, Winter, Spring };
```

In this enumeration, the values of the successive elements are indicated below:

```
enum Seasons
{
    Summer = 1,
    Fall,     // 2
    Winter,   // 3
    Spring    // 4
};
```

You can assign a value to any element — not necessarily the first one:

```
enum WeekDays { Sat, Sun, Mon = 9, Thu, Wed, Thu, Fri };
```

This will make the values of the elements that follow Mon 10, 11, 12, and 13. However, Sat and Sun will still be 0 and 1.

You can also assign integers to the elements as appropriate. In this example, scores that correspond to grades are assigned:

```
enum Grades { Pass = 65, Good = 75, VeryGood = 85, Distinct = 100 };
```

You can choose another underlying type rather than **int**, such as **long**, if you need to use numbers in that range for the elements:

```
enum Color: long { Red, Green, Blue };
```

The enumeration identifier is followed by a colon and then the underlying type.

7-4-2 Using Enumerations

In order to use one of the enumerators, you must qualify it with the enumeration name. For example, the elements of the WeekDays enumeration are WeekDays.Sun, WeekDays.Mon, and so forth.

However, to convert an enum element to an integral type you must use a cast. For example:

```
int monday = (int) WeekDays.Mon;
long monday = (long) WeekDays.Mon;
```

In the following example, you declare three enumerations for *WeekDays*, *Seasons*, and *Grades*. This example demonstrates the various enumeration rules explained in the preceding sections.

Example 7-4

```
// Example 7-4
// enum example

using System;

enum WeekDays { Sun, Mon, Tue, Wed, Thu, Fri, Sat };
enum Seasons { Summer = 1, Fall, Winter, Spring };
enum Grades { Pass = 65, Good = 75, VeryGood = 85, Distinct = 100 };

class MyClass
{
    static void Main()
    {
        int sunday = (int) WeekDays.Sun;
        short summer = (short) Seasons.Summer;
        byte vGood = (byte) Grades.VeryGood;
        Console.WriteLine("Sunday = {0}", sunday);
        Console.WriteLine("Summer = {0}", summer);
        Console.WriteLine("Very Good = {0}", vGood);
    }
}
```

Output:

```
Sunday = 0
Summer = 1
Very Good = 85
```

7-4-3 Using .NET Methods with enums

If you have an enum like this one:

```
enum Color { Red = 1, Green, Blue }
```

you can declare a blue color object using the following statement:

```
Color c = Color.Blue;
```

You can display the name of this element simply by using the **ToString** method like this:

```
Console.WriteLine(c);
```

This statement displays the string Blue.

You can also use the methods of the **System.Enum** structure. This structure includes various methods to process enums. One useful method, which is used to display the name of any enum element, is **GetName**. If you declare a general Color object like this:

```
Color c = new Color();
```

you can use this method to display a specific element by using its numeric value. For example, you can display the name of the element whose value is 2 by using the following statement:

```
Console.WriteLine(Enum.GetName(c.GetType(), 2));
```

This statement displays the string Green.

Another useful method is **GetNames**. It stores the names of the enum elements in a **string** array. For example, you can store all the Color names in an array like this:

```
string[] colorNames = Enum.GetNames(c.GetType());
```

You can then display this array by using a repetition loop.

These methods are demonstrated in the following example.

Example 7-5

```
// Example 7-5.cs
// Using System.Enum methods

using System;

// Declare the Color enum:
enum Color { Red = 1, Green, Blue }

class MyClass
{
    static void Main()
    {
        // Declare a blue color object:
        Color myColor = Color.Blue;

        // Display the color name using ToString:
        Console.WriteLine("My color is: {0}", myColor);   // Blue
```

```
      // Declare a color object:
      Color yourColor = new Color();

      // Display the color whose value is 2 by using the GetName method:
      Console.WriteLine("Your color is: {0}",
              Enum.GetName(yourColor.GetType(), 2));  // Green

      // Display all the color names using the GetNames method:
      Console.WriteLine("Your colors are:");
      // Declare a string array for colors:
      string[] colorNames = Enum.GetNames(yourColor.GetType());
      foreach (string s in colorNames)
         Console.WriteLine("{0} ", s);
   }
}
```

Output:

```
My color is: Blue
Your color is: Green
Your colors are:
Red
Green
Blue
```

Drill 7-3

Enumerations can be used as selector expressions in the switch constructs. Declare the enum Color, which contains the three basic colors (red, green, and blue). Then enter a color number from the keyboard. Use a switch construct to display the color name according to the entered number along with the appropriate message. If the entered number is not one of the enum values, display an appropriate message.

7-5 Attributes

Attributes are additional declarative information that can modify the declarations of program entities (types, members, parameters, and so forth). At run time the compiler can retrieve this information through a process called *reflection*. Attributes can be either predefined or user-defined. In most cases, programmers use the predefined attributes. The user-defined attributes are not covered in this book. Attributes serve different purposes, such as marking a method as deprecated, indicating conditional compilation, setting a type layout, and so forth.

Attributes are derived from the abstract class **System.Attribute**, which defines the services of attributes. By convention, all attributes have the suffix Attribute, such as **DllImportAttribute**. You can skip the suffix and just use the attribute *alias*, which is **DllImport**.

The attribute is written between brackets like this example:

```
[method: DllImport("user32.dll")]
```

Notice that the brackets are part of the attribute syntax. Do not confuse these brackets with those that indicate the optional part of the syntax.

The word "method" in this attribute represents the *target* to which the attribute is applied. In this example, the attribute applied is to a method in the library user32.dll. In most cases, the target is optional; it is necessary only if there is ambiguity. For instance, add the target if the attribute can be applied to a method or a return type.

In this example, the attribute is written without the target element:

```
[DllImport("user32.dll")]
```

Target elements can be any of the following:

- assembly
- field
- event
- method
- parameter
- property
- return
- type

When using an attribute, either qualify its name or use the appropriate **using** directive. The following are some commonly used attributes that exist in various namespaces:

- System.ObsoleteAttribute
- System.Diagnostics.ConditionalAttribute
- System.Runtime.InteropServices.DllImportAttribute
- System.Xml.Serialization.XmlArrayAttribute

7-5-1 **Attribute Parameters**

Consider this example, which indicates a deprecated method by applying the **ObsoleteAttribute** attribute:

```
[Obsolete]
public static void MyMethod()
{
    // The body of the obsolete method.
}
```

When MyMethod is executed, you get the warning:

'MyClass.MyMethod()' is obsolete.

Some attributes such as **Obsolete** allow the programmer to provide extra information on using the deprecated method. You can do this by using the following modified version, which includes two parameters:

```
[System.Obsolete ("Use MyNewMethod instead.", false)]
public static void MyMethod()
{
    // The body of the obsolete method.
}
```

When you compile this method, the compiler generates the warning:

'MyClass.MyMethod()' is obsolete: 'Use MyNewMethod instead.'

The first parameter contains the string message that you would like to add. The second parameter causes the compilation to generate either an error or a warning, depending on whether it is false or true. The default value is false.

7-5-2 **The Conditional Attribute**

This attribute is in the namespace **System.Diagnostics**. It is used to execute a method if a specific constant is defined in the program. For example:

```
[Conditional("MYCONSTANT")]
public void MyMethod(string s) {}
```

MyMethod is only executed if the constant MYCONSTANT is defined in the program with a preprocessor directive:

```
#define MYCONSTANT
```

If the constant is not defined, the execution resumes and the attribute is ignored. The target method must be of the **void** type.

7-5-3 Combining Attributes

Attributes can be grouped or combined. For example, you can group the two attributes **Obsolete** and **Conditional** as shown in this example:

```
[Obsolete]
[Conditional ("TRACE")]
```

You can also combine the attributes by listing them inside a pair of square brackets and separating them with commas:

```
[Obsolete, Conditional ("TRACE")]
```

You can also combine the two styles together as shown in this example, which uses three attributes:

```
[Serializable]
[Obsolete, Conditional ("TRACE")]
```

The following example demonstrates combining attributes.

Example 7-6

```
Example 7-6.cs
// Attribute example

#define TRACE
using System;
using System.Diagnostics;

public class MyClass
{
    [Obsolete("Please use MyNewMethod.", false)]
    [Conditional("TRACE")]
    public void MyMethod(string s)
    {
        Console.WriteLine(s);
    }
    static void Main()
    {
        MyClass mc = new MyClass();
        mc.MyMethod("The conditional method is executed.");
        Console.WriteLine("End execution.");
    }
}
```

Output:

The output shows the result of the compilation and the output of execution.

```
Compilation:
warning CS0618: 'MyClass.MyMethod(string)' is obsolete: 'Please use
                MyNewMethod.'
Output:
The conditional method is executed.
End execution.
```

Drill 7-4

Make some changes to the above example by misspelling the word "TRACE" in the attribute or by removing the preprocessor directive, and see the result.

7-5-4 Calling Native Functions

To call a native function (outside the .NET Framework), such as **MessageBoxA**, use the **DllImportAttribute** attribute like this example:

```
[DllImport("user32.dll")]
```

To use this function in your C# program, do the following:

1. Declare the function as a C# method by using the two modifiers **extern** and **static**:

```
static extern int MessageBoxA(int h, string m, string c, int type);
```

 Note　If you don't remember the syntax of the function, use the IDE's IntelliSense feature.

2. Add the attribute **DllImport** right before the declaration:

```
[DllImport("user32.dll")]
static extern int MessageBoxA(int h, string m, string c, int type);
```

This attribute tells the program that the required function exists in the library user32.dll.

3. Add the following directive to your program:

```
using System.Runtime.InteropServices;
```

Example 7-7 shows the complete program, which results in a message box titled "My Message Box" that contains the phrase "Hello, World!"

Example 7-7

```
// Example 7-7.cs
// Calling native functions

using System.Runtime.InteropServices;

class PlatformInvokeTest
{
   [method: DllImport("user32.dll")]
   static extern int MessageBoxA(int h, string m, string c, int type);
   static int Main()
   {
      return MessageBoxA(0, "Hello, World!", "My Message Box", 0);
   }
}
```

Output:

This program will result in the message box shown in Figure 7-1.

Figure 7-1: The message box.

Drill 7-5

Write a program to call one of the native functions of C++, such as puts, which lives in the library msvcrt.dll.

Note: The function puts is used to display its string parameter, for example, puts(myString).

7-5-5 **Emulating Unions**

It is possible to use attributes to emulate unions in C++, as shown in the following example:

```
[type: StructLayout(LayoutKind.Explicit)]
public struct UnionStruct
{
    [field: FieldOffset(0)]    // offset #0
    public int i;
    [field: FieldOffset(0)]    // offset #0
    public double d;
}
```

In this example, two attributes are used:

```
[type: StructLayout(LayoutKind.Explicit)]
[field: FieldOffset(0)]
```

The first attribute targets the struct, and the second targets a field of the struct. Notice that the words "type" and "field" in these attributes can be omitted because they are obvious.

Using these two attributes, it is possible to store two numbers, an **int** and a **double**, in the same memory location. The two numbers are different in size but they both start at offset 0. It is possible, of course, to use any offset, such as FieldOffset(2) or FieldOffset(5). It is also possible to store any number of different types in the same location as long as you don't use them at the same time. In the following example, more types are added to the union.

Example 7-8

```
// Example 7-8.cs
// Union emulation

using System;
using System.Runtime.InteropServices;

[StructLayout(LayoutKind.Explicit)]
public struct UnionStruct
{
    [FieldOffset(0)]
    public int i;
    [FieldOffset(0)]
    public double d;
    [FieldOffset(0)]
    public char c;
```

```csharp
    [FieldOffset(0)]
    public byte b;
}

class MyClass
{
    static void Main()
    {
        UnionStruct u = new UnionStruct();

        u.i = 13;
        Console.WriteLine("Integer = {0}", u.i);

        u.d = 12.34;
        Console.WriteLine("Double = {0}", u.d);

        u.c = (char)65;
        Console.WriteLine("Character = {0}", u.c);

        u.b = 127;
        Console.WriteLine("Byte = {0}", u.b);
    }
}
```

Output:

```
Integer = 13
Double = 12.34
Character = A
Byte = 127
```

Drill 7-6

You already know that a long number is stored in 8 bytes and an integer is stored in 4 bytes. This means that two integers can be stored in the space of the long number. Write a program to demonstrate this fact. Display the results in hexadecimal in order to indicate the content of each byte. For example, if the first integer is 5 and the second is 7, the long number becomes:

```
700000005
```

This means that the two integers occupy the first and the fifth bytes (notice that one byte is represented by two digits).

Summary

In this chapter:

■ Structures were described in detail and you know how to declare and use structs. You also know the difference between passing a struct and passing a class to a method.

■ You were introduced to the enumerations type and used it in various examples. You also used some of the **System.Enum** structure to display the names of the enum elements.

■ Finally, you saw a tour of attributes and learned how to use many predefined attributes in your program in order to better control the program entities.

Chapter 8

Interfaces

Contents:
- Declaring and using interfaces
- Using the is operator
- Using the as operator
- Hiding base class members
- Versioning
- Hiding interface members

8-1 What Is an Interface?

In daily life we deal with the interfaces of many electronic devices such as TVs, iPods, and mobile phones. When you browse in a store looking for a mobile phone, you don't need to see inside to know its capabilities. By looking at its interface you can see what it can do. For example, you can tell if the phone has the ability to take pictures or record video clips. Also, if the manufacturer decides to add or remove some features, it should be reflected on the interface. Similarly, in programming you can tell by looking at the interface what is contained in the class that implements this interface. In other words, the interface is a contract that describes the behavior of the class that implements this interface. Describing an interface as a contract implies obligation. That means that a manufacturer cannot add a camera button to a mobile phone without adding the implementing electronic circuit that does the actual job internally. Similarly, if an interface contains the name of a method, the class implementing this interface is obligated to include the implementation of this method.

8-2 Declaring an Interface

Declare an interface by using the **interface** keyword as shown in this example:

```
interface IMyInterface
{
    // interface members
}
```

The declaration can be modified with a valid combination of access modifiers or the **new** keyword. It can also be preceded by attributes. The members of an interface can include:

- Methods
- Properties
- Indexers
- Events

The interface cannot, however, contain fields. Interface members are public by default. You cannot use accessibility modifiers on them.

The members of an interface are the signatures of methods, properties, indexers, or events. For example:

```
interface ICounter
{
    void Count(int i);
    int SetCounter();
}
```

As you can see in this declaration, the interface contains only the names, types, and parameters of methods. This is similar to function prototypes in C++. In the actual implementation, we will discuss the types that implement this interface.

An interface might implement one or more interfaces, as shown in the following example:

```
interface IMyInterface: Interface1, Interface2
{
    // interface members
}
```

In this example, IMyInterface implements both **Interface1** and **Interface2**.

8-3 **Interface Implementation**

The interface can be implemented by a class or a struct as shown in this example:

```
class MyClass: IMyInterface1
{
    // class implementation
}
```

By this declaration the class MyClass is obligated to implement all members of the interface IMyInterface.

It is also possible for a class to implement more than one interface:

```
class MyClass: IMyInterface1, IMyInterface2
{
    // class implementation
}
```

A class can also implement another class in addition to the interfaces:

```
class MyClass: MyBaseClass, IMyInterface1, IMyInterface2
{
    // class implementation
}
```

In the following example, the class **Point** implements the interface **IPoint**. Notice that all the fields are included in the class but none are included in the interface.

Example 8-1

```
// Example 8-1.cs
// Interface example

using System;

interface IPoint
{
    // Property signatures:
    int Myx
    {
        get; set;
    }
```

```
   int Myy
   {
      get; set;
   }
}

class Point: IPoint
{
   // Fields:
   private int x;
   private int y;

   // Constructor:
   public Point(int x, int y)
   {
      this.x = x;
      this.y = y;
   }

   // Property implementation:
   public int Myx
   {
      get {return x;}
      set {x = value;}
   }

   public int Myy
   {
      get {return y;}
      set {y = value;}
   }
   public static void DisplayMyPoint(IPoint myPoint)
   {
      Console.WriteLine("({0},{1})", myPoint.Myx, myPoint.Myy);
   }
}

class MyClass
{
   static void Main()
   {
      Point myPoint = new Point(12,300);
      Console.Write("My point is created at: ");
      Point.DisplayMyPoint(myPoint);
   }
}
```

Output:

```
My point is created at: (12,300)
```

Notes about the preceding example:

1. If you don't implement all the members of the interface, you get a compilation error. Try commenting the properties (Myx and Myy) in the class to see the compiler error message.

2. Notice that the class can contain members other than the members of the interface, such as the method DisplayMyPoint.

3. Notice also that it is possible to pass a parameter of the type **IPoint** to the method DisplayMyPoint. You can, of course, pass a parameter of the type **Point** instead.

8-4 Explicit Interface Implementation

Consider a class, MyClass, that implements an interface, IMyInterface. It is possible to implement the interface member, MyMethod, like this:

```
string IMyInterface.MyMethod()
{
    // interface implementation
}
```

In this example, MyMethod is qualified by the interface name, IMyInterface:

```
IMyInterface.MyMethod()
```

This is called *explicit interface implementation*. Assume that you created an object from MyClass using the following statement:

```
MyClass mc = new MyClass();
```

You can also create an interface object by casting the class object:

```
IMyInterface mi = (IMyInterface) mc;
```

In this case, you can only access MyMethod through the interface object mi. For example:

```
Console.Write(mi.MyMethod());
```

Attempting to access MyMethod through the class member mc would generate a compilation error:

```
Console.Write(mc.MyMethod());    // error
```

So, when do you need to use this code? There are cases in which the use of explicit interface implementation becomes necessary, such as when the class is implementing two interfaces and both interfaces contain a method named MyMethod. If the first interface object is mi1 and the second interface object is mi2, accessing MyMethod through interface objects does not cause any ambiguity. That is:

```
Console.Write(mi1.MyMethod());
Console.Write(mi2.MyMethod());
```

In fact, using the class object to access the method will cause ambiguity.

The following example demonstrates a temperature converter that converts from Fahrenheit to Celsius and vice versa. The program contains two interfaces: **ITemp1** and **ITemp2**. Each contains a method named **Convert**. The class **TempConverter** explicitly implements the two interfaces. In the **Main** method, two interface objects, iFC and iCF, are used to access the **Convert** method.

Example 8-2

```
// Example 8-2.cs
// Explicit interface implementation

using System;

public interface ITemp1
{
    double Convert(double d);
}

public interface ITemp2
{
    double Convert(double d);
}

public class TempConverter: ITemp1, ITemp2
{
    double ITemp1.Convert(double d)
    {
        // Convert to Fahrenheit:
        return (d * 1.8) + 32;
    }
```

```
    double ITemp2.Convert(double d)
    {
        // Convert to Celsius:
        return (d - 32) / 1.8;
    }
}

class MyClass
{
    public static void Main()
    {
        // Create a class instance:
        TempConverter cObj = new TempConverter();

        // Create instances of interfaces
        // Create a From-Celsius-to-Fahrenheit object:
        ITemp1 iCF = (ITemp1) cObj;
        // Create From-Fahrenheit-to-Celsius object:
        ITemp2 iFC = (ITemp2) cObj;

        // Initialize variables:
        double F = 32;
        double C = 20;

        // Print results:
        Console.WriteLine("Temperature {0} C in Fahrenheit: {1:F2}",
                          C, iCF.Convert(C));
        Console.WriteLine("Temperature {0} F in Celsius: {1:F2}", F,
                          iFC.Convert(F));
    }
}
```

Output:

```
Temperature 20 C in Fahrenheit: 68.00
Temperature 32 F in Celsius: 0.00
```

Drill 8-1

Modify the preceding example to accept a temperature from the keyboard in one of the two systems and then convert it and display it in the other system.

8-5 **Using is to Test Types**

The operator **is** is used to test the type of various objects at run time. It is used in the following form:

> *expression* **is** *type*

where:

type is a reference type.
expression is the object to be tested.

The result of this operation is either true or false.

For example, the following expression:

```
myObj is MyClass
```

is used to check if the object myObj is an instance of the class MyClass. The result of the expression renders true if it is an instance of MyClass; false otherwise.

Also, the expression:

```
myObj is IMyInterface
```

is used to check if the object myObj is an instance of a class that implements the interface IMyInterface. The result is either true or false.

In the following example, the operator **is** is used to check if the type of an object is an instance of MyClass and the two interfaces **I1** and **I2**.

Example 8-3

```
// Example 8-3.cs
// The is operator

using System;

interface I1
{
}

interface I2
{
}

class Class1: I1, I2
{
}
```

```
class MyClass
{
    static bool TestType(object obj)
    {
        if (obj is I1 & obj is I2 & obj is Class1)
            return true;
        else
            return false;
    }
    public static void Main()
    {
        Class1 c = new Class1();
        Console.WriteLine("The result of the test: {0}", TestType(c));
    }
}
```

Output:

```
The result of the test: True
```

Drill 8-2

In the above example, change the declaration of Class1 from:

```
class Class1: I1, I2
```

to:

```
class Class1: I1
```

and see the result of the program run.

Also, replace "&" in the following condition:

```
(obj is I1 & obj is I2 & obj is Class1)
```

with "|":

```
(obj is I1 | obj is I2 | obj is Class1)
```

and see the result.

8-6 **Using as to Test Types**

The operator **as** is used to convert an expression to a specified reference type. It is used according to the form:

expression **as** *type*

where:

type is a reference type.
expression is the object to be converted.

If the conversion is successful, it returns the value of the expression; null otherwise.

This expression is equivalent to casting *expression* with *type* except that it doesn't throw an exception if the conversion fails. The expression is equivalent to the following conditional expression:

expression is *type* ? (*type*) *expression* : (*type*) null;

In the following example, the method **TestType** is used to test objects of various types. Notice that only reference-type objects are converted.

Example 8-4

```csharp
// Example 8-4.cs
// The as operator

using System;

public class MyClass
{
    static void TestType(object o)
    {
        if (o as MyClass != null)
            Console.WriteLine ("The object \"{0}\" is a class.", o);
        else if (o as string != null)
            Console.WriteLine ("The object \"{0}\" is a string.", o);
        else
            Console.WriteLine ("The object \"{0}\" is not a reference
                                type.", o);
    }

    static void Main()
    {
        MyClass mc = new MyClass();
        string myString = "Hello, World!";
        int myInt = 123;
```

```
        TestType(mc);
        TestType(myString);
        TestType(myInt);
    }
}
```

Output:

```
The object "MyClass" is a class.
The object "Hello, World!" is a string.
The object "123" is not a reference type.
```

Drill 8-3

Modify the preceding example to display the following output:

```
The object "Hello, World!" is a string.
The object "123" is not a string. It is System.Int32.
The object "12.34" is not a string. It is System.Double.
```

8-7 Hiding Members of the Base Class

You've already used the **new** operator to create objects. Another use of the **new** operator is to modify declarations of the inherited members in order to hide members with the same names in the base class. Suppose that you have a base class that contains a method called MyMethod:

```
public class MyBaseClass
{
    public int myInt;
    public void MyMethod()    // MyMethod on the base class
    {
        // ...
    }
}
```

When this class is inherited, the derived class will inherit all its members. Suppose that you would like to declare a new member with the same name, MyMethod, in the derived class. You can do that by using the **new** modifier, as shown in this example:

```
public class MyDerivedClass: MyBaseClass
{
    new public void MyMethod()    // MyMethod on the derived class
    {
        // ...
```

```
    }
}
```

The job of the **new** modifier here is to hide the member with the same name in the base class. A method that uses the **new** modifier hides properties, fields, and types with the same name. It also hides the methods with the same signatures. In general, declaring a member in the base class would hide any members in the base class with the same name. If you declare MyMethod in the above example without the **new** modifier, it still works, but you will get a compiler warning:

'MyDerivedClass.MyMethod()' hides inherited member 'MyBaseClass.MyMethod()'. Use the new keyword if hiding was intended.

Notice the following when you use the **new** modifier:

- You cannot use **new** and **override** in the same declaration. If you do that you get the compiler error:

  A member 'MyDerivedClass.MyMethod()' marked as override cannot be marked as new or virtual.

- It is possible, though, to use **virtual** and **new** in the same declaration. This emphasizes your intention to hide the member in the base class and start a new point of specialization in the inheritance hierarchy.

8-8 Versioning

Using the **new** modifier to hide the inherited members is similar to overriding methods using the **override** modifier. Both are used to design a new version of a program while maintaining backward compatibility with previous versions of the program. For example, assume that you are inheriting a class produced by Acme Company called **AcmeClass**:

```
public class AcmeClass    // Acme class
{
    // ...
}
public class MyClass: AcmeClass    // your class
{
    // ...
}
```

Suppose that you needed to add a method of your own named MyMethod, like this:

```
public class MyClass: AcmeClass
{
    public virtual MyMethod()
    {
        // The new method in your program.
    }
    // ...
}
```

Your program was working just fine until Acme produced a new version of its program that includes a method called MyMethod, which does the same work:

```
public class AcmeClass
{
    public virtual MyMethod()
    {
        // The new method in Acme's program v2.0.
    }
    // ...
}
```

Now you have a problem. The solution is to just use the **new** modifier to declare MyMethod in your program. This will emphasize your intention to hide the method MyMethod in the second version of **AcmeClass**. For example:

```
public class MyClass: AcmeClass
{
    public new virtual MyMethod()
    {
        // ...
    }
}
```

Problem solved.

You can, as an alternative, use the **override** modifier if you plan to override MyMethod in the base class.

In the following example, the class MyDerivedClass inherits the class MyBaseClass. Each class contains a member class called MyClass. In order to hide MyClass in the base class, the **new** modifier is used in the class declaration. This way, it becomes possible to access members in both classes and use their members.

Example 8-5

```csharp
// Example 8-5.cs
// Hiding members using the new modifier

using System;

public class MyBaseClass
{
   public class MyClass
   {
      public int myInt = 123;

      public virtual string MyMethod()
      {
         return "Hello from the base class!";
      }
   }
}

public class MyDerivedClass: MyBaseClass
{
   // The following nested class hides the base class member:
   new public class MyClass    // notice the new modifier
   {
      public int myInt = 321;

      public virtual string MyMethod()
      {
         return "Hello from the derived class!";
      }
   }

   static void Main()
   {
      // Create an object from the "new" MyClass:
      MyClass myObj1 = new MyClass();

      // Create an object from the hidden MyClass:
      MyBaseClass.MyClass myObj2 = new MyBaseClass.MyClass();

      Console.WriteLine("Value from the 'new' MyClass: {0}",
                        myObj1.myInt);
      Console.WriteLine("Value from the 'hidden' MyClass: {0}",
                        myObj2.myInt);
      Console.WriteLine("Message from the 'new' MyClass: {0}",
                        myObj1.MyMethod());
```

```
        Console.WriteLine("Message from the 'hidden' MyClass: {0}",
                          myObj2.MyMethod());
    }
}
```

Output:

```
Value from the 'new' MyClass: 321
Value from the 'hidden' MyClass: 123
Message from the 'new' MyClass: Hello from the derived class!
Message from the 'hidden' MyClass: Hello from the base class!
```

In the preceding example you created an object of each of the classes named MyClass. Although each class contains a field and a method with the same name as those in the other class, the **new** modifier was used only once in declaring the class.

8-9 Hiding Interface Members

It is also possible to apply the same principle of hiding base class members on interfaces. Suppose that you have two interfaces: **IBase** and **IDerived**. As the name indicates, **IDerived** is derived from **IBase**. The following is a declaration of a property **M1** on the interface **IBase**.

```
interface IBase
{
    int M1 { get; set; }
}
```

In the same program, you can declare a method with the same name, **M1**, on the interface **IDerived**:

```
interface IDerived: IBase
{
    new int M1();
}
```

With this declaration, the member **M1** on the derived interface hides the member **M1** on the base interface. In this case, it is necessary to use explicit interface implementation in any class that implements these interfaces:

```
class MyClass: IDerived
{
    private int m1;
    // Explicit implementation of the property M1:
    int IBase.M1
    {
```

```
      get { return m1; }
      set { m1 = value; }
   }

   // Explicit implementation of the method M1:
   void IDerived.M1() { }
}
```

It is also possible to implement the property explicitly and the method normally, as shown in this example:

```
class MyClass: IDerived
{
   private int m1;
   // Explicit implementation of the property:
   int IBase.M1
   {
      get { return m1; }
      set { m1 = value; }
   }

   // Normal implementation of the method:
   public void M1() { }
}
```

A third possibility is to implement the method explicitly and the property normally, as shown below:

```
class MyClass: IDerived
{
   private int m1;
   // Normal implementation of the property:
   public int M1
   {
      get { return m1; }
      set { m1 = value; }
   }

   // Explicit implementation of the method:
   void IDerived.M1() { }
}
```

In the following example, one of the explicit alternative implementations of method and property is demonstrated.

Example 8-6

```
// Example 8-6.cs
// Hiding interface members

using System;

interface IBase
{
   int M1 { set; get; }
}

interface IDerived: IBase
{
   // Declare a method that hides the property
   // on the IBase interface:
   new void M1();
}

class MyClass: IDerived
{
   private int x;

   // Explicit implementation of the property:
   int IBase.M1
   {
      get { return x; }
      set { x = value; }
   }

   // Explicit implementation of the method:
   void IDerived.M1()
   {
      Console.WriteLine("Hi, I am the M1 method!");
   }
}

class MainClass
{
   static void Main()
   {
      // Create a class object:
      MyClass mc = new MyClass();

      // Create an IDerived object:
      IDerived mi1 = (IDerived)mc;
```

```
        // Create an IBase object:
        IBase mi2 = (IBase)mc;

        // Use the property:
        mi2.M1=123;

        // Call the method:
        mi1.M1();

        // Display the property:
        Console.WriteLine("I am the M1 property. My value is {0}.",
                        mi2.M1);
    }
}
```

Output:

```
Hi, I am the M1 method!
I am the M1 property. My value is 123.
```

Drill 8-4

Modify the preceding example to use an explicit implementation of the property and normal implementation of the method. The output should be the same as for the example.

Summary

In this chapter:

- You learned how to declare interfaces and interface members.
- You also learned how to implement an interface by a type or by another interface.
- You now know when you need to use the explicit implementation of interfaces and how to do so.
- You also learned how to use the **is** operator to test types, and how to use the **as** operator to convert and test types.
- You now know how to design a new version of a program while maintaining backward compatibility with previous versions.
- Finally, you learned about hiding members of base classes and interfaces and how to use the hidden members in your code.

Chapter 9

Exceptions

Contents:
- *Errors and exceptions*
- *Throwing an exception*
- *Handling an exception*
- *Exceptions in file processing*
- *Using a finally block*
- *Defining your own exceptions*
- *Rethrowing an exception*
- *Tracing exceptions*

9-1 Errors and Exceptions

Exceptions are run-time errors that can stop the program execution unless they are handled properly. Exceptions are generated when certain conditions occur in your program, such as dividing by zero, trying to open a file that was erased, incorrect casting, or running out of memory. In such cases, you deal with the exception by using the appropriate handler in order to prevent the program from stopping. The handler is a block of code that catches the exception and tries to continue the program execution. If the appropriate handler is not available in your code, the default handler is used and the program is terminated.

In C#, an exception is an object of the class **System.Exception** or one of its subclasses, which represents an error that occurred during the program execution. The keywords used in handling exceptions are **throw**, **catch**, and **finally**. Handling exceptions requires using a special construct that uses one of the following statements:

- *throw*: To throw or rethrow an exception.
- *try-catch*: To catch and handle the exception.

- *try-finally*: To clean up the resources after throwing the exception regardless of whether or not the exception was caught.
- *try-catch-finally*: To catch and handle the exception and clean up resources.

These statements are explained in the following sections.

9-2 **Throwing an Exception**

In this section, we deliberately throw an exception to show you what one looks like. You can do this using the **throw** statement.

The **throw** statement takes the following form:

```
throw [expression];
```

where:

expression is the exception object.

Some of the exceptions that can be thrown by an application are:

- InvalidCastException
- OverFlowException
- ArgumentNullException
- ArithmeticException
- DivideByZeroException

When an exception is thrown, the execution pauses momentarily, searching for the appropriate exception handler. If one is found, it handles the exception and the execution resumes; otherwise, the execution is terminated at this point.

In the following example, you throw an exception object of the class **ArgumentNullException** after assigning the value null to the variable myString.

Example 9-1

```
// Example 9-1.cs
// Throw an exception

using System;

public class MyClass
```

```
{
   static void Main()
   {
      string myString = "Hello.";

      // Print the first statement:
      Console.Write("The string is {0}", myString);

      myString = null;

      if (myString == null)
      {
         throw new ArgumentNullException();   // throwing the exception
      }

      // The following line will not be executed:
      Console.Write("myString is null.");
   }
}
```

When you run this program, it first displays the text:

```
The string is Hello.
```

It then displays the following window:

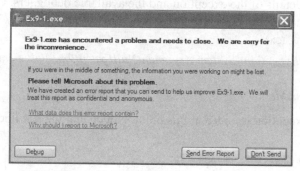

Figure 9-1: The error window.

This window contains the regular options that are available when a run-time error occurs. When you click **Debug**, the following Just-in-Time Debugger window appears on the screen.

Figure 9-2: The Just-in-Time Debugger window.

As you can see in Figure 9-2, the name of the exception that caused the termination of the application (ArgumentNullException) and the name of the application (Ex9-1.exe) are indicated in the first two lines. This screen also contains some details of the exception and the available debuggers. Click **No** to skip the debugger and return to the program execution. You will then see the following text:

Unhandled Exception: System.ArgumentNullException: Value cannot be null.
*   at MyClass.Main()*

The program execution is ended at this point. Notice that the last line of code:

```
Console.Write("myString is null.");
```

will not be executed because it followed throwing the exception.

You can use the class **System.Exception** instead of the class **ArgumentNullException**, in which case you get another message from the program that says:

Unhandled Exception: System.Exception: Exception of type 'System.Exception' was thrown.
*   at MyClass.Main()*

The name of the exception object always shows up in the result. This example demonstrates the default handler, which is used when you don't catch the exception. In the following sections, you will learn how to catch an exception and use the appropriate handler to deal with it in order to continue executing the application.

9-3 Catching an Exception

You can catch exceptions by using the **try-catch** statement, which contains two blocks. The first is the try block, inside which the suspicious code is inserted. It takes the form:

```
try
{
    // The code to be tried.
}
```

The second block is the catch block, which handles the exception. It takes the form:

```
catch [(declaration)]
{
    // The handler code.
}
```

where:

declaration is the exception object declaration and is optional.

The two blocks are used together to build one statement. If you attempt to use the try block alone, you will get the compilation error:

error CS1524: Expected catch or finally.

The catch block can be used without any parameters at all, in which case it is used to catch any exceptions. It is also possible to use more than one catch block. In this case, the **try-catch** statement takes the form:

```
try
{
    //
}
catch (declaration-1)
{
    // first handler
}
catch (declaration-2)
{
    // second handler
}
```

```
catch (declaration-3)
{
    // third handler
}
...
```

When the program throws an exception, the run-time engine starts looking for the suitable catch block that matches the exception. If the catch block is found, the program resumes execution after handling the problem or displaying the appropriate message that explains the problem that took place during the program execution.

Example 9-2 demonstrates the following:

- Throwing the exception.
- Trying the suspicious code using the try block.
- Handling the exception by using the catch block.

Example 9-2

```
// Example 9-2.cs
// Handling an exception

using System;

class MyClass
{
    public void MyMethod(string myString)
    {
        if (myString == null)
        // Throwing the exception
        throw(new ArgumentNullException());
    }

    public static void Main()
    {
        MyClass myClass = new MyClass();
        // Trying the suspicious code:
        try
        {
            string myString = null;
            myClass.MyMethod(myString);
        }
        // Handling the exception:
        catch (Exception e)
```

```
        {
            Console.WriteLine("The following exception is caught: \n{0}", e);
        }

        // Continue after handling the exception:
        Console.WriteLine("Now the program continues...");
    }
}
```

Output:

```
The following exception is caught:
System.ArgumentNullException: Value cannot be null.
    at MyClass.Main()
Now the program continues...
```

Notice in the above example that the existence of the catch block itself was enough to resume the program execution, regardless of the code it contains. As you can see in the program, the catch block contains only a printing statement to display some information about the exception and that was enough to handle it and resume the execution. In real applications, however, it becomes necessary to fix the problem that took place. If the problem was, for example, running out of memory, it might be suitable to warn the user to close some of the open applications and retry the operation.

 Note Using the Exception class as a parameter in a catch block is equivalent to not using a parameter at all.

That means:

```
catch (Exception) {}
```

is equivalent to:

```
catch {}
```

You can use a parameter, such as Exception e, if you would like to display the exception text that is associated with the object e.

9-3-1 Organizing the Handlers

When you use more than one catch block, it is important to catch the most specific exceptions before the least specific ones. If, for example, the most specific exception is ArithmeticException, this exception should be the first one to catch. Then you organize the rest of the handlers in order, ending with the most general exception. For example:

```
catch (ArithmeticException e)    // first handler
{
    //...
}
...
...
catch (Exception e)              // last handler
{
    // ...
}
```

Although the sequence of the exception handlers is totally up to your judg-ment, you cannot have the general handler before the specific ones. If you do that, you get the following compiler error:

error CS0160: A previous catch clause already catches all exceptions of this or of a super type ('System.Exception').

In the following example, you try the expression y/x (where y = 0), which throws the divide-by-zero exception. Two handlers are used, one that is a specific exception (ArithmeticException) and another that is the general exception (Exception).

Example 9-3

```csharp
// Example 9-3.cs
// Exception hierarchy

using System;

class MyClass
{
    static void Main()
    {
        int x = 0;
        int y = 10;

        try
        {
            int z = y/x;
        }

        // Catch the most specific exception:
        catch (ArithmeticException e)
        {
            Console.WriteLine("Arithmetic Exception Handler: {0}", e);
        }
```

```
        // Catch the general exception:
        catch (Exception e)
        {
            Console.WriteLine("General Exception Handler: {0}", e);
        }

        // Continue the program:
        Console.WriteLine("Program continues...");
    }
}
```

Output:

```
Arithmetic Exception Handler: System.DivideByZeroException: Attempted to
divide by zero.
   at MyClass.Main()
Program continues...
```

Try removing the ArithmeticException handler in the above example and see the result when the general handler deals with the exception.

Drill 9-1

Although it is possible to catch the divide-by-zero exception by using the handler ArithmeticException, there is a more specific class to deal with such exceptions — the DivideByZeroException class.

Try using this class in the preceding example with the other classes. Change the order of the handlers to get the best sequence that the compiler doesn't complain about.

9-3-2 Sequence of Events in Handling Exceptions

When an exception is thrown, the run-time engine stops executing the code and starts searching for a catch block with a matching handler. It then selects the most suitable handler and executes its code. If the handler does not exist in the current method, it looks for it in the other methods.

The following examples demonstrate two scenarios that are worth comparing. In the first one (9-4A), an exception is thrown and handled in the same method (MyMethod2). In the second example (9-4B), an exception is thrown in MyMethod1 and is handled in MyMethod2. Therefore, in the second example, you can see how the methods are searched for the appropriate handler.

Example 9-4A

```
// Example 9-4A.cs
// Sequence of events

using System;

class MyClass
{
   static void Main()
   {
      Console.WriteLine("Main starts...");
      MyClass mc = new MyClass();
      mc.MyMethod1();

      // Continue the program:
      Console.WriteLine("Program ends.");
   }

   void MyMethod1()
   {
      Console.WriteLine("Starting MyMethod1.");
      MyMethod2();
      Console.WriteLine("Exiting MyMethod1.");
   }

   void MyMethod2()
   {
      // Entering MyMethod1:
      Console.WriteLine("Starting MyMethod2.");

      try
      {
         Console.WriteLine("Starting the try block.");
         throw new Exception();
         Console.WriteLine("Exiting the try block.");
      }

      catch
      {
         Console.WriteLine("Handling the exception.");
      }

      // Exiting MyMethod2:
      Console.WriteLine("Exiting MyMethod2.");
   }
}
```

Output:

In the following text, you can see the output of the statements that marked the start and end of each method. This enables you to keep track of all the events that took place in the program. Notice in this example that entering MyMethod2 is followed by entering the try and catch blocks, and then exiting the method.

```
Main starts...
Starting MyMethod1.
Starting MyMethod2.              → entering the method
Starting the try block.
Handling the exception.
Exiting MyMethod2.              → exiting the method
Exiting MyMethod1.
Program ends.
```

The following example demonstrates stack unwinding to search for a handler.

Example 9-4B

```
// Example 9-4B.cs
// Sequence of events

using System;

class MyClass
{
    static void Main()
    {
        Console.WriteLine("Main starts...");
        MyClass mc = new MyClass();
        mc.MyMethod1();
        Console.WriteLine("Program ends.");
    }

    void MyMethod1()
    {
        Console.WriteLine("Starting Method1.");

        try
        {
            Console.WriteLine("Starting the try block.");
            MyMethod2();
            Console.WriteLine("Exiting the try block.");
        }
```

```
        catch
        {
            Console.WriteLine("Handling the exception.");
        }

        Console.WriteLine("Exiting Method1.");
    }

    void MyMethod2()
    {
        Console.WriteLine("Starting Method2.");
        throw new Exception();
        Console.WriteLine("Exiting Method2.");
    }
}
```

Notice in the output that after entering the try block in MyMethod1, the execution jumped to MyMethod2, looking for a handler.

Output:

```
Main starts...
Starting Method1.
Starting the try block.
Starting Method2.
Handling the exception.
Exiting Method1.
Program ends.
```

Notice in Examples 9-4A and 9-4B that the execution entered the try block and displayed the sentence:

```
Starting the try block.
```

However, you don't see the exiting statement from the try block that was supposed to display:

```
Exiting the try block.
```

This means that the execution never returns back to the point where the exception was thrown.

➲ **Note** When you compile these programs, you get a warning that there is unreachable code in the program, which is expected. This code usually follows the statement:

```
throw new Exception();
```

9-4 Expected Exceptions in File Processing

In the following sections, the file protocols are introduced as well as the expected exceptions that might occur when processing files.

9-4-1 Reading Text Files

There are specific protocols for opening and closing files using the .NET methods. For example, to open a text file named "test.txt" for reading, do the following:

1. Use the **using** directive **System.IO**.

2. Declare a file variable by using the **StreamReader** type:
   ```
   StreamReader myFile;
   ```

3. Open the file using one of the following methods:
   ```
   myFile = File.OpenText("test.txt");
   ```
   OR
   ```
   myFile = new StreamReader("test.txt");
   ```

4. Read the file using one of the following methods:
   - Either line by line using the method **ReadLine**, and store each line in a variable using a suitable loop:
     ```
     string line = myFile.ReadLine();
     ```
   - Or by reading the whole file as one string by using the method **ReadToEnd**:
     ```
     string file = myFile.ReadToEnd();
     ```

5. Display the content of the file by using one of the following methods:
   - Either line by line using a suitable loop:
     ```
     Console.WriteLine(line);
     ```
   - Or as one string:
     ```
     Console.WriteLine(file);
     ```

6. Close the file using the **Close** method:
   ```
   myFile.Close();
   ```

9-4-2 Writing and Appending Text Files

You can open a file for writing by using the **StreamWriter** class, as shown in the following declaration:

```
StreamWriter myFile = new StreamWriter("test.txt");
```

You can also open a file for appending by using the following declaration:

```
StreamWriter myFile = new StreamWriter("test.txt", true);
```

Note There are other ways to read or write files besides those mentioned above. We only introduced the most common methods. You can read more information about the StreamReader and StreamWriter classes on the Microsoft web site at http://msdn.microsoft.com.

9-4-3 Expected Exceptions

When you process files, an exception can be thrown if the file was not found (FileNotFoundException). Therefore, it is recommended that you put the file processing statements inside a try block. In the following example, you read a text file called "test.txt," and then you display it, line by line, using a **while** loop. To handle the exceptions, two handlers are used: one to handle the most specific exception, FileNotFoundException, and one to handle the general exception.

Example 9-5

```
// Example 9-5.cs
// Processing files

using System;
using System.IO;

class MyClass
{
    static void Main()
    {
        int counter = 0;
        string line;

        try
        {
            StreamReader file = File.OpenText("test.txt");
            while((line = file.ReadLine()) != null)
```

```
        {
            Console.WriteLine (line);
            counter++;
        }
        file.Close();
    }
    catch (FileNotFoundException)
    {
        Console.WriteLine(
        "The file you are trying to open is not found.");
    }
    catch
    {
        Console.WriteLine("General catch statement.");
    }
  }
}
```

Assuming that the file is not on the hard disk, the program will display the sentence in the first catch block.

Output:

```
The file you are trying to open is not found.
```

After you run the program, create the file "test.txt" or copy the source code file to "test.txt" by using the following command:

```
Copy Ex9-5.cs test.txt
```

Then run the program again to see the result.

Note The variables declared inside the try block cannot be accessed from outside the block. Therefore, it is recommended that you declare your variables in the Main method. You can then initialize them in the try block.

Drill 9-2

Write a program that performs the same tasks shown in Example 9-5 by reading the file with the statement ReadToEnd.

9-5 **The finally Block**

The finally block is used with the try block, in which case, the statement is called the **try-finally** statement. It can also be used with both **try** and **catch**, in which case, the statement is called the **try-catch-finally** statement. When using the finally block in your program, control is transferred to that block regardless of whether or not the exception was handled. The finally block is used to clean up the resources, such as closing the open files.

9-5-1 **The try-finally Statement**

The **try-finally** statement takes the form:

```
try
{
    // try-block
}
finally
{
    // finally-block
}
```

where:
try-block contains the suspicious code to be tried.
finally-block contains the cleanup statements to be executed regardless of the exception.

The following example demonstrates how the statements in the finally block are executed. This program throws the exception InvalidCastException because it uses the cast **int** with an object of the type **string** (which is an invalid cast). The finally block contains some statements that are executed regardless of the thrown exception.

Example 9-6

```
// Example 9-6.cs
// try-finally example

using System;

public class MyClass
{
    static void Main()
```

```
{
    string myString = "Finally";
    object myObject = myString;

    try
    {
        // The following conversion is invalid.
        // It throws an exception.
        int myInt = (int)myObject;
    }

    finally
    {
        // The code in this block is always executed:
        Console.WriteLine("The program continues and ends here:");
        Console.WriteLine("My String is: {0}", myString);
    }

    // The following code will not be executed:
    Console.WriteLine("Hello again!");
}
}
```

When you run the above example, the execution stops and the error-reporting window pops up. Click **Debug** and then click **No** when the exception window pops up. This will take you back to the command-line environment to see the output message.

Output:

```
Unhandled Exception: System.InvalidCastException: Specified cast is not
valid.
    at MyClass.Main()
The program continues and ends here:    → the finally block is executed
                                           here
My String is: Finally
```

Notice in the output that the code in the finally block was executed after throwing the exception. However, the last statement in the program that followed the finally block was not executed. This means that the exception prevents control from being transferred to any part of the program except the finally block.

9-5-2 The try-catch-finally Statement

The **try-catch-finally** statement takes the form:

```
try
{
    // try-block
}
catch
{
    // catch-block
}
finally
{
    // finally-block
}
```

where:

try-block contains the suspicious code to be tried.

catch-block contains the exception handler.

finally-block contains the cleanup statements to be executed regardless of
the exception.

This is the common form for using the **finally** keyword. As long as an
exception is expected to be thrown, it is best to handle it with the catch
block. You can, of course, use one or more catch blocks, as mentioned
earlier.

In the following example, a catch block is added to Example 9-6. This
way the scenario is completed by catching the exception and continuing
the program execution.

Example 9-7

```
// Example 9-7.cs
// try-catch-finally example

using System;

public class MyClass
{
    static void Main()
    {
        string myString = "Try-Catch-Finally.";
        object myObject = myString;

        try
```

```
        {
            // The following conversion is invalid.
            // It throws an exception.
            int myInt = (int)myObject;
        }
        catch(InvalidCastException ex)
        {
            Console.WriteLine("The exception \"{0}\" was handled.", ex);
        }

        catch
        {
            Console.WriteLine("Unknown exception handled.");
        }

        finally
        {
            // The code in this block is always executed:
            Console.Write("The program continues here: ");
            Console.WriteLine("My String is: {0}", myString);
        }

        // The following code will always be executed:
        Console.WriteLine("Goodbye!");
    }
}
```

Output:

```
The exception "System.InvalidCastException: Specified cast is not valid.
    at MyClass.Main()" was handled.
The program continues here: My String is: Try-Catch-Finally.
Goodbye!
```

Notice in this example:

1. The first catch block handled the exception InvalidCastException and displayed the description of the exception.

2. The second catch block is the general catch block. It is used without parameters this time, but because the job was accomplished by the first catch block, it wasn't executed.

3. The finally block displayed the continuation message in addition to the value of the variable myString.

4. After handling the exception, the last statement was executed and displayed the message "Goodbye!" This is the main difference between Example 9-6 and Example 9-7.

> ## Drill 9-3
>
> As you now know, the main purpose of the finally block is to clean up resources. Write a program that reads a text file and uses the finally block to close the open file.

9-6 User-defined Exceptions

You can create an exception of your own by declaring it as a class derived from the **ApplicationException** class. The benefit to the programmer is the ability to add to the handlers whatever text is needed to explain in detail the error that took place. It is obvious that the run-time engine doesn't know anything about the user-defined exception that your program threw.

You can inherit the **ApplicationException** as shown in this example:

```
class MyCustomException: ApplicationException
```

A constructor with a string parameter is used to send it as a message to the inherited class:

```
MyCustomException(string message): base(message)
{
}
```

The string parameter contains the message you would like to display when the exception is thrown.

The following example demonstrates how to throw and handle user-defined exceptions.

Example 9-8

```
// Example 9-8.cs
// Custom Exceptions

using System;

public class MyCustomException: ApplicationException
{
    // The MyCustomException class constructor:
    public MyCustomException(string message): base(message)
    {
    }
}
```

```
class MyClass
{
    static void Main()
    {
        // Create an instance of MyCustomException:
        MyCustomException e = new MyCustomException(
        "which includes my custom message");
        try
        {
            // Throwing the exception:
            throw e;
        }

        catch(MyCustomException)
        {
            // Catching the exception:
            Console.WriteLine(
            "The exception \"{0}\" was handled successfully.", e);
        }

        catch
        {
            Console.WriteLine("Unknown exception handled.");
        }

        finally
        {
            // The code in this block is always executed:
            Console.WriteLine("The program continues here.");

        }

        // Display a message after the finally block:
        Console.Write("Execution ends.");
    }
}
```

Output:

```
The exception "MyCustomException: which includes my custom message
at MyClass.Main()" was handled successfully.
The program continues here.
Execution ends.
```

As you can see in the program output, the custom message was displayed with the exception. (Note that a real custom message should explain more about the error.) Notice also that after the finally block was executed, the statement at the end of the program was also executed to indicate that the problem was solved successfully.

9-7 **Rethrowing Exceptions**

Sometimes you need to rethrow an exception. Consider this scenario: An exception handler is taking care of an exception inside some method, but in order to get more information on the error, it has to throw the exception to another method or back to the **Main** method to get this information or to do further handling.

To rethrow an exception, use the keyword **throw** without parameters, as shown in this example:

```
catch
{
    throw;
}
```

It is also possible for the catch block to throw the same exception associated with a message that adds additional information about the problem:

```
catch (DivideByZeroException e)
{
    throw (new DivideByZeroException("Dividing by zero occurred in
        MyMethod()", e));
}
```

9-7-1 **Rethrowing the Exception Back to Main**

One of the possible situations is to throw the exception back to the **Main** method. In Example 9-9 the following scenario takes place:

1. MyMethod1 is first invoked in **Main**.
2. MyMethod1 calls the method MyMethod2.
3. MyMethod2 throws the exception for the first time.
4. The exception is caught in MyMethod1, where some handling is done.
5. MyMethod1 rethrows the exception.
6. The exception is caught in **Main**, where more handling is done.

You can see these events in the output of the example.

Example 9-9

```
// Example 9-9.cs
// Rethrowing exceptions

using System;

class MyClass
```

```
{
   static void Main()
   {
      MyClass mc = new MyClass();

      try
      {
         mc.MyMethod1();                                    // event #1
      }
      catch(Exception e)
      {
         Console.WriteLine("Caught in Main: {0}", e);       // event #6
         Console.WriteLine("More cleanup ...");

      }
   }

   public void MyMethod1()
   {
      try
      {
         MyMethod2();                                       // event #2
      }
      catch(Exception)
      {
         Console.WriteLine("Caught in MyMethod1");          // event #4
         Console.WriteLine("Cleanup chores ...");
         // Rethrow the same exception:
         throw;                                             // event #5
      }
   }

   public void MyMethod2()
   {
      throw new Exception("thrown by MyMethod2");           // event #3
   }
}
```

Output:

```
Caught in MyMethod1
Cleanup chores ...
Caught in Main: System.Exception: thrown by MyMethod2
   at MyClass.MyMethod2()
   at MyClass.MyMethod1()
   at MyClass.Main()
More cleanup ...
```

9-7-2 **Rethrowing by the Handler Block**

In the following example, the exception is handled and rethrown back to **Main** for more processing. In the example, you see the following events:

1. MyMethod is invoked from **Main**.
2. MyMethod generates the exception DivideByZeroException.
3. MyMethod catches the exception and rethrows it back to **Main**.
4. The exception is caught and handled in **Main**.

Example 9-10

```
// Example 9-10.cs
// Rethrowing exceptions by the handler

using System;

class MainClass
{
    static void Main()
    {
        MyClass mc = new MyClass();
        try
        {
            mc.MyMethod();
        }
        catch (Exception ex)
        {
            // Catch the rethrown exception:
            Console.WriteLine("Rethrown exception is caught in
                        Main:\n{0}", ex);
        }
    }
}

class MyClass
{
    int x = 0, y = 0;
    public void MyMethod()
    {
        try
        {
            int z = x / y;    // dividing by zero
        }
```

```
        catch (DivideByZeroException ex)
        {
            // Catch and Rethrow the same exception:
            throw (new DivideByZeroException
                ("Dividing by zero occurred in MyMethod\n", ex));
        }
    }
}
```

Output:

```
Rethrown exception is caught in Main:
System.DivideByZeroException: Dividing by zero occurred in MyMethod
---> System.DivideByZeroException: Attempted to divide by zero.
   at MyClass.MyMethod()
   --- End of inner exception stack trace ---
   at MyClass.MyMethod()
   at MainClass.Main()
```

Notice that the sequence of events in the output starts from the moment the rethrown exception was caught.

9-8 Using the StackTrace Property

StackTrace, a property of the **Exception** class, lets you keep track of the exception object as it travels up the call stack looking for a matching handler. The property retrieves a string that represents the trace of the method calls when the current exception is thrown.

As you can see in the following example, which is a rewrite of Example 9-9, the output is simple and clear. We removed all the printing statements whose purpose was to keep track of the program execution. Instead, the following method is used:

```
Console.WriteLine("Caught exception:\n{0}", e.StackTrace);
```

The text "Caught exception" is the only text that you need to write. The rest is generated by the StackTrace:

```
   at MyClass.MyMethod2()
   at MyClass.MyMethod1()
   at MyClass.Main()
```

When you examine the program, you can see that this is the way exception handling in a real application should be written.

Example 9-11

```csharp
// Example 9-11.cs
// Using the StackTrace property

using System;

class MyClass
{
   static void Main()
   {
      MyClass mc = new MyClass();

      try
      {
         mc.MyMethod1();          // event #1
      }

      catch(Exception e)
      {
         Console.WriteLine("Caught exception:\n{0}", e.StackTrace);
         // event #6
      }
   }

   public void MyMethod1()
   {
      try
      {
         MyMethod2();             // event #2
      }

      catch(Exception)
      {
         // Rethrow the same exception:
         throw;                   // event #5
      }
   }

   public void MyMethod2()
   {
      throw new Exception();      // event #3
   }
}
```

Output:

```
Caught exception:
    at MyClass.MyMethod2()
    at MyClass.MyMethod1()
    at MyClass.Main()
```

Drill 9-4

It is possible to use the handler to fix the problem that takes place when the code throws an exception. Write a program that catches the exception DivideByZeroException and solve the problem in the catch block. Part of the handling should be reading a new number from the keyboard to use as the denominator of the division and retry evaluating the expression $z = x/y$. The output of the program should be something like this:

```
A divide-by-zero occurred:
    at MyClass.MyMethod(Int32 x)
Please enter the denominator of the division 'x': 2
The division: 10 / 2 = 5
```

Summary

In this chapter:

- You started by examining an exception and went through the succes-sive screens that describe it.
- You learned how to use the try block to see if a suspicious code seg-ment would throw an exception.
- You also learned how to use catch blocks that catch exceptions and handle them so that the program can resume execution.
- You took a tour of file protocols and learned how to open a file for reading, writing, or appending. You also learned about the expected exceptions in file processing and how to catch them.
- You now know the purpose of using the finally block in exception han-dling and how to build the exception construct by using the keywords **try**, **catch**, and **finally**.

- You learned how to create your own exceptions in order to include detailed text about the caught exception.
- You also learned how to rethrow an exception and how to make use of this feature to do further handling of the exceptions.
- Finally, you learned about the **StackTrace** property and how to use it in displaying the call stack.

Chapter 10

Delegates and Events

Contents:
- Delegate definition
- Declaring and using delegates
- Adding and deleting delegates
- Anonymous methods
- Covariance and contravariance
- Events
- Using events in applications

10-1 What Is a Delegate?

A *delegate* is one of the reference types in C#. It is used to encapsulate a method of a specific signature and pass it as its parameter. It is similar to a function pointer in C++ except it is type-safe like all the elements of the managed languages under the umbrella of .NET.

As the name indicates, the delegate does not work alone, but it delegates the associated method to do its work.

10-2 Declaring Delegates

You can declare a delegate using the following form:

```
[modifiers] delegate result identifier ([parameters])
```

where:

modifiers is a valid combination of access modifiers in addition to the **new** modifier.

result is the type of the delegate, which is the same as the type of the encapsulated method.

identifier is the delegate name.
parameters is an optional list of parameters.

For example:

```
delegate void MyDelegate(object o1, object o2);
```

This delegate can encapsulate methods with the same signature, such as:

```
static void MyMethod(object o1, object o2) { ... }
```

Notice that with the new delegate features, *covariance* and *contravariance*, some flexibility is provided in matching delegates and the associated methods. Covariance and contravariance are explained in Sections 10-8 and 10-9.

10-3 **Creating a Delegate**

To create a delegate, follow these steps:

1. Declare the delegate where you usually declare types (in a namespace or a class). For example:

   ```
   delegate void MyDelegate(object o1, object o2);
   ```

2. Declare the method that will be associated with the delegate. For example:

   ```
   public static void MyMethod(object id, object name) { ... }
   ```

   Notice that the return type and parameter types are identical for both the methods and the delegate (they are indicated by the boldface).

3. Create a delegate object:

   ```
   MyDelegate delegObj = new MyDelegate(MyMethod);
   ```

   Notice that the parameter of the delegate is the name of the encapsulated method.

   You can also create a delegate object without using the **new** operator, simply by assigning the method to the delegate:

   ```
   MyDelegate delegObj = MyMethod;
   ```

10-4 **Invoking the Delegate**

Invoke the delegate using the same parameters you would use when calling the associated method. You can invoke the delegate created in the preceding section like this:

```
delegObj(119, "Jane Doe");
```

Alternatively, you can invoke the delegate from a method, as shown in the following example:

```
public static void CallDelegate(MyDelegate meth)
{
    meth(119, "Jane Doe");
}
```

Notice that this method is using a parameter, meth, of the type MyDelegate. It is obvious that the name of the method is not important, but the signature is; it must have the same signature as the encapsulated method, MyMethod.

You can also invoke the delegate by using the .NET method **Invoke** like this:

```
delegObj.Invoke(119, "Jane Doe");
```

In this specific example, we used the modifier **static**, just to make things simpler. However, delegates can use both instance and static methods.

In the following example, delegates are brought into action.

Example 10-1

```
// Example 10-1.cs
// Using delegates

using System;

// Declare a delegate:
delegate void MyDelegate(int n, string s);

class MainClass
{
    static void Main()
    {
        // Instantiate the class:
        MyClass obj = new MyClass();

        // Instantiate the delegate:
        MyDelegate d = new MyDelegate(obj.MyMethod);

        // Invoke the delegate:
        obj.CallDelegate(d);
    }
}

class MyClass
{
    // A method to invoke the delegate:
```

```
public void CallDelegate(MyDelegate meth)
{
    meth(119, "Jane Doe");
}

// The encapsulated method:
public void MyMethod(int id, string name)
{
    Console.WriteLine("ID = {0}\nName = {1}", id, name);
}
}
```

Output:

```
ID = 119
Name = Jane Doe
```

Drill 10-1

Rewrite the preceding example without using the extra method:

```
public void CallDelegate(MyDelegate meth)
```

Instead, invoke the delegate directly by using the parameters of the associated method.

10-5 Associating a Delegate with More Than One Method

The association between a delegate and a method is defined dynamically at run time. In other words, the delegate doesn't know, during the compilation, which method it will encapsulate. What matters is the signature and the return type of that method. This means that you can associate the same delegate with more than one method in your program.

In the following example, two **double** methods are declared, one to calculate the average and one to calculate the sum. A delegate of the type **double** is declared and instantiated. The delegate object is associated with each method and invoked, one at a time.

Example 10-2

```
// Example 10-2.cs
// Delegates

using System;

public class Calc
{
    // Declare a delegate:
    public delegate double Calculation(int x, int y, int z);

    // Declare methods:
    public static double Sum(int n1, int n2, int n3)
    {
        return n1 + n2 + n3;
    }

    public static double Average(int n1, int n2, int n3)
    {
        return (n1 + n2 + n3)/3;
    }

    public static void Main()
    {
        double result;

        // Instantiate the delegate, associate it with Average:
        Calculation myCalc = new Calculation(Average);

        // Invoke the delegate:
        result = myCalc(3,6,9);
        Console.WriteLine("Average: {0}", result);

        // Instantiate another object and associate it with Sum:
        myCalc = new Calculation(Sum);

        // Invoke the delegate:
        result = myCalc(3,6,9);
        Console.WriteLine("Sum: {0}", result);
    }
}
```

Output:

```
Average: 6
Sum: 18
```

10-6 **Adding and Removing Delegates**

Delegates can be combined by using the + operator to create a compound delegate. Invoking the compound delegate invokes the constituent delegates. The purpose of combining delegates is to encapsulate more than one method by the same delegate. This operation is called *multicasting*. It is also possible to remove a delegate from a compound delegate by using the – operator. You can use += and –= to do the same thing.

Similarly, you can add and remove delegates by using the .NET methods **Combine** and **Remove**, which are members of the class **System.Delegate**.

The following example demonstrates delegate multicasting.

Example 10-3

```
// Example 10-3.cs
// Adding and removing delegates

using System;

// Declare a delegate:
delegate void MyDelegate();

class MyClass
{
    public void MyMethod1()
    {
        Console.Write("MyMethod #1 ");
    }

    public void MyMethod2()
    {
        Console.Write("MyMethod #2 ");
    }
}

class MainClass
{
    static void Main()
    {
        // Instantiate MyClass:
        MyClass mc = new MyClass();
```

```
        // Declare delegate object and reference MyMethod1:
        MyDelegate d1 = new MyDelegate(mc.MyMethod1);

        // Declare delegate object and reference MyMethod2:
        MyDelegate d2 = new MyDelegate(mc.MyMethod2);

        // Declare delegate d3 by adding d1 and d2.
        // This will invoke both MyMethod1 and MyMethod2:
        MyDelegate d3 = d1 + d2;

        // Declare delegate d4 by removing d1 from d3.
        // This will invoke MyMethod2 only:
        MyDelegate d4 = d3 - d1;

        Console.Write("Invoking d1, referencing ");
        d1();
        Console.Write("\nInvoking d2, referencing ");
        d2();
        Console.Write("\nInvoking d3, referencing ");
        d3();
        Console.Write("\nInvoking d4, referencing ");
        d4();
    }
}
```

Output:

```
Invoking d1, referencing MyMethod #1
Invoking d2, referencing MyMethod #2
Invoking d3, referencing MyMethod #1 MyMethod #2
Invoking d4, referencing MyMethod #2
```

Notes on the preceding example:

- In this example, the delegate d1 encapsulated MyMethod1. Also, the delegate d2 encapsulated MyMethod2.

- Adding d1 to d2 to create d3 resulted in calling MyMethod1 and MyMethod2 when d3 was invoked.

- Removing d1 from d3 resulted in calling MyMethod2 only when d3 was invoked.

- It is possible to use the shorthand assignment operators, += and -=, to add and remove delegates. For example:

```
d1 += d2;   // add d1 to d2 and assign the result to d1.
d3 -= d1    // subtract d1 from d3 and assign the result to d3.
```

10-6-1 Using .NET Methods to Add and Remove Delegates

To add or remove delegates by using the .NET methods, use the following statements:

```
// Combine d1 and 2, giving d3:
MyDelegate d3 = (MyDelegate)Delegate.Combine(d1, d2);
// Remove d1 from d3, giving d4:
MyDelegate d4 = (MyDelegate)Delegate.Remove(d3, d1);
```

When using .NET methods it is necessary to use casting to convert the result to the **delegate** type.

 Note Using void as the delegate type in the previous examples was not by accident. In fact, it is recommended over any other type as long as the delegate encapsulates more than one method; otherwise, you cannot control the returned values from methods when you invoke the delegate.

Drill 10-2

Rewrite Example 10-3 using static methods and make sure you get the same results.

10-7 Anonymous Methods

Anonymous methods, a new feature of C# 2005, enables you to pass a code segment as a delegate parameter directly without declaring a separate method. Consider the following delegate declaration:

```
delegate void MyDelegate(string s);
```

Instead of declaring a separate method, MyMethod, like this:

```
public void MyMethod(string s)
{
    Console.WriteLine(s);
}
```

you can directly associate the delegate with the method's code:

```
MyDelegate delegObject = delegate(string s) { Console.WriteLine(s); };
```

Notice the semicolon at the end of the block.

In the following example, a delegate using an anonymous method with two object parameters is demonstrated.

Example 10-4

```
// Example 10-4.cs
// Anonymous methods

using System;

class MyClass
{
   // Declare a delegate:
   delegate void MyDelegate(object o1, object o2);

   static void Main()
   {
      // Instantiate the delegate using an anonymous method:
      MyDelegate delegObject = delegate(object o1, object o2)
      {
         Console.WriteLine("{0} {1}", o1, o2);
      };

      // Invoke the delegate:
      delegObject("My number is: ", 123);
   }
}
```

Output:

```
My number is:  123
```

10-7-1 Outer Variables

Local variables that are used inside anonymous methods are called *outer* or *captured* variables. The lifetime of an outer variable is the same as the lifetime of the delegate. While a regular local variable is removed from memory right after the method exits, an outer variable is removed when the delegate is garbage collected.

In the following example, a local variable is declared and captured by a delegate; therefore, its lifetime is extended during the successive calls of the delegate. The outer variable maintains its value across the multiple calls of the delegate.

Example 10-5

```
// Example 10-5.cs
// Anonymous methods and outer variables

using System;

class MyClass
{
    // Declare a delegate:
    delegate void MyDelegate();

    static void Main()
    {
        // Declare an outer variable:
        int outerVar = 0;

        // Instantiate the delegate using an anonymous method:
        MyDelegate delegObject = delegate()
        {
            Console.WriteLine("My outer variable is now: {0}", ++outerVar);
        };

        // Invoke the delegate object several times:
        for (int n=1; n <= 10; n++)
            delegObject();
    }
}
```

Output:

```
My outer variable is now: 1
My outer variable is now: 2
My outer variable is now: 3
My outer variable is now: 4
My outer variable is now: 5
My outer variable is now: 6
My outer variable is now: 7
My outer variable is now: 8
My outer variable is now: 9
My outer variable is now: 10
```

10-7-2 **Restrictions on Using Anonymous Methods**

When using anonymous methods, you should be aware of the following restrictions:

- The scope of an anonymous method is limited to its block. This means that you cannot use any jump statements to transfer control outside the method's block. The opposite is not allowed either.
- An anonymous method cannot use the $-=$ operator. If you need to remove a named method from a multicast delegate, you must use named methods.
- An anonymous method cannot use unsafe code inside its block.
- An anonymous method cannot be a function member.
- An anonymous method cannot use attributes.
- Anonymous methods cannot use **ref** or **out** with an outer variable.

➲ **Note** In Chapter 14, you will learn about lambda expressions, which provide a concise syntax for writing anonymous methods. Lambda expressions are known as a superset of anonymous methods.

10-8 **Covariance**

Covariance is a new feature that was added to C# 2005 to provide some flexibility in matching the delegate type and the return type of the encapsulated method. Instead of using the same type for both the delegate and the method's return value, covariance permits using a return type for the method that specializes (is derived from) the type of the delegate.

In the following example, a delegate of the type Person encapsulates two methods, MyMethodP and MyMethodE. MyMethodP has the return type Person, which is the same type as the delegate. MyMethodE has the return type Employee, which specializes Person — this is covariance.

Example 10-6

```
// Example 10-6.cs
// Covariance

using System;

public class Employee: Person {}
```

```
public class Person {}

class MyClass
{
   // Declare a delegate:
   delegate Person MyDelegate();

   // The encapsulated method of type Person:
   public Person MyMethodP()
   {
      Console.WriteLine("MyMethodP is called.");
      return null;
   }

   // The encapsulated method of type Employee:
   public Employee MyMethodE()
   {
      Console.WriteLine("MyMethodE is called.");
      return null;
   }

   static void Main()
   {
      // Instantiate the class:
      MyClass mc = new MyClass();

      // Instantiate the delegate (regular case):
      MyDelegate d1 = mc.MyMethodP;

      // Instantiate the delegate (covariance case):
      MyDelegate d2 = mc.MyMethodE;

      // Invoke both delegates:
      d1.Invoke();
      d2.Invoke();
   }
}
```

Output:

```
MyMethodP is called.
MyMethodE is called.
```

Notice in the preceding example the different way of instantiating delegates without the **new** operator:

```
MyDelegate d1 = mc.MyMethodP;
```

Keep in mind that if the method is static, you don't need to qualify it with the object mc.

10-9 **Contravariance**

Contravariance is another new feature added to C# 2005 in order to give more flexibility in matching the signatures of the delegate and the encapsulated method. Instead of using the same type of parameters, contravariance allows using a method's parameter of a type that specializes (is derived from) the parameter of delegate.

The following example demonstrates both covariance and contravariance. Four classes are declared: **Person**, **Employee**, **Resident**, and **Citizen**. The class **Employee** specializes Person, and the class **Citizen** specializes Resident. A delegate and the associated method are declared like this:

```
delegate Person MyDelegate(Citizen c);
public static Employee MyMethod(Resident r)
```

The return type of the method (**Employee**) specializes the type of the delegate (Person), which is covariance. The parameter of the delegate (Citizen) specializes the parameter of the method (**Resident**), which is contravariance.

Example 10-7

```
// Example 10-7.cs
// Contravariance

using System;

public class Person { }
public class Employee: Person { }
public class Resident { }
public class Citizen: Resident { }

class MyClass
{
    // Declare a delegate:
    delegate Person MyDelegate(Citizen c);

    // The encapsulated method.
    // Notice the return type and the parameters:
    public static Employee MyMethod(Resident r)
    {
        Console.WriteLine("MyMethod is called.");
        return null;
    }

    static void Main()
```

```
    {
        // Instantiate the Citizen class:
        Citizen citizen = new Citizen();

        // Instantiate the delegate:
        MyDelegate d = MyMethod;

        // Invoke the delegates:
        d.Invoke(citizen);
    }
}
```

Output:

```
MyMethod is called.
```

Notice the declaration of the delegate object by assigning the method to it:

```
MyDelegate d = MyMethod;
```

which is an alternative to:

```
MyDelegate d = new MyDelegate(MyMethod);
```

10-10 **Events**

One of the most important uses of delegates is programming events, especially in the Windows environment. When you click a button in a window, an event is fired. The response to that event may take several forms. It is your job as a programmer to write the appropriate response to that event in your application. For example, if you created a Windows forms application and you started by adding a button to the application form, you can associate the button click to a specific result, such as writing some text in a text box. In the following figure, you see the phrase "Hello, World!" written in a text box as a result of clicking the button.

Figure 10-1: Firing an event with a button click.

The code written in the background of this operation is the following method:

```
private void button1_Click(object sender, EventArgs e)
{
    textBox1.Text = "Hello, World!";
}
```

If you are familiar with programming Windows applications, you know that the only piece of code you are required to provide here is:

```
textBox1.Text = "Hello, World!";
```

This line of code means, "When you click the button, write the phrase "Hello, World!" in the text box object textBox1." The method itself is provided by the IDE environment when you double-click the button in the design mode.

When we discuss events, we use the terms *sending* (or *firing*) the event and *receiving* (or *handling*) the event.

In the Windows environment there are many events that can be fired, such as changing the text in a text box, moving to another control element, and so forth. Receiving the event depends totally on the application you are developing. The result can be playing a tune or sending a text message in a message box.

10-10-1 Using Events in Applications

In the command-line environment, it is possible to use events in a variety of applications, such as to simulate the action of clicking a mouse button. To do that, follow these steps:

1. Declare a delegate to be used as a handler (or a receiver).

    ```
    delegate void RightButtonDown(object sender, EventArgs e);
    ```

2. Then use this delegate name (RightButtonDown) as the type for the event, which is declared with the **event** keyword. For example, call the event (the sender) PressDown:

    ```
    event RightButtonDown PressDown;
    ```

This registers the delegate as an event. When the event occurs, the delegate is invoked.

The following example is a simulation of a bookstore's sales to analyze the sales situation by measuring the stock changes. The output of the program gives a report like this:

```
2007 Sales Rate:
    C# Books are up by 20
```

```
C++ Books are down by 11
...
```

This report is based on the inventory change of C# books by –20 (sales) and C++ books by +11 (returns).

Example 10-8

```
// Example 10-8.cs
// Bookstore

using System;

class MyEventArgs: EventArgs
{
    // Fields:
    private string stock;
    private int change;

    // Properties:
    public string MyStock
    {
        get { return stock; }
        }
        public int MyChange
        {
        get { return change; }
    }

    // Constructor:
    public MyEventArgs(string s, int c)
    {
        stock = s;
        change = c;
    }
}

class Sender
{
    public delegate void EventHandler(object source, MyEventArgs e);
    public event EventHandler OnChange;

    // Update database:
    public void Update(string s, int c)
    {
        MyEventArgs e = new MyEventArgs(s,c);
        if (OnChange != null)
            OnChange(this, e);
    }
```

```
    }

class Receiver
{
    public Receiver(Sender s)
    {
        // Add the event:
        s.OnChange += new Sender.EventHandler(OnStockChange);
    }
    void OnStockChange(object source, MyEventArgs e)
    {
        string upOrDown;
        if (e.MyChange > 0)
            upOrDown = "down";
        else upOrDown = "up";
            int ch = Math.Abs(e.MyChange);
        Console.WriteLine("{0} {1} by {2}", e.MyStock, upOrDown, ch);
    }
}

class MyClass
{
    public static void Main()
    {
        Sender s = new Sender();
        Receiver r = new Receiver(s);
        // Print Results:
        Console.WriteLine("2007 Sales Rate:");
        s.Update("\tC# Books:", -20);
        s.Update("\tC++ Books:", 11);
        s.Update("\tVB .NET Books:", -15);
        s.Update ("\tScience Fiction Books:", 120);
    }
}
```

Output:

```
2007 Sales Rate:
C# Books: up by 20
C++ Books: down by 11
VB .NET Books: up by 15
Science Fiction Books: down by 120
```

Notes about the above example:

- The classes of the program are divided into **Sender** and **Receiver** in addition to the class MyEventArgs.

■ The MyEventArgs class is derived from the **EventArgs** class:

```
class MyEventArgs: EventArgs
{
    // Fields:
    private string stock;
    private int stockChange;
    ...
}
```

In order to build this class, it is necessary to pass the arguments stock and stockChange as shown in the constructor:

```
public MyEventArgs(string s, int c)
{
    stock = s;
    stockChange = c;
}
```

■ The delegate is declared like this:

```
public delegate void EventHandler(object source, MyEventArgs e);
```

This way, the parameter e is holding the necessary information of the sender when the inventory level changes. The event is declared by using the delegate:

```
public event EventHandler OnstockChange;
```

■ Notice that the **Receiver** class contains an object of the **Sender** class (s). This object is used to add the event like this:

```
s.OnstockChange += new Sender.EventHandler(OnStockstockChange);
```

Notice that the only allowed operators are += and —=. For example, you cannot use the following statement to add the event:

```
s.OnstockChange = new Sender.EventHandler(OnStockstockChange);
```

This statement releases any previous association of the event. What is actually required is to add a new association.

■ The method **OnStockstockChange** is used to receive and analyze the inventory data. It also uses the parameters e and source:

```
void OnStockstockChange(object source, MyEventArgs e)
```

■ The role of **Main** in this example is to pass the changes that took place in the inventory to the **Update** method, which fires the event and handles it.

Drill 10-3

Write a program to simulate the mouse right-click and respond by displaying an appropriate text message.

 Note In Chapter 14, you learn about generic delegate types (a new feature of C# 3.0), which can be used to construct delegates without the need to explicitly declare them.

Summary

In this chapter:

- You learned how to declare, create, and invoke a delegate.
- You also know how to combine delegates to create a compound delegate that encapsulates more than one method. You also learned how to add delegates to and remove them from a compound delegate.
- You now know that you can use a delegate that encapsulates an unnamed method (anonymous method).
- You learned about covariance and contravariance, new features that were introduced with C# 2005.
- You took a tour of events and learned how to use them in your applications.

Chapter 11

Collections and Iterators

Contents:
- Collections classes
- The Stack collection
- The Queue collection
- The ArrayList collection
- The SortedList collection
- The Hashtable collection
- Specialized collections
- The Linked List collection
- Using enumerators
- Iterators

11-1 Collections Classes

The namespaces **System.Collections** and **System.Collections.Generic** introduced a large number of commonly used collections you can choose from according to your application. Selecting the right collection is very important to avoid problems that may arise when your application is nearing completion.

The array has historically been the most common collection used by developers. However, it has some disadvantages. The biggest disadvantage of an array is that it is a static collection with a fixed size. Before .NET 2005, programmers, especially beginners, struggled when trying to change the size of the array in the middle of a project. The only way to do that was to copy the array to a new one and discard the old one. With .NET 2005, the method **Array.Resize** solved this problem by doing this work for you in the background. Arrays also have advantages over other collection types. For example, you can access any element of the array randomly and quickly by using the index of the element. Also, when you use dynamic

241

collections such as **LinkedList** and **ArrayList** collections, you can add elements at run time without any size restrictions.

In the following sections, some of the most commonly used collections of the **System.Collections** are introduced:

- Stack
- Queue
- ArrayList
- SortedList
- Hashtable
- ListDictionary

These collections implement the interface **IEnumerable**; therefore, you can iterate over their members using the **foreach** loop, as explained later in this chapter. Section 11-8 also introduces the non-generic Linked List collection. In order to use **foreach** with this collection, you have to manually enumerate the collection; this will be discussed in Section 11-10. In Chapter 12, the generic **LinkedList** collection is introduced.

11-2 **The Stack Collection**

The *Stack* collection is distinguished as being "last-in, first-out" (LIFO collection classes). When you insert some elements in the stack, the last element pushed in is the first one that pops out. The *capacity* of a **Stack** collection is the number of elements that can be stored in the collection. The default initial capacity is 10. When you add more elements to the collection, the capacity is automatically increased.

To try a simple and quick Stack program, use the following procedure:

1. Add the following directive to your application:
   ```
   using System.Collections;
   ```
2. Declare the **Stack** collection with one of the constructors listed in Table 11-1, such as:
   ```
   Stack <stack-name> = new Stack();
   ```
3. Add elements to the collection by using the method **Push**.
4. Use the method **Pop** to remove and display the elements of the stack.
5. Use the method **Peek** to display the element at the top of the stack.
6. Display the elements by using a **foreach** loop, which is designed to work with collections.

The following table shows other **Stack** methods and properties that you can use in your applications.

➲ **Note**   The Stack class implements the following interfaces:

```
IClonable
ICollection
IEnumerable
```

11-2-1 **Stack Members**

The following are the commonly used members of the **Stack** collection.

Table 11-1: Commonly used members of the Stack class

Property/Method	Description	Syntax
Public constructors	Creates and initializes an empty Stack collection with the default capacity.	Stack()
	Creates and initializes a Stack collection with the elements of a specified *collection*.	Stack(ICollection *collection*)
	Creates and initializes a Stack collection with an initial specified *capacity* or the default capacity, whichever is greater.	Stack(int *capacity*)
Clear	Removes all items from the collection.	public virtual void Clear()
Contains	Checks if a specific *item* is in the collection.	public virtual bool Contains(object *item*)
Count	Retrieves the number of items in the collection.	public virtual int Count {get;}
Peek	Returns the item at the top of the collection without removing it.	public virtual object Peek()
Pop	Removes and returns the item at the top of the collection.	public virtual object Pop()
Push	Inserts an *item* in the Stack collection.	public virtual void Push(object *item*)
ToArray	Copies all the items in the collection to an object array.	public virtual object[] ToArray()

For a list of all the members of the collection, see the Stack help file.

Example 11-1

In the following example, a **Stack** collection is initialized with four **string** objects and then displayed using **foreach**. As you can see, the first inserted item is the last one displayed.

```
// Example 11-1.cs
// Stack1

using System;
using System.Collections;

public class MyClass
{
    public static void Main()
    {
        // Create a stack object:
        Stack myStack = new Stack();

        // Insert elements:
        myStack.Push("out");
        myStack.Push("first");
        myStack.Push("in");
        myStack.Push("Last");

        // Display the elements:
        foreach(object item in myStack)
        {
            Console.Write("{0} ", item);
        }
    }
}
```

Output:

```
Last in first out
```

Example 11-2

In the following example, a **Stack** collection is initialized with an array. The items in the collection are removed one by one until it is empty. The number of the remaining items and the item on the top of the collection are displayed after each removal.

```
// Example 11-2.cs
// Stack2

using System;
using System.Collections;
```

```csharp
public class MyClass
{
    public static void Main()
    {
        // Declare an array collection:
        string[] myArr = {"Tom", "Dick", "Harry"};

        // Use the array to initialize a stack object:
        Stack myStack = new Stack(myArr);

        // Display the number of elements:
        Console.WriteLine("The number of elements is: {0} ",
                        myStack.Count);

        // Display all:
        Console.Write("Elements: ");
        foreach (object obj in myStack)
            Console.Write(obj + " ");
        Console.WriteLine();

        // Display and remove items one by one:
        for (int i = myStack.Count; i > 0; i--)
        {
            Console.WriteLine("\nTop element on the stack is now: {0}",
                            myStack.Peek());
            Console.WriteLine("The number of elements is now: {0}",
                            myStack.Count);
            Console.WriteLine("Element '{0}' has been removed from the
                            stack.", myStack.Pop());
        }

        // Display the number of elements:
        Console.WriteLine("\nThe number of elements is now: {0} ",
                        myStack.Count);
    }
}
```

Output:

```
The number of elements is: 3
Elements: Harry Dick Tom

Top element on the stack is now: Harry
The number of elements is now: 3
Element 'Harry' has been removed from the stack.

Top element on the stack is now: Dick
The number of elements is now: 2
Element 'Dick' has been removed from the stack.
```

```
Top element on the stack is now: Tom
The number of elements is now: 1
Element 'Tom' has been removed from the stack.

The number of elements is now: 0
```

Drill 11-1

Create a Stack collection that contains four elements. Display its items, display and remove the item on the top, and then check if the fourth element is in the stack. Finally, copy the remaining items to an array and display it.

11-3 The Queue Collection

The *Queue* collection represents a "first-in, first-out" (FIFO) collection of objects. When you insert some elements in the queue, the first element inserted is the first one to be extracted. The *capacity* of a **Queue** collection is the number of elements that can be stored in the collection. The default initial capacity is 32. When you add elements to the collection, the capacity is automatically increased. The *growth factor* is the number by which the current capacity is multiplied when the capacity increases. Unless it is set by the appropriate constructor, the growth factor takes the default value 2.0.

To create a simple and quick **Queue** collection program, use the following procedure:

1. Add the following directive to your program:
   ```
   using System.Collections;
   ```
2. Declare an empty **Queue** collection with the statement:
   ```
   Queue <queue-name> = new Queue();
   ```
3. Add elements to the collection by using the method **Enqueue**.
4. Use the method **Dequeue** to remove and display the elements of the queue.
5. Use the method **Peek** to display the element at the beginning of the queue.
6. Display the elements by using a **foreach** loop, which is designed to work with collections.

The following table lists other **Queue** methods and properties that you can use in your applications.

⊖ **Note**   The Queue class implements the following interfaces:
```
IClonable
ICollection
IEnumerable
```

11-3-1 **Queue Members**

Table 11-2 lists the commonly used members of the **Queue** collection.

Table 11-2: Commonly used members of the Queue class

Property/Method	Description	Syntax
Public constructors	Creates and initializes an empty Queue collection with the default capacity (32) and default growth factor (2.0).	Queue()
	Creates and initializes a Queue collection with the elements of a specified *collection*.	Queue(ICollection *collection*)
	Creates and initializes a Queue collection with an initial specified *capacity* or the default capacity.	Queue(int *capacity*)
	Creates and initializes a Queue collection with an initial specified *capacity* and a specified *growth* factor.	Queue(int *capacity*, float *growth*)
Clear	Removes all items from the collection.	public virtual void Clear()
Contains	Checks if a specific *item* is in the collection.	public virtual bool Contains(object *item*)
Count	Retrieves the number of items in the collection.	public virtual int Count {get;}
Dequeue	Removes and returns the item at the beginning of the collection.	public virtual object Dequeue()
Enqueue	Inserts an *item* at the end of the collection.	public virtual void Enqueue(object *item*)
Peek	Returns the item at the beginning of the collection.	public virtual object Peek()
ToArray	Copies all the items in the collection to an object array.	public virtual object[] ToArray()
TrimToSize	Sets the capacity of the collection to the existing number of items.	public virtual void TrimToSize()

For a list of all the members of the collection, see the Queue help file.

Example 11-3

In the following example, a **Queue** collection is initialized with four elements and then displayed by using the **foreach** statement.

```
// Example 11-3.cs
// Queue1

using System;
using System.Collections;

public class MyClass
{
    public static void Main()
    {
        // Create an empty Queue collection:
        Queue myQueue = new Queue();

        // Add items to the collection:
        myQueue.Enqueue("First");
        myQueue.Enqueue("in");
        myQueue.Enqueue("first");
        myQueue.Enqueue("out");

        // Display the contents:
        foreach(string item in myQueue)
        {
            Console.Write("{0} ", item);
        }
    }
}
```

Output:

```
First in first out
```

Example 11-4

In the following example, a **Queue** collection is initialized from an array collection. The collection items are removed and displayed by using the **Dequeue** method until the collection is empty. The number of items is displayed before and after the removal.

```
// Example 11-4.cs
// Queue2

using System;
using System.Collections;
```

```
public class MyClass
{
    public static void Main()
    {
        // Declare an array collection:
        string[] myArr = {"Tom", "Dick", "Harry"};

        // Use the array to initialize a Queue object:
        Queue myQueue = new Queue(myArr);

        // Display the number of items:
        Console.WriteLine("The number of items is: {0}",
            myQueue.Count);

        // Display and remove items:
        while(myQueue.Count != 0)
        {
            Console.Write(myQueue.Dequeue() + " ");
        }
        Console.WriteLine("\nThe number of items is now: {0}",
            myQueue.Count);
    }
}
```

Output:

```
The number of items is: 3
Tom Dick Harry
The number of items is now: 0
```

Drill 11-2

The Queue collection is a collection of objects, which means that it can contain both numbers and strings. To demonstrate this, create a Queue collection and initialize it from an int array, and then create a string array and add its elements to the collection. Copy the collection to an object array and display it.

11-4 **The ArrayList Collection**

An *ArrayList* collection is a dynamic array. You can add items to and remove items from the collection at run time. The elements of an **ArrayList** collection are not sorted automatically, but you can use the **ArrayList.Sort** method to do that. The *capacity* of an **ArrayList** collection is the number of elements that can be stored in the collection. The default capacity is 16. When you add more elements to the collection, the capacity is automatically increased. You can set the capacity by using the appropriate method shown in Table 11-3.

To create a simple and quick **ArrayList** collection program, use the following procedure:

1. Add the following directive to your program:

       using System.Collections;

2. Declare an empty **ArrayList** collection with the statement:

       ArrayList <ArrayList-name> = new ArrayList();

3. Add elements to the collection by using the method **Add**.

4. Display the elements by using a **foreach** loop, which is designed to work with collections.

Table 11-3 lists other **ArrayList** methods and properties that you can use in your applications.

Note   The ArrayList class implements the following interfaces:

    IClonable
    ICollection
    IEnumerable
    IList

11-4-1 **ArrayList Members**

The following table contains the commonly used members of the **ArrayList** collection.

Table 11-3: Commonly used members of the ArrayList class

Property/Method	Description	Syntax
Public constructors	Creates and initializes an empty ArrayList with the default capacity.	ArrayList()
	Creates and initializes an ArrayList with the elements of a specified *collection*.	ArrayList(ICollection *collection*)
	Creates and initializes an ArrayList with an initial specified *capacity*.	ArrayList(int *capacity*)
Add	Adds an *item* to the end of the collection.	public virtual int Add(object *item*)
Capacity	Retrieves or sets the number of items in the collection.	public virtual int Capacity {get; set;}
Clear	Removes all items from the collection.	public virtual void Clear()
Contains	Checks if a specific *item* is in the collection.	public virtual bool Contains(object *item*)
Count	Retrieves the number of items in the ArrayList collection.	public virtual int Count {get;}
IndexOf	Retrieves the index of the first matching *item*.	public virtual int IndexOf(object *item*)
	Retrieves the index of the first matching *item* in the portion of the collection starting at the specified *startingIndex*.	public virtual int IndexOf(object *item*, int *startingIndex*)
	Retrieves the index of the first matching *item* in the portion of the collection starting at the specified *startingIndex* and contains the specified *number* of items.	public virtual int IndexOf(object *item*, int *startingIndex*, int *number*)
Insert	Inserts an *item* into the ArrayList collection at the specified *index*.	public virtual void Insert(int *index*, object *item*)
Item	Retrieves or sets the value of an item that corresponds to a specified *index* (e.g., myList["003"]).	public virtual object this [int *index*] {get; set;}
Remove	Removes the first item that matches the specified *item*.	public virtual void Remove(object *item*)
RemoveAt	Removes the item at the specified *index*.	public virtual void RemoveAt(int *index*)
RemoveRange	Removes a range of items specified by *count* and starting at the specified *index*.	public virtual void RemoveRange(int *index*, int *count*)

Property/Method	Description	Syntax
Reverse	Reverses the order of the items in the ArrayList collection.	public virtual void Reverse()
	Reverses the order of the items in a range specified by *count* and starting at *index*.	public virtual void Reverse(int *index*, int *count*)
Sort	Sorts the items in the collection.	public virtual void Sort()
	Sorts the items in the collection by using a *comparer*.	public virtual void Sort(IComparer *comparer*)
	Sorts the items in the collection by using a *comparer*, *index*, and *count*.	public virtual void Sort(int *index*, int *count*, IComparer *comparer*)
ToArray	Copies all the items in the collection to an object array.	public virtual object[] ToArray()
TrimToSize	Sets the capacity of the collection to the existing number of items.	public virtual void TrimToSize()

For a list of all the members of the collection, see the ArrayList help file.

Example 11-5

In the following example, you initialize an empty ArrayList collection and display its capacity. You then add five items to the collection and display the number of items and the new capacity. You also sort the collection and display the items before and after the sorting.

```
// Example 11-5.cs
// ArrayList

using System;
using System.Collections;

public class MyClass
{
    public static void Main()
    {
        // Create an ArrayList:
        ArrayList myArrayList = new ArrayList();

        // Display the initial capacity:
        Console.WriteLine("The initial capacity is: {0}",
                          myArrayList.Capacity);

        // Initialize the list with some elements:
        myArrayList.Add("SNL");
        myArrayList.Add("Mad TV");
        myArrayList.Add("Seinfeld");
```

```
            myArrayList.Add("Everybody Loves Raymond");
            myArrayList.Add("Married with Children");

            // Display the number of items:
            Console.WriteLine("The number of items: {0}", myArrayList.Count);

            // Display the new capacity:
            Console.WriteLine("The capacity is now: {0}",
                            myArrayList.Capacity);

            // Display the elements in the list:
            Console.WriteLine("\nThe contents of the ArrayList: ");
            DisplayIt(myArrayList);

            // Sort and display the list:
            myArrayList.Sort();
            Console.WriteLine("\nThe contents of the sorted ArrayList: ");
            DisplayIt(myArrayList);
        }

        public static void DisplayIt(ArrayList myList)
        {
            foreach (object item in myList)
                Console.WriteLine("{0}", item);
        }
    }
```

Output:

```
The initial capacity is: 0
The number of items: 5
The capacity is now: 8

The contents of the ArrayList:
SNL
Mad TV
Seinfeld
Everybody Loves Raymond
Married with Children

The contents of the sorted ArrayList:
Everybody Loves Raymond
Mad TV
Married with Children
Seinfeld
SNL
```

Drill 11-3

Add a second "SNL" item to the end of the collection in Example 11-5, and then use the method IndexOf to search for this item starting at index 2.

11-5 The SortedList Collection

The *SortedList* collection is similar to the **ArrayList**, but it is sorted by a key. The data in the **SortedList** consists of key/value entries. The data can be accessed either by keys or indexes. The default capacity of the **SortedList** is 16.

To create a simple and quick **SortedList** collection, use the following procedure:

1. Add the following directive to your program:
   ```
   using System.Collections;
   ```

2. Declare an empty **SortedList** collection with the statement:
   ```
   SortedList <SortedList-name> = new SortedList();
   ```

3. Add elements to the collection by using the method **Add**.

4. Display the elements by using a **foreach** loop, which is designed to work with collections.

Table 11-4 lists other **SortedList** methods and properties that you can use in your applications.

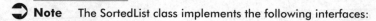

Note   The SortedList class implements the following interfaces:
```
IClonable
ICollection
IEnumerable
IDictionary
```

11-5-1 SortedList Members

The following table contains the commonly used members of the **SortedList** class.

Table 11-4: Commonly used members of the SortedList class

Property/Method	Description	Syntax
Public constructors	Creates and initializes an empty SortedList collection with the default capacity.	SortedList()
	Creates and initializes a SortedList with the elements of a specified dictionary *collection* and sorted according to the IComparable interface implemented by each key.	SortedList(IDictionary *collection*)
	Creates and initializes an empty SortedList collection with an initial default capacity and sorted according to the specified *comparer*.	SortedList(IComparer *comparer*)
Add	Adds an *item* to the collection with the specified *key*.	public virtual void Add(object *key*, object *item*)
Capacity	Retrieves or sets the capacity of a collection.	public virtual int Capacity {get; set;}
Clear	Removes all items from the collection.	public virtual void Clear()
Contains	Checks if a specific *key* is in the SortedList collection.	public virtual bool Contains(object *key*)
ContainsKey	Same as Contains.	public virtual bool ContainsKey(object *key*)
ContainsValue	Checks if a specific *item* is in the collection.	public virtual bool ContainsValue(object *item*)
Count	Retrieves the number of items in the collection.	public virtual int Count {get;}
GetByIndex	Retrieves the item at the specified *index*.	public virtual object GetByIndex(int *index*)
GetKey	Retrieves the key at the specified *index*.	public virtual object GetKey(int *index*)
IndexOfKey	Retrieves the index of a *key*.	public virtual int IndexOfKey(object *key*)
Item	Retrieves or sets the item at the specified *key* (e.g., myList["003"]).	public virtual object this [object *key*] {get; set;}
Remove	Removes the first item that matches the specified *key*.	public virtual void Remove(object *key*)
RemoveAt	Removes the item at the specified *index*.	public virtual void RemoveAt(int *index*)

For a list of all the members of the collection, see the SortedList help file.

Note SortedList does not allow duplicate keys. If you use the same key for two elements, the program throws an exception.

Example 11-6

In the following example, you create a **SortedList** collection and initialize it with the keys and names of five TV shows. You then display the number of items and the capacity. You also display the items of the list, which are sorted according to the key.

```csharp
// Example 11-6.cs
// SortedList

using System;
using System.Collections;

public class MyClass
{
    public static void Main()
    {
        // Create an ArrayList:
        SortedList myList = new SortedList();

        // Initialize the list with some items:
        myList.Add("003","SNL");
        myList.Add("002","Mad TV");
        myList.Add("004","Seinfeld");
        myList.Add("001","Married with Children");
        myList.Add("006","Everybody Loves Raymond");

        // Display the number of items:
        Console.WriteLine("The number of items is: {0}", myList.Count);

        // Display the capacity:
        Console.WriteLine("The capacity is: {0}", myList.Capacity);

        // Display the items in the list:
        Console.WriteLine("The contents of the list: ");
        Console.WriteLine("Key\t Name");
        for (int i = 0; i < myList.Count; i++)
        {
            Console.WriteLine("{0}:\t {1}",
                myList.GetKey(i), myList.GetByIndex(i));
        }
        Console.WriteLine();
    }
}
```

Output:

```
The number of items is: 5
The capacity is: 16
The contents of the list:
Key       Name
001:      Married with Children
002:      Mad TV
003:      SNL
004:      Seinfeld
006:      Everybody Loves Raymond
```

Drill 11-4

Create a collection similar to the collection in the above example and then do the following:

1. Use the method IndexOfKey to get the index of a specific key.
2. Find the item that corresponds to that key by using the Item method.
3. Search for a specific item by using the method ContainsValue.

11-6 The Hashtable Collection

The *Hashtable* collection is a collection of key/value entries. The entries are sorted according to the hash code of the key. Items in a **Hashtable** are of the type **DictionaryEntry**, where each entry has a key and a value. The capacity of a **Hashtable** is the number of items that can be stored in the **Hashtable**. The default initial capacity for a **Hashtable** is zero. When you add items to it, the capacity is automatically increased.

To create a simple and quick **Hashtable** program, use the following procedure:

1. Add the following directive to your program:
   ```
   using System.Collections;
   ```
2. Declare an empty **Hashtable** collection with the statement:
   ```
   Hashtable <Hashtable-name> = new Hashtable();
   ```
3. Add elements to the collection by using the method **Add**.

4. Display the elements by using a **foreach** loop, which is designed to work with collections. When you display items of a **Hashtable**, you can use the **DictionaryEntry** object like this example (see also the **ListDictionary** example in the next section):

```
foreach (DictionaryEntry de in myHashtable)
    Console.WriteLine("{0} {1}", de.Key, de.Value);
```

You can also use the **Keys** property to display values that correspond to each key. For example:

```
foreach (string k in myHashtable.Keys)
    Console.WriteLine("{0} {1}", k, myHashtable[k]);
```

The following table lists other **Hashtable** methods and properties that you can use in your applications.

➔ **Note**   The Hashtable class implements the following interfaces:

```
IClonable
ICollection
IDictionary
IEnumerable
ISerializable
IDeserializationCallback
```

11-6-1 **Hashtable Members**

The following table contains the commonly used members of the **Hashtable** class.

Table 11-5: Commonly used members of the Hashtable class

Property/Method	Description	Syntax
Public constructors	Creates and initializes an empty Hashtable collection with the default capacity and load factor.	Hashtable()
	Creates and initializes a Hashtable collection with an initial specified *capacity* and the default load factor.	Hashtable(int *capacity*)
	Creates and initializes a Hashtable collection with an initial specified *capacity* and specified *loadFactor*.	Hashtable(int *capacity*, float *loadFactor*)
Add	Adds an item with a specified *key* and *value* to the collection.	public virtual void Add(object *key*, object *value*)
Clear	Removes all items from the collection.	public virtual void Clear()

Property/Method	Description	Syntax
Contains	Checks if a specified *key* is in the collection.	public virtual bool Contains(object *key*)
ContainsKey	Same as Contains.	public virtual bool ContainsKey(object *key*)
ContainsValue	Checks if a specified *value* is in the collection.	public virtual bool Contains(object *value*)
Count	Retrieves the number of items in the collection.	public virtual int Count {get;}
Item	Retrieves or sets the value of an item that corresponds to a specified *key* (e.g., myList["003"]).	public virtual object this [object *key*] {get; set;}
Keys	Retrieves an ICollection containing the keys in the collection.	public virtual ICollection Keys {get;}
Remove	Removes an item with a specified *key* from the collection.	public virtual void Remove(object *key*)
Values	Retrieves an ICollection containing the values in the collection.	public virtual ICollection Values {get;}

For a list of all the members of the collection, see the Hashtable help file.

Example 11-7

In the following example, a **Hashtable** collection is initialized with the area codes for some of the states in the U.S. The area codes and the states are displayed.

```
// Example 11-7.cs
// Hashtable

using System;
using System.Collections;
public class MyClass
{
    public static void Main()
    {

        // Creates a Hashtable object:
        Hashtable AreaCodeHash = new Hashtable();

        // Initializes the Hashtable.
        AreaCodeHash.Add("201", "New Jersey");
        AreaCodeHash.Add("337", "Louisiana");
        AreaCodeHash.Add("425", "Washington");
        AreaCodeHash.Add("415", "California");
        AreaCodeHash.Add("503", "Oregon");
```

```
        AreaCodeHash.Add("489", "Texas");

        // Displays the contents of the Hashtable.
        DisplayIt(AreaCodeHash);

        // Display the number of elements:
        Console.WriteLine("Number of elements: {0}", AreaCodeHash.Count);
    }

    public static void DisplayIt(Hashtable AreaCodeHash)
    {
        Console.WriteLine("Area Code\tState");
        foreach (string k in AreaCodeHash.Keys)
            Console.WriteLine("{0, -16}{1}", k, AreaCodeHash[k]);
    }
}
```

Output:

```
Area Code       State
337             Louisiana
489             Texas
425             Washington
503             Oregon
415             California
201             New Jersey
Number of elements: 6
```

Drill 11-5

Create a Hashtable collection for the zip codes of cities in your state, then display all the entries and the city that corresponds to a specified zip code in this format: ZipCodeHash["98006"]. The output should look something like:

```
Zip Code        City
98501           Olympia
98101           Seattle
98006           Bellevue
98201           Everett
98040           Mercer Island
98033           Kirkland

The city that corresponds to zip code "98006": Bellevue
```

11-7 **Specialized Collections**

There are some specialized collections in the .NET Framework class library that are used for specific purposes. They are available in the **System.Collections.Specialized** namespace.

The following table lists some of the common specialized collections.

Table 11-6: Commonly used specialized collections

Collection	Description
HybridDictionary	Implements the IDictionary interface by using a ListDictionary while the collection contains a small number of elements (10 or less). When the number of elements increases, it switches to a Hashtable.
NameValueCollection	A collection of keys and values that can be accessed either with the key or with the index. Both keys and values are strings.
OrderedDictionary	A collection of key/value entries. The items in this collection are DictionaryEntry type objects.
StringCollection	A collection of strings whose items can be accessed using a zero-based integer index.
StringDictionary	A string collection that implements a Hashtable. Both keys and values are strings.

The **ListDictionary** (a **HybridDictionary** with a few items) collection is demonstrated in the following section.

11-7-1 **The ListDictionary Collection**

The *ListDictionary* collection implements the **IDictionary** interface using a singly-linked list. It is recommended for small collections that contain less than 10 items.

11-7-2 **ListDictionary Members**

The following table lists the commonly used members of the **ListDictionary** class.

Table 11-7: Commonly used members of the ListDictionary class

Property/Method	Description	Syntax
Public constructors	Creates an empty ListDictionary collection with the default comparer.	ListDictionary()
	Creates an empty ListDictionary collection with a specified *comparer*.	ListDictionary(IComparer *comparer*)
Add	Adds an item with a specified *key* and *value* to the collection.	public void Add(object *key*, object *value*)

Property/Method	Description	Syntax
Clear	Removes all items from the collection.	public void Clear()
Contains	Checks if a specified *key* is in the collection.	public bool Contains(object *key*)
CopyTo	Copies the collection to a one-dimensional *array* at the specified *index*.	void CopyTo(Array *array*, int *index*)
Count	Retrieves the number of entries in the collection.	public int Count {get;}
Item	Retrieves or sets the value of an item that corresponds to a specified *key* (e.g., myLD["Learn J#"]).	public object this [object *key*] {get; set;}
Keys	Retrieves an ICollection of the keys contained in the collection.	public ICollection Keys {get;}
Remove	Removes an item with a specified *key* from the collection.	public void Remove(object *key*)
Values	Retrieves an ICollection of the values contained in the collection.	public ICollection Values {get;}

For a list of all the members of the collection, see the ListDictionary help file.

Example 11-8

In this example, you create a **ListDictionary** collection and initialize it with names of books and their corresponding prices, and then you display its contents by using a **foreach** statement. Notice that the foreach loop is using the **DictionaryEntry** structure that contains both the key and the value of the current dictionary entry.

```
// Example 11-8.cs
// ListDictionary collection

using System;
using System.Collections;
using System.Collections.Specialized;

public class LDClass
{
    public static void Main(string[] args)
    {
        // Create an empty ListDictionary object:
        ListDictionary myLD = new ListDictionary();

        // Initialize the ListDictionary collection:
        myLD.Add("Learn Pascal", "$39.95");
```

```
        myLD.Add("Learn Pascal in Three Days", "$19.95");
        myLD.Add("Learn C in Three Days", "$19.95");
        myLD.Add("Learn J#", "$35.95");
        myLD.Add("Learn C#", "$39.95");

        // Display the contents:
        DisplayIt(myLD);
    }

    public static void DisplayIt(ListDictionary myLD)
    {
        string s = "\t\t\t\t";
        Console.WriteLine("Book{0}Price\n", s);
        foreach (DictionaryEntry book in myLD)
            Console.WriteLine("{0,-32}{1}", book.Key, book.Value);
    }
}
```

Output:

Book	Price
Learn Pascal	$39.95
Learn Pascal in Three Days	$19.95
Learn C in Three Days	$19.95
Learn J#	$35.95
Learn C# 2005	$39.95

Drill 11-6

Modify the example above to use the Values and Keys properties to do the following:

1. Display all the values in the collection. Use a foreach statement like this:

   ```
   foreach (string value in myLD.Values) ...
   ```

2. Display all the keys in the collection. Use a foreach statement like this:

   ```
   foreach (string key in myLD.Keys) ...
   ```

3. Use the Keys property as an index for the items in the collection. Use a statement like the following to display the same output as that of Example 11-8:

   ```
   foreach (string key in myLD.Keys)
       Console.WriteLine("{0, -32}{1}", key, myLD[key]);
   ```

11-8 **The Linked List Collection**

Before .NET 2005, the linked list was not part of the **System.Collections** namespace. Programmers had to design the linked list from scratch. After .NET 2005, the generic doubly-linked list became part of the **System.Collection.Generic** namespace, providing programmers with a number of methods and properties that made their jobs easier.

Example 11-9

This example demonstrates how to build and display a non-generic linked list. The linked list class contains a class called *Node* and a field of the type **Node** (*head*), which represents the head of the linked list. The **Node** class contains two fields: one field that points to the next node in the linked list (*next*) and another that contains the data (*item*). Remember that this linked list collection cannot use the **foreach** statement to iterate through its items without using an enumerator. In the next section, the same example will be revisited to demonstrate how to use iterators with this linked list.

```
// Example 11-9.cs
// Linked list

using System;

public class LL
{
    public Node head, current;
    public class Node
    {
        public Node next;
        public int item;
    }
}
class MyClass
{
    static void Main(string[] args)
    {
        // Create a linked list with a null pointer:
        LL ll = new LL();
        ll.head = null;

        // Build the linked list:
        Console.WriteLine("Building the list:");
        for (int i = 1; i <= 5; i++)
        {
            // Create the current node:
```

```
            ll.current = new LL.Node();
            // Assign to current node:
            ll.current.item = i * 10;
            ll.current.next = ll.head;
            // Move current to head:
            ll.head = ll.current;
            Console.WriteLine(ll.current.item + " ");
        }

        // Traverse the linked list:
        ll.current= ll.head;
        Console.WriteLine("\nTraversing the list:");
        while (ll.current != null)
        {
            // Move to next node:
            Console.WriteLine(ll.current.item + " ");
            ll.current = ll.current.next;
        }
    }
}
```

Output:

```
Building the list:
10
20
30
40
50

Traversing the list:
50
40
30
20
10
```

11-9 Using Enumerators

Enumerators are used to iterate through a collection. They can only be used to read data from a collection and cannot modify the collection. Enumerators are created by implementing the interfaces **IEnumerable** and **IEnumerator**. As you noticed in the previous sections, all **System.Collections** collections implement the **IEnumerable** interface. That is why you can iterate through these collections using a **foreach** loop. In fact, the **foreach** loop is recommended for reading data from collections because it hides the complexity of enumerators.

To enumerate a collection, implement the **IEnumerable** interface, which exposes the enumerator. The method **GetEnumerator**, the only public member of the **IEnumerable** interface, returns an enumerator of the type **IEnumerator**, which is used to iterate through the collection.

The **IEnumerator** interface contains two abstract methods, **MoveNext** and **Reset**, and a property called **Current**:

```
object Current {get;}
bool MoveNext()
void Reset()
```

Here is a brief description of the **IEnumerator** interface members:

- The **Current** property retrieves the current item in the collection.
- The **MoveNext** method moves the enumerator to the next item in the collection.
- The **Reset** method moves the enumerator to the initial position before the first item in the collection.

To read the collection, start by calling **MoveNext** in order to move the enumerator to the first item in the collection, then use **Current** to read the item. Each consequent read should be preceded by calling **MoveNext**. When the enumerator is located before the first item or after the last element in the collection, **MoveNext** returns false and the value of **Current** becomes undefined. Using **Current** in one of these positions throws an exception. If the collection is changed (by another thread, for instance) during this process by adding, deleting, or modifying items, the enumerator is invalidated.

The following example applies these rules to enumerate a user-defined collection.

Example 11-10

```csharp
// Example 11-10.cs
// Using enumerators

using System;
using System.Collections;

// Declare the collection:
public class MyCollection: IEnumerable
{
    string[] items;
    public MyCollection()
    {
        items = new string[4] {"This", "is", "my", "collection."};
    }
```

```csharp
    // Implement the GetEnumerator() method:
    IEnumerator IEnumerable.GetEnumerator()
    {
        return new MyEnumerator(this);
    }

    // Implement the members of IEnumerator:
    public class MyEnumerator: IEnumerator
    {
        int pointer;
        MyCollection myColl;
        public MyEnumerator(MyCollection c)
        {
            myColl = c;
            pointer = -1;
        }

        // Implement Reset:
        public void Reset()
        {
            pointer = -1;
        }

        // Implement MoveNext:
        public bool MoveNext()
        {
            pointer++;
            if (pointer > myColl.items.Length - 1)
                return false;
            return true;
        }

        // Implement the Current property on IEnumerator:
        object IEnumerator.Current
        {
            get
            {
                return (myColl.items[pointer]);
            }
        }
    }
}

class MyClass
{
    public static void Main(string[] args)
```

```
    {
        MyCollection myColl = new MyCollection();

        // Display the collection:
        foreach (string item in myColl)
        {
            Console.Write(item + " ");
        }
        Console.WriteLine();
    }
}
```

Output:

```
This is my collection.
```

Example 11-11

This example is a rewrite of Example 11-8 that uses an enumerator based on the **IDictionaryEnumerator** interface. The **IDictionaryEnumerator** is used to enumerate the elements of a non-generic dictionary. It contains the **Entry** property that gets both the key and the value of the current dictionary entry.

```
// Example 11-11.cs
// Using enumerators with collections.

using System;
using System.Collections;
using System.Collections.Specialized;

public class LDClass
{
    public static void Main(string[] args)
    {
        // Create an empty ListDictionary object:
        ListDictionary myLD = new ListDictionary();

        // Initialize the ListDictionary collection.
        myLD.Add("Learn Pascal", "$39.95");
        myLD.Add("Learn Pascal in Three Days", "$19.95");
        myLD.Add("Learn C in Three Days", "$19.95");
        myLD.Add("Learn J#", "$35.95");
        myLD.Add("Learn C#", "$39.95");

        // Display the contents of the collection:
        DisplayIt(myLD);
    }
```

```
    // Display the contents by using the enumerator:
    public static void DisplayIt(IDictionary myLD)
    {
        IDictionaryEnumerator myEnumerator = myLD.GetEnumerator();
        string s = "\t\t\t\t";
        Console.WriteLine("Book{0}Price\n", s);
        while (myEnumerator.MoveNext())
            Console.WriteLine("{0,-32}{1}", myEnumerator.Key,
                              myEnumerator.Value);
    }
}
```

Output:

Book	Price
Learn Pascal	$39.95
Learn Pascal in Three Days	$19.95
Learn C in Three Days	$19.95
Learn J#	$35.95
Learn C#	$39.95

11-10 Iterators

As you might have noticed in the previous section, implementing the **IEnumerator** interface can be difficult, especially with complex enumerations. For this reason, C# 2005 introduced iterators to solve the problem by standardizing the enumerator implementation.

An iterator is used to iterate through a collection and return an ordered sequence of values of the same type. The backbone of an iterator is the **yield** statement, which specifies the returned value. One way to create an iterator is to implement the **GetEnumerator** method of the **IEnumerable** interface as shown in the following example:

```
class MyClass
{
    public string[] item = {"One", "Two", "Three"};
    public IEnumerator GetEnumerator()
    {
        for (int i = 0; i < item.Length; i++)
            yield return item[i];
    }
}
```

The **yield return** statement here is used to return the **Current** property of the item. The **MoveNext** method calls the next **yield return** until all the items of the enumeration are returned. The presence of the **GetEnumerator** method makes the class enumerable, which means that you can use the **foreach** statement to display the enumeration values:

```
MyClass mc = new MyClass();
foreach (string item in mc)
{
    Console.WriteLine(item);
}
```

Another way to create an iterator is to use a *named iterator* by declaring a method that returns the **IEnumerable** interface. In this case, there is no need to implement the **GetEnumerator** method. For example:

```
public string[] item = {"One", "Two", "Three"};
public IEnumerable MyIterator()   // named iterator
{
    for (int i = 0; i < item.Length; i++)
      yield return item[i];
}
```

With this *iterator block*, you can use the iterator method MyIterator to display the items of the collection:

```
MyClass mc = new MyClass();
foreach (string item in mc.MyIterator())
{
    Console.WriteLine(item);
}
```

11-10-1 **The Iterator Blocks**

The iterator block, which can be a method, property, or operator method, contains the logic for enumerating a collection. The iterator block contains **yield return** statements, but no **return** statements are allowed in the block. The iterator block has some restrictions, though:

- It cannot be an anonymous method.
- It cannot appear in a **try** block with a **catch** clause or in a **finally** block.
- An iterator method must return an **IEnumerable** or **IEnumerator** interface.
- An iterator method cannot have **ref** or **out** parameters.
- An iterator method cannot exist in an unsafe block.

11-10-2 **The yield Statement**

The **yield** statement is used in an iterator block to iterate through a collection. It takes one of the following forms:

```
yield return expression;
yield break;
```

In the first form, the **yield return** is used to evaluate and return *expression*, which is the value of the iterator object. The **yield return** statement is used to return the **Current** property of the item.

In the second form, **yield break** is used to end the enumeration.

It is possible to use more than one **yield return** in the same iterator to return several values, as shown in this example:

```
public class MyClass
{
    public IEnumerable MyIterator()
    {
        yield return "Hi there!";
        yield return "I am your iterator.";
        yield return "I can return";
        yield return "as many items as required.";
    }
    public static void Main()
    {
        MyClass mc = new MyClass();
        foreach (string item in mc.MyIterator())
        Console.Write(item + " ");
    }
```

Example 11-12

This example is a modification of Example 11-9, which contained a non-generic linked list. In this example, an iterator is used to enumerate the linked list and traverse it using the **foreach** loop.

```
// Example 11-12.cs
// Using an iterator with non-generic linked list

using System;
using System.Collections;

public class LL
{
    public Node head, current;
    public class Node
```

```csharp
{
   public Node next;
   public int item;
}

// Create a named iterator:
public static IEnumerable myColl(LL ll)
{
   while (ll.current != null)
   {
      yield return ll.current.item;

      // Move to next node:
      ll.current = ll.current.next;
   }
}
static void Main(string[] args)
{
   // Create a LL with a null pointer:
   LL ll = new LL();
   ll.head = null;

   // Build the list:
   Console.WriteLine("Building the list:");
   for (int i = 1; i <= 5; i++)
   {
      // Create the current node:
      ll.current = new LL.Node();
      // Assign to current node:
      ll.current.item = i * 10;
      ll.current.next = ll.head;
      // Move current to head:
      ll.head = ll.current;
      Console.WriteLine(ll.current.item + " ");
   }
   // Traverse the list using foreach:
   Console.WriteLine("\nTraversing the list:");
   foreach(int i in myColl(ll))
      Console.WriteLine(i);

}

}
```

Output:

```
Building the list:
10
20
30
40
50

Traversing the list:
50
40
30
20
10
```

Drill 11-7

Rewrite Example 4-7 from Chapter 4 to create an iterator that iterates through the collection of prime numbers between 1 and 10 and display its items.

Summary

In this chapter:

- You learned about the collection classes in the namespace **System.Collections**.

- You learned how to use the most common collection classes such as **Stack, Queue, ArrayList, SortedList**, and **Hashtable**.

- You were introduced to the specialized collections in the namespace **System.Collections.Specialized** and used the **ListDictionary** collection.

- You learned how to build and traverse a non-generic linked list collection.

- You also learned how to create enumerators by implementing the interfaces **IEnumerable** and **IEnumerator**, and how to use them to iterate through a collection.

- You learned about iterators, and used them to enumerate a non-generic linked list and traverse it using the **foreach** loop.
- In working with iterator blocks, you learned how to use the **yield return** statement to return the **Current** property of an item, and the **yield break** statement to end the enumeration.

Chapter 12

Generics

Contents:

- *Definition of generics*
- *The common generic collection classes in the .NET class library*
- *The common generic collection interfaces in the .NET class library*
- *Creating generic classes*
- *Creating generic methods*
- *Using the default keyword*
- *Using constraints*
- *Generic delegates*
- *Generic interfaces*
- *Benefits and limitations of generics*

12-1 What Are Generics?

Generics, a new feature that was added to C# 2005, enable the programmer to design classes or function members and postpone the definition of types until the class is instantiated. By adding this feature, C# made a big step in code reuse, especially in the field of collections.

When you use a collection such as **ArrayList**, you store the items as objects because the type **object** can hold any kind of data. Consider this example where you store some **double** numbers in a **Stack** collection:

```
Stack myStack = new Stack ();
myStack.Push (4.5);
myStack.Push (2.1);
myStack.Push (3.2);
```

275

When you create this list, the compiler automatically boxes the **double** numbers to convert them to the **object** type. When you retrieve the data, you have to cast the numbers to the **double** type. For example:

```
foreach(object obj in myList)
    Console.WriteLine((double)obj * 3.14);
```

If the elements of the stack include mixed types, such as **double** and **string**, casting would be a problem. For example, you can add the following item to the **Stack** collection:

```
myStack.Push ("This is my string item");
```

When you try to cast this item as you did with the previous item, the program throws an InvalidCastException exception.

Before generics, if you needed a stack of integers or strings, you had to create a collection for each type. Now, you can create one generic collection useful for any type, and postpone specifying the actual type until you create your objects. Instead of using the namespace **System.Collections**, use the namespace **System.Collections.Generic**, which includes a generic **Stack**.

Here is an example of using the generic Stack collection:

```
Stack<double> myStack = new Stack<double>();
Stack<int> myStack = new Stack<int>();
Stack<string> myStack = new Stack<string>();
```

In these examples, you just determined the type on instantiating the **Stack** class.

The syntax of the generic **Stack** class looks like this:

```
public class Stack<T> { }
```

The letter T, which is called the *type parameter*, can be replaced on instantiating the class with a *type argument*, which can be any strong type such as **int**, **double**, and so forth. It is a common convention to use the letter T for a type parameter. If a type is using more than one type parameter, the name of each type starts with a T, such as <T1, T2> or <TKey, TValue>.

You can create generic types, methods, properties, delegates, and interfaces.

> **Note** A type can be either generic or *concrete*. Concrete types do not use type parameters, while generic types are distinguished by using type parameters.

12-2 Using Generic Collections

Before you learn how to create your own generic classes, interfaces, methods, and delegates, you may want to take a look at some of the generic collection classes in the .NET Framework class library and learn how to use them.

In addition to the non-generic collections you learned about in Chapter 11, the namespace **System.Collections.Generic** provides interfaces, classes, and structures that allow you to create strongly typed collections that provide more type safety and performance than their counterparts of the non-generic collections. It is recommended that you use generic collections whenever possible since all the non-generic collections have equivalent generic collections.

In the following sections, you are introduced to the following generic collections:

- List<T>
- Dictionary<TKey, TValue>
- LinkedList<T>

You also learn about the following interfaces:

- ICollection<T>
- IDictionary<TKey, TValue>

12-3 List<T>

The **List** generic collection is equivalent to **ArrayList**. They both behave like an array as they both use indexes for their elements.

The generic List collection implements the following generic interfaces:

- IList<T>
- ICollection<T>
- IEnumerable<T>

It also implements the following non-generic interfaces:

- IList
- ICollection
- IEnumerable

To create a simple generic List collection, use the following procedure:

1. Add the following directive to your program:

   ```
   using System.Collections.Generic;
   ```

2. Declare an empty **List** collection with the statement:

   ```
   List <type-argument> list-name = new List<type-argument>();
   ```

   The *type-argument* can be any value or reference data type, such as **string**, or any of the value types. For example:

   ```
   List <string> list-name = new List<string>();
   ```

3. Add elements to the collection by using the method **Add**.

4. Display the elements by using a **foreach** loop, which is designed to work with collections.

5. To access a specific item, use its index number. For example:

   ```
   Console.Write(list-name[3]);
   ```

Table 12-1 lists other **List<T>** methods and properties that you can use in your applications.

12-3-1 **List<T> Members**

The following table contains the commonly used members of the **List<T>** class.

Table 12-1: Commonly used members of the List<T> class

Property/Method	Description	Syntax
Public constructors	Creates and initializes an empty List with the default capacity.	public List()
	Creates and initializes a List with the elements of a specified *collection*.	public List(IEnumerable<T> *collection*)
	Creates and initializes a List with an initial specified *capacity*.	public List(int *capacity*)
Add	Adds an *item* to the end of the collection.	public void Add(T *item*)
Capacity	Retrieves or sets the number of items in the collection.	public int Capacity {get; set;}
Clear	Removes all items from the collection.	public void Clear()
Contains	Checks if a specific *item* is in the collection.	public bool Contains(T *item*)
Count	Retrieves the number of items in the List collection.	public int Count {get;}

Property/Method	Description	Syntax
IndexOf	Retrieves the index of the first matching item.	List.IndexOf (T)
	Retrieves the index of the first matching item in the portion of the collection starting at the specified index to the end of the list.	List.IndexOf (T, Int32)
	Retrieves the index of the first matching item in the portion of the collection starting at the specified index and contains the specified number of items.	List.IndexOf (T, Int32, Int32)
Insert	Inserts an *item* into the List collection at the specified *index*.	public void Insert(int *index*, T *item*)
Item	Retrieves or sets the value of an item that corresponds to a specified *index* (e.g., myList["003"]).	public T this [int *index*] {get; set;}
Remove	Removes the first item that matches the specified *item*.	public bool Remove(T *item*)
RemoveAt	Removes the item at the specified *index*.	public void RemoveAt(int *index*)
RemoveRange	Removes a range of items specified by *count* and starting at the specified *index*.	public void RemoveRange(int *index*, int *count*)
Reverse	Reverses the order of the items in the List collection.	public void Reverse()
	Reverses the order of the items in a range specified by *count* and starting at *index*.	public void Reverse(int *index*, int *count*)
Sort	Sorts the items in the collection by using the default comparer.	public void Sort()
	Sorts the items in the collection by using a specified System.Comparison.	public void Sort(Generic Comparison)
	Sorts the items in the collection by using a specified comparer.	public void Sort(Generic IComparer)
	Sorts the items in the range specified by *index*, and *count* using a specified comparer.	public void Sort(int *index*, int *count*, Generic IComparer)
ToArray	Copies all the items in the collection to an array.	public T[] ToArray()
TrimExcess	Sets the capacity of the collection to the existing number of items.	public void TrimExcess()

Example 12-1

In the following example, you create an empty generic **List** collection and initialize it with some **string** items, and then you display the collection. You also use the methods **Insert** and **Remove** to insert and remove items from the collection, and you use the **Item** property to display an item at a specific index.

```
// Example 12-1.cs
// List<T> example

using System;
using System.Collections.Generic;

class MyClass
{
    static void Main()
    {
        // Declare the list:
        List<string> myList = new List<string>();

        // Build the list:
        myList.Add("Dylan");
        myList.Add("Isabella");
        myList.Add("Eve");
        myList.Add("Angelina");

        // Display items:
        DisplayIt(myList);

        // Add a new item:
        myList.Insert(3,"Bill");
        Console.WriteLine("Adding Bill...");

        // Display items:
        DisplayIt(myList);

        // Search the list for the item "Bill":
        bool test = myList.Contains("Bill");
        Console.WriteLine("Is \"Bill\" in the list? {0}", test);

        // Remove "Bill" and then search for it:
        myList.Remove("Bill");
        Console.WriteLine("Removing Bill...");

        test = myList.Contains("Bill");
        Console.WriteLine("Is \"Bill\" in the list now? {0}", test);
        Console.WriteLine();
```

```csharp
      // Display items:
      DisplayIt(myList);

      // Display item #2:
      Console.WriteLine("Item number 2: {0}", myList[2]);
   }

   // Display the list:
   static void DisplayIt(List<string> myL)
   {
      foreach(string name in myL)
      {
         Console.WriteLine(name);
      }
      Console.WriteLine();
   }
}
```

Output:

```
Dylan
Isabella
Eve
Angelina

Adding Bill...
Dylan
Isabella
Eve
Bill
Angelina

Is "Bill" in the list? True
Removing Bill...
Is "Bill" in the list now? False

Dylan
Isabella
Eve
Angelina

Item number 2: Eve
```

Drill 12-1

Create a List collection that contains some strings, then sort the list and display it. Next, copy the List to an array and display it.

12-4 Dictionary<TKey, TValue>

The generic **Dictionary** collection resembles the non-generic **Hashtable** collection. The collection stores entries in the form of key/value pair objects by using the generic structure **KeyValuePair<TKey, TValue>**. The Dictionary collection stores values in a sub-collection called **ValueCollection** and the keys in a sub-collection called **KeyCollection**. You can retrieve each sub-collection separately. Keys must be unique and cannot be null; values don't have to be unique and can be null.

The **Dictionary** class implements the following generic interfaces:

- IDictionary<TKey, TValue>
- ICollection<KeyValuePair<TKey, TValue>>
- IEnumerable<KeyValuePair<TKey, TValue>>

It also implements the following non-generic iterfaces:

- IDictionary
- ICollection
- IEnumerable
- ISerializable
- IDeserializationCallback

To create a simple generic **Dictionary** collection, follow this procedure:

1 Add the following directive to your program:

```
using System.Collections.Generic;
```

2. Declare an empty Dictionary collection with the statement:

```
Dictionary<type-argument1, type-argument2 > dictionary-name =
new Dictionary<type-argument1, type-argument2>();
```

The *type-argument1* and *type-argument2* represent the key and the value type for the items in the **Dictionary** collection. They can be any value or reference data type. For example:

```
Dictionary<int, string> myDictionary = new Dictionary
<int, string>();
```

3. Add elements to the collection by using the **Add** method. For example:

```
myDictionary.Add(10, "Apples");
```

4. Display the elements by using a **foreach** loop and the **KeyValuePair** element type. For example:

```
foreach(KeyValuePair<int, string> mD in myDictionary)
{
    Console.WriteLine("Key = {0}, Value = {1}",
    mD.Key, mD.Value);
}
```

5. To access a specific value, use its **Item** property. For example:

```
Console.Write(myDictionary[3]);
```

The following table lists other **Dictionary<TKey, TValue>** methods and properties that you can use in your applications.

12-4-1 **Dictionary<TKey, TValue> Members**

Table 12-2: Commonly used members of the Dictionary<TKey, TValue> class

Property/Method	Description	Syntax
Public constructors	Creates and initializes an empty generic Dictionary collection with the default equality comparer for the key type.	public Dictionary()
	Creates and initializes an empty generic Dictionary collection with an initial specified $capacity$ and the default equality comparer for the key type.	public Dictionary(int $capacity$)
	Creates and initializes a generic Dictionary collection with the elements of a specified IDictionary and the default equality comparer for the key type.	public Dictionary(IDictionary<TKey, TValue> $dictionary$)
Add	Adds an item with a specified key and $value$ to the collection.	public void Add(TKey key, TValue $value$)
Clear	Removes all items from the collection.	public virtual void Clear()
ContainsKey	Checks if a specified key is in the collection.	public bool ContainsKey(TKey key)
ContainsValue	Checks if a specified $value$ is in the collection.	public bool ContainsValue(TValue $value$)
Count	Retrieves the number of key/value entries in the collection.	public int Count {get;}
Item	Retrieves or sets the value of an item that corresponds to a specified key (e.g., myDictionary[33] or yourDictionary["Cherry"]).	public TValue this [TKey key] {get; set;}

Property/Method	Description	Syntax
Keys	Retrieves the KeyCollection that contains the keys of the collection.	public KeyCollection Keys {get;}
Remove	Removes an item with a specified key from the collection.	public bool Remove(TKey key)
TryGetValue	Retrieves the value associated with a specified key.	public bool TryGetValue(TKey key, out TValue value)
Values	Retrieves the ValueCollection that contains the values of the collection.	public ValueCollection Values {get;}

Example 12-2

This example creates an empty Dictionary collection and initializes it with some key/value entries. Keys represent fruit types and values represent the corresponding prices. The contents of the collection are displayed, and then the collection is searched for two types of fruit: cherries and oranges. The oranges are then removed and the collection is searched again for oranges; the appropriate message is displayed in each case.

```
// Example 12-2.cs
// Dictionary collection example

using System;
using System.Collections.Generic;

public class Example
{
    public static void Main()
    {
        // Create an empty Dictionary collection:
        Dictionary<string, double> myDictionary =
            new Dictionary<string, double>();

        // Add some elements to the dictionary.
        // Assume keys are fruit and values are prices.
        // Prices can be duplicates.
        myDictionary.Add("Apples", 0.30);
        myDictionary.Add("Oranges", 0.50);
        myDictionary.Add("Cherries", 0.44);
        myDictionary.Add("Peaches", 0.50);

        // Display items by using the KeyValuePair type:
        foreach(KeyValuePair<string, double> mD in myDictionary)
        {
            Console.WriteLine("{0,-20}{1:C}", mD.Key, mD.Value);
```

```
        }

        // Search for "Cherries," and if found display the price:
        SearchForItem(myDictionary, "Cherries");

        // Search for "Oranges," and if found display the price:
        SearchForItem(myDictionary, "Oranges");

        // Remove "Oranges":
        myDictionary.Remove("Oranges");
        Console.WriteLine("Oranges removed...");

        // Search for "Oranges," and if found display the price:
        SearchForItem(myDictionary, "Oranges");
    }

    // A method to search for a specific key in the Dictionary collection:
    static void SearchForItem(Dictionary<string, double> myDictionary,
              string s)
    {
        if (myDictionary.ContainsKey(s))
            Console.WriteLine("{0} are in the store. The price is {1:C}.",
                  s, myDictionary[s]);
        else
            Console.WriteLine("{0} are not in the store now. Please check
                  back later.", s);
    }
}
```

Output:

```
Apples          $0.30
Oranges         $0.50
Cherries        $0.44
Peaches         $0.50
Cherries are in the store. The price is $0.44.
Oranges are in the store. The price is $0.50.
Oranges removed...
Oranges are not in the store now. Please check back later.
```

Drill 12-2

Create a generic Dictionary collection that contains some key/value entries, and then create two collections from the Dictionary collection, one that contains the values and one that contains the keys. Display the contents of each collection.

12-5 **LinkedList<T>**

The generic linked list is a doubly-linked list where each node points to the next node and to the previous node. When you compare this linked list to the non-generic linked list introduced in Chapter 11, you realize that although it's more sophisticated than the non-generic version, the generic linked list is easier to build and manipulate. (Remember also that you have to build the non-generic linked list from scratch because it is not supported by the .NET class library.) The nodes of the generic linked list are of the type **LinkedListNode<T>**. Each element of the LinkedListNode collection contains a value and a reference to its **LinkedList**. It also contains a reference to the next node and to the previous node.

The **LinkedList<T>** collection implements the following generic interfaces:

- ICollection<T>
- IEnumerable<T>

It also implements the following non-generic interfaces:

- ICollection
- IEnumerable
- ISerializable
- IDeserializationCallback

To create a simple generic **LinkedList** collection, follow this procedure:

1. Add the following directive to your program:
   ```
   using System.Collections.Generic;
   ```
2. Declare an empty **LinkedList** collection with the statement:
   ```
   LinkedList<type-argument> list-name = new
   LinkedList<type-argument>();
   ```
   The *type-argument* can be any value or reference data type such as **string**, or any of the value types. For example:
   ```
   LinkedList<string> myLinkedList = new LinkedList<string>();
   ```
3. Add nodes to the collection by using the methods **AddBefore**, **AddAfter, AddFirst**, or **AddLast**.
4. You can also remove nodes from the collection by using the methods **Remove, RemoveFirst**, or **RemoveLast**.

5. Display the elements by using a **foreach** loop. For example:
```
foreach (string name in myLinkedList)
{
    Console.WriteLine(name);
}
```

6. To check for the existence of a specific value, use the method **Contains**. For example:
```
Console.Write(myLinkedList.Contains("Tom"));
```

Tables 12-3 and 12-4 list other **LinkedList<T>** and **LinkedListNode<T>** methods and properties that you can use in your applications.

12-5-1 **LinkedList<T> Members**

The following table contains the commonly used members of the **LinkedList<T>** class.

Table 12-3: Commonly used members of the LinkedList<T> class

Property/Method	Description	Syntax
Public constructors	Creates and initializes an empty LinkedList.	public LinkedList()
	Creates and initializes a LinkedList with the elements of a specified *collection*.	public LinkedList(IEnumerable<T> *collection*)
AddAfter	Adds a node containing the specified *value* after a specified existing node.	public LinkedListNode<T> AddAfter(LinkedListNode<T> node, T *value*)
AddBefore	Adds a node containing the specified *value* before a specified existing node.	public LinkedListNode<T> AddBefore(LinkedListNode<T> node, T *value*)
AddFirst	Adds a node containing the specified *value* at the beginning of the LinkedList.	public LinkedListNode<T> AddFirst(T *value*)
AddLast	Adds a node containing the specified *value* at the end of the LinkedList.	public LinkedListNode<T> AddLast(T *value*)
Clear	Removes all the nodes from the LinkedList.	public void Clear()
Contains	Determines if a specific *value* is in the LinkedList.	public bool Contains(T *value*)
Count	Retrieves the number of nodes in the LinkedList collection.	public int Count {get;}
Find	Finds the first node that contains the matching *value*.	public LinkedListNode<T> Find(T *value*)
FindLast	Finds the last node that contains the matching *value*.	public LinkedListNode<T> FindLast(T *value*)

Property/Method	Description	Syntax
First	Retrieves the first node in the LinkedList.	public LinkedListNode<T> First {get;}
Remove	Removes the first occurrence of *value* from the LinkedList.	public bool Remove(T *value*)
RemoveFirst	Removes the first node from the LinkedList.	public void RemoveFirst()
RemoveLast	Removes the last node from the LinkedList.	public void RemoveLast()
Last	Retrieves the last node in the LinkedList.	public LinkedListNode<T> Last {get;}
ToArray	Copies the LinkedList to an *array* starting at the specified *index*.	public void CopyTo(T[] *array*, int *index*)

12-5-2 **LinkedListNode<T> Members**

The following table contains the commonly used members of the **LinkedListNode<T>** class.

Table 12-4: Commonly used members of the LinkedListNode<T> class

Property/Method	Description	Syntax
Public constructors	Creates and initializes a new instance of the LinkedListNode class with the specified *value*.	public LinkedListNode(T *value*)
List	Retrieves the LinkedList object to which the LinkedListNode points.	public LinkedList<T> List {get;}
Next	Retrieves the next node in the LinkedList.	public LinkedListNode<T> Next {get;}
Previous	Retrieves the previous node in the LinkedList.	public LinkedListNode<T> Previous {get;}
Value	Retrieves or sets the value stored in the node.	public T Value {get; set;}

Example 12-3

The following example demonstrates the use of the **LinkedList<T>** and **LinkedListNode<T>** collections. An empty linked list is created and initialized with some names, and then some nodes are removed and added. The example also shows how to search and display the contents of a specific node by using the properties of the **LinkedListNode<T>** class.

```
// Example 12-3.cs
// Generic LinkedList

using System;
using System.Collections.Generic;
```

```
public class LinkedList
{
   public static void Main()
   {
      // Create an empty LinkedList collection that stores strings:
      LinkedList<string> myLinkedList = new LinkedList<string>();

      // Build the list:
      myLinkedList.AddFirst("Tom");
      myLinkedList.AddAfter(myLinkedList.First, "Dick");
      myLinkedList.AddLast("Harry");
      myLinkedList.AddBefore(myLinkedList.Last, "and");

      // Display the list:
      Display(myLinkedList);

      // Remove and add nodes:
      myLinkedList.Remove("Dick");
      myLinkedList.Remove("and");
      myLinkedList.AddBefore(myLinkedList.Last, "and");

      // Display it after removing 2 nodes:
      Display(myLinkedList);

      // Find the LinkedListNode that contains "Harry":
      LinkedListNode<string> myNode = myLinkedList.Find("Harry");

      // Display the value in the current node:
      Console.WriteLine(
         "The value in the current node is \"{0}.\"", myNode.Value);
   }

   // Display a LinkedList object:
   private static void Display(LinkedList<string> myLL)
   {
      foreach (string name in myLL)
      {
         Console.Write(name + " ");
      }
      Console.WriteLine();

      // Display the number of items:
      Console.WriteLine(
         "The number of nodes is now {0}.", myLL.Count);
   }
}
```

Output:

```
Tom Dick and Harry
The number of nodes is now 4.
Tom and Harry
The number of nodes is now 3.
The value in the current node is "Harry."
```

Drill 12-3

Create a string array with three names, such as John, Paul, and Mary, and then initialize a LinkedList collection from the array elements. Add to the collection three other names, such as Tom, Dick, and Harry. Display the collection and the number of nodes. The output should be something like:

```
Paul John Mary Tom Dick and Harry
The number of nodes is 7.
```

12-6 ICollection<T>

The generic **ICollection** interface defines methods that manipulate generic collections. It is the base interface for generic classes in the namespace **System.Collections.Generic**. The **ICollection** interface implements the following interfaces:

- IEnumerable<T>
- IEnumerable

12-6-1 ICollection Members

The following table lists the public properties and methods of the **ICollection** interface.

Table 12-5: The members of the ICollection<T> interface

Property/Method	Description	Syntax
Add	Adds an *item* to the ICollection.	void Add(T *item*)
Clear	Removes items from the ICollection.	void Clear()
Contains	Checks if an ICollection contains a specific *item*.	bool Contains(T *item*)
CopyTo	Copies the items of an ICollection to an *array* starting at the specified *index*.	void CopyTo(T[] *array*, int *index*)

Property/Method	Description	Syntax
Count	Retrieves the number of objects contained in an ICollection.	int Count {get;}
IsReadOnly	A Boolean value that indicates if the ICollection is read-only.	bool IsReadOnly {get;}
Remove	Removes the first occurrence of an *item* from the ICollection.	bool Remove(T *item*)

12-7 IDictionary<TKey, TValue>

The **IDictionary** interface defines methods that manipulate generic collections that contain key/value pairs. The **IDictionary** interface implements the following interfaces:

- ICollection<KeyValuePair<TKey, TValue>>
- IEnumerable<KeyValuePair<TKey, TValue>>
- IEnumerable

Elements of **IDictionary** are stored in the form of **KeyValuePair** objects. Key/value pairs are enumerated, but there is no particular sort order. A key must be unique and may or may not be permitted to be null depending on the implementation. A value can be a null and does not have to be unique.

12-7-1 IDictionary Members

The following table lists the public properties and methods of the **IDictionary** interface.

Table 12-6: The members of the IDictionary<TKey, TValue> interface

Property/Method	Description	Syntax
Add	Adds an item with the specified *key* and *value* to the IDictionary collection.	void Add(TKey *key*, TValue *value*)
ContainsKey	Checks if an IDictionary collection contains an item with a specified *key*.	bool ContainsKey(TKey *key*)
Item	Retrieves or sets the item corresponding to a specific *key*.	TValue this [TKey *key*] {get; set;}
Keys	Retrieves the ICollection that contains the Keys of the IDictionary collection.	ICollection<TKey> Keys {get;}
Remove	Removes the item with a specified *key* from the IDictionary collection.	bool Remove(TKey *key*)

Property/Method	Description	Syntax
TryGetValue	Retrieves a Boolean value that indicates whether the *value* associated with the specified *key* exists in the IDictionary collection.	bool TryGetValue(TKey *key*, out TValue *value*)
Values	Retrieves the ICollection that contains the *Values* of the IDictionary collection.	ICollection<TValue> *Values* {get;}

12-8 Creating Your Own Generic Classes

You can create a generic class by using one or more *type parameters*. For example, you can declare a class like this:

```
class MyClass<T>
```

where:

T is the type parameter.

The type parameter, as mentioned earlier, is a placeholder for a type. When you instantiate the class, replace the type parameter with a *type argument* (a strong type). For example:

```
MyClass<string> c1 = new MyClass<string>();
MyClass<int> c2 = new MyClass<int>();
```

In the first instance the type parameter T is replaced with **string**; in the second instance it is replaced with **int**.

The type parameter can be used inside the class to define members. For example:

```
private T myField;
```

When you create instances of the class, such as c1 and c2 above, the field myField of the instance c1 can accept strings, while myField of the instance c2 accepts integers.

Note The generic types are also called *constructed types*. A constructed type that is using type parameters is called an *open constructed type*, while a constructed type that is using type arguments is called a *closed constructed type*. The type parameters of an open constructed type are called *unbound generic parameters*, while the type arguments of a closed constructed type are called *bound generic parameters*.

Example 12-4

The following is a complete example of a generic class with a field and
property that use its type parameter.

```
// Example 12-4.cs
// Generic classes

using System;

class MyClass<T>
{
    // Generic field:
    private T myField;

    // Generic property:
    public T MyProperty
    {
        get { return myField; }
        set { myField = value; }
    }
}

class MainClass
{
    static void Main()
    {
        // Instantiate a string object:
        MyClass<string> c1 = new MyClass<string>();

        // Instantiate an int object:
        MyClass<int> c2 = new MyClass<int>();

        // Assign values to properties:
        c1.MyProperty = "John";
        c2.MyProperty = 123;

        // Display results:
        Console.WriteLine("{0}, {1}", c1.MyProperty, c2.MyProperty);
    }
}
```

Output:

```
John, 123
```

As you can see in the above example, using type parameters enabled you
to create one class that does the work of two classes. When you
instantiated the class, you created two versions: one for integers and one

for strings. In other words, you were able to reuse the class code without using casts or boxing. Using generics increases the efficiency and type-safety of code.

12-9 **Generic Methods**

You can create a generic method by using one or more type parameters after the method's name. For example:

```
void MyMethod<T>(T var1, T var2) { ... }
```

The type parameter can be used in the method's parameters or inside the method's body. The following generic method swaps two variables of the type T, which can be replaced by any strong type when you use the method.

```
void Swap<T>(ref T var1, ref T var2)
{
    T temp;
    temp = var1;
    var1 = var2;
    var2 = temp;
}
```

12-9-1 **Generic Methods inside Generic Classes**

A generic method can live inside a generic or non-generic class. However, if the generic method lives inside a generic class and uses the same type parameter as the containing class, its type parameter will hide the type parameter of the class. The compiler will issue a warning in this case. To avoid this warning, you can use a different identifier for each type parameter. For example:

```
class MyClass<T>
{
    ...
    void MyMethod<U>()
    {
        ...
    }
}
```

> **Note**   Non-generic methods that belong to generic classes can use the
> type parameters of the class. For example:

```
class<T> MyClass
{
    void MyMethod(T var1, T var2) { ... }
}
```

12-9-2 Overloading Generic Methods

Generic methods can be overloaded based on signature or *arity* (the number of type parameters on a method). You can also overload generic and non-generic methods of the same name if the methods are different in type parameters. For example, the following methods can exist in the same class:

```
MyMethod<U>() { ... }
MyMethod<U, V>() { ... }
MyMethod() { ... }
```

> **Note**   If you have two overloaded methods, one non-generic and one
> using type parameters, the non-generic method will be called in case of
> possible ambiguity.

Example 12-5

This example demonstrates the generic **Swap** method used to swap two variables of any type. As you can see in the example, the method is used once to swap two integers (x and y) and once to swap two strings (a and b).

```
// Example 12-5.cs
// The generic "Swap" method

using System;

class MyClass
{
    // Generic method to swap two variables:
    static void Swap<T>(ref T var1, ref T var2)
    {
        T temp;
        temp = var1;
        var1 = var2;
        var2 = temp;
    }
```

```
static void Main()
{
    int x = 33;
    int y = 44;
    string a = "Hello";
    string b = "World!";

    // Display the integer variables before and after swapping:
    Console.WriteLine("Before swapping: x = {0}, y = {1}", x, y);
    Swap<int>(ref x, ref y);
    Console.WriteLine("After swapping: x = {0}, y = {1}", x, y);

    // Display the string variables before and after swapping:
    Console.WriteLine("Before swapping: a = {0}, b = {1}", a, b);
    Swap<string>(ref a, ref b);
    Console.WriteLine("After swapping: a = {0}, b = {1}", a, b);
}
}
```

Output:

```
Before swapping: x = 33, y = 44
After swapping: x = 44, y = 33
Before swapping: a = Hello, b = World!
After swapping: a = World!, b = Hello
```

Notice that the **Swap** method is used here as a member of a non-generic class. This is one way to do it, but you can also declare it like this:

```
public class MyClass<T>
{
    public void Swap(ref T var1, ref T var2)
    {
        ...
    }
}
```

You should notice, however, that you cannot place the **Main** method in this class; otherwise, you get the warning: *'MyClass<T>.Main()': an entry point cannot be generic or in a generic type*. You can, in this case, create a second class to contain the **Main** method.

12-10 **Using the default Keyword**

If you don't know in advance whether the type you are creating will be a reference or value type, you might run into some problems. Consider this example:

```
void MyMethod<T>(T myVar)
{
    myVar = null;
    ...
}
```

When you compile this code, the compiler will issue the following error: *Cannot convert null to type parameter 'T' because it could be a value type. Consider using 'default(T)' instead*. To resolve this issue, you can use the **default** keyword, like this:

```
void MyMethod<T>(T myVar)
{
    myVar = default(T);
    ...
}
```

If T is going to be a reference type, it will be assigned the default value for reference types, which is null. If T is going to be a value type, it will be assigned the default value of value types, which is zero for all numeric types. If T will be a struct, its members are treated in the same way and will be initialized either with zero or null, depending on whether the member is a value type or a reference type.

12-11 **Using Constraints**

It is possible to enforce rules on type parameters by defining constraints. When you instantiate the class by using a type argument that does not conform to the rules specified in the constraint, the compiler will issue an error. You can specify a constraint by using the contextual keyword **where**, as shown in the following examples:

```
class MyClass<T> where T: IEnumerable { ... }
class MyClass<T, U> where T: IComparable
                    where U: MyBaseClass { ... }
class MyClass<T> where T: class, IComparable<T>, new() { ... }
```

The first example indicates that the parameter type, T, implements the **IEnumerable** interface. The second example uses two type parameters, with a constraint on each one. The constraint on T indicates that it will implement **IComparable**; the constraint on U indicates that it will use objects of the type MyBaseClass or objects derived from it.

The third example uses three constraints on the same type parameter T. Constraints are applied to both generic types and generic methods.

12-11-1 Types of Constraints

Constraints are divided into several types, as shown in the following table.

Table 12-7: Types of constraints

Constraint	Comment
where T: struct	T must be a value type (except the nullable types).
where T: class	T must be a reference type.
where T: <base class>	T must be, or inherit from, a base class.
mult1where T: <interface>	T must be, or implement, an interface (generic or non-generic). Implementing more than one interface is allowed.
where T: new()	T must have a public parameterless constructor. The new constraint, if used with other constraints, must be the last one specified in the list.
where T: T1	T1 must be the same as, or derived from, T. This is called a *naked type constraint*.

12-11-2 When to Use Constraints

When you use type parameters with a generic type, it can be replaced by any type that inherits from **System.Object**. This is fine if you are not planning to do any operations other than simple method calls or variable assignment. In some cases, you may plan to use the type parameter in a specific way. For example, by using the following base class constraint:

```
public MyClass<T> where T: MyBaseClass { ... }
```

you can use objects of MyBaseClass, or objects inherited from it, as type arguments. Another example is when you would like to use the type parameter as an **Array** type and enumerate it using the **foreach** loop. In this case, you need to use a constraint on the type parameter to make it implement the **IEnumerable** interface, which is required by the **foreach** loop:

```
public class MyClass<T> where T: IEnumerable { ... }
```

Using this constraint defines your plan in using the type parameter T. Without using this constraint, the compiler cannot automatically predict this plan. In general, using constraints enables you to do more specialized operations on type parameters.

Example 12-6

This example demonstrates the scenario of using the type parameter as an **Array** type, and enumerating the array by using the **foreach** loop. Notice that if you remove the constraint, the program won't compile and you get the compiler error: *foreach statement cannot operate on variables of type 'T' because 'T' does not contain a public definition for 'GetEnumerator.'*

```
// Example 12-6.cs
// Constraints

using System;
using System.Collections;

public class MyClass<T> where T: IEnumerable
{
    public void MyMethod(T myArray)
    {
        Console.Write("The array elements are: ");
        foreach(int x in myArray)
        {
            Console.Write("{0} ", x);
        }
    }
}
public class MainClass
{
    static void Main()
    {
        int[] myArray = { 11, 22, 33, 44 };
        MyClass<int[]> mc = new MyClass<int[]>();
        mc.MyMethod(myArray);
    }
}
```

Output:

```
The array elements are: 11 22 33 44
```

Drill 12-4

Create a generic class whose type parameter is using a class, Employee, as a constraint. Employee has two properties: Name and ID. The generic class contains two members: a stack of strings and a non-generic method that uses the type parameter of the class. The method is used to push and pop the properties of an Employee object. Store the properties of two employees and display them.

12-12 **Generic Delegates**

You can create a generic delegate that uses its own type parameters. For example:

```
delegate void MyDelegate<T1, T2>(T1 id, T2 name);
```

The encapsulated method can be a non-generic method:

```
public void MyMethod(int id, string name) { ... }
```

As with other generic types or methods, when you instantiate the delegate, you must provide the type arguments:

```
MyDelegate<int, string> d =
    new MyDelegate<int, string>(mc.MyMethod);
```

You can also create a delegate that uses the type parameters of the enclosing class:

```
class MyClass<T1, T2>
{
    // Declare a delegate:
    delegate void MyDelegate(T1 id, T2 name);
    ...
}
```

Again, provide the type arguments on instantiating the delegate:

```
// Instantiate the class:
MyClass<int, string> mc = new MyClass<int, string>();
// Instantiate the delegate:
MyClass<int, string>.MyDelegate delg =
    new MyClass<int, string>.MyDelegate(mc.MyMethod);
```

Example 12-7

This example, which demonstrates generic delegates, is a rewrite of Example 10-1. It declares a delegate, MyDelegate, defined within a generic class, MyClass. The delegate and the associated method, MyMethod, use the T1 and T2 type parameters of the class.

```
// Example 11-7.cs
// Generic delegates

using System;

class MyClass<T1, T2>
{
    // Declare a delegate:
    public delegate void MyDelegate(T1 n, T2 s);
```

```
    // Declare the encapsulated Method:
    public void MyMethod(T1 id, T2 name)
    {
        Console.WriteLine("ID number = {0}\nName = {1}", id, name);
    }
}

class MainClass
{
    static void Main()
    {
        // Instantiate the class:
        MyClass<int, string> mc = new MyClass<int, string>();

        // Instantiate the delegate:
        MyClass<int, string>.MyDelegate delg =
            new MyClass<int, string>.MyDelegate(mc.MyMethod);

        // Invoke the delegate:
        delg.Invoke(911, "Angelina Abolrous");
    }
}
```

Output:

```
ID number = 911
Name = Angelina Abolrous
```

Drill 12-5

Rewrite the above example using a delegate with type parameters.

12-13 Generic Interfaces

Declaring a generic interface is similar to declaring a generic class. When you implement a generic interface you must follow the same rules for inheriting a generic class. You saw earlier some of the generic interfaces implemented by generic types or used as constraints. You can also use multiple interface constraints on the same type. For example:

```
class Queue<T> where T: IEnumerable<T>, IComparable<T>
```

Closed constructed interfaces can be implemented by concrete classes. For example:

```
interface MyInterface<T>
class MyClass: MyInterface<double>
```

Generic interfaces can also use one or more type parameters:

```
interface MyInterface<T1, T2>
```

It is possible for generic classes to implement open or closed constructed interfaces. For example:

```
interface MyInterface<T>
interface YourInterface<U>
class YourClass<T>: MyInterface<T>, YourInterface<string>
```

Example 12-8

This example demonstrates a simple application for generic interfaces using an array with type parameters. Notice that when you implement the **IEnumerable<T>** interface, you have to implement both generic and non-generic **GetEnumerator**. For example:

```
IEnumerator IEnumerable.GetEnumerator()
```

and

```
IEnumerator<T> GetEnumerator()
```

This is because **IEnumerable<T>** inherits from **IEnumerable**.

```
// Example 12-8.cs
// Generic interfaces

using System;
using System.Collections;
using System.Collections.Generic;

public class MyClass<T>: IEnumerable<T>
{
    public T[] myArray = new T[5];

    // Implementation of the IEnumerable.GetEnumerator()
    IEnumerator IEnumerable.GetEnumerator()
    {
        return GetEnumerator();
    }

    // Implementation of IEnumerator<T> GetEnumerator()
    public IEnumerator<T> GetEnumerator()
```

```csharp
        {
            for (int i = 0; i < myArray.Length; i++)
                yield return myArray[i];
        }
        public void Initialize(int[] myArray)
        {
            for (int i = 0; i < myArray.Length; i++)
            {
                myArray[i] = i * 2;
            }
        }
        public void Initialize(double[] myArray)
        {
            // Initialize:
            for (int i = 0; i < myArray.Length; i++)
            {
                myArray[i] = i * 3.14;
            }
        }
    }
    public class MainClass
    {
        static void Main()
        {
            // Create instances:
            MyClass<int> mc = new MyClass<int>();
            MyClass<double> mc1 = new MyClass<double>();

            // Initialize objects:
            mc.Initialize(mc.myArray);
            mc1.Initialize(mc1.myArray);

            // Display results:
            Console.WriteLine("The integer array elements are: ");
            foreach (int i in mc.myArray)
                Console.Write("{0} ", i);
            Console.WriteLine("\nThe double array elements are: ");
            foreach (int i in mc1.myArray)
                Console.Write("{0:F2} ", i);
        }
    }
```

Output:

```
The integer array elements are:
0 2 4 6 8
The double array elements are:
0.00 3.00 6.00 9.00 12.00
```

12-14 Benefits of Using Generics

- With generic types, the items do not require boxing when added to the collection or casting when retrieved.
- Using generics eliminated a lot of programming overhead. For example, you don't need to create a class for each item type. Type parameters are dynamically replaced at run time.
- Using generic types increases performance by eliminating the boxing and unboxing of collection items. The difference is significant with large collections.
- Generic types reduce the memory consumption as a result of fewer boxing operations.
- Generic code is easier to read and maintain.
- Generics provide a code pattern implementation that is reusable.
- In general, using generic types maximizes type safety and performance.

12-15 Limitations of Using Generics

The following are some limitations when using generics:
- You cannot use a generic **Main** method.
- Properties, indexers, and attributes cannot be generic.
- You cannot use generic types in the unsafe code.
- Operator methods cannot be generic methods.

Summary

In this chapter:
- You were introduced to generics, an important feature of C# 2005.
- You had a tour of the most common collection classes and interfaces in the namespace **System.Collections.Generic**.
- You learned how to create you own generic classes, methods, delegates, and interfaces.
- In working with generics, you learned how to use the **default** keyword to add more flexibility to type parameters.
- You also learned how to define and use constraints to enforce rules on your type parameters.
- Finally, you learned about the benefits and limitations of generics.

Chapter 13

Visual Studio Essentials

Contents:

- Using the integrated development environment (IDE)
- Starting a new application
- Creating and using console applications
- The main features of the IDE
- Compiling and executing a project
- Creating and building library projects
- Referencing a library in an application
- Using Windows applications
- Using web site applications
- Important features of the Code Editor

13-1 Using the Integrated Development Environment

In this chapter, you'll get a quick introduction to Visual Studio, which is the tool for building and compiling projects in the integrated development environment (IDE).

You will learn about the important features of the IDE and types of applications you can develop in Visual Studio. The tour will not cover everything because Visual Studio capabilities cannot be covered in one chapter. This tour, however, is enough for you to learn how to use Visual Studio in building C# applications.

When you run Visual Studio, you start with the Start Page, which contains the following main sections:

- Recent Projects
- MSD SQL Server

- Getting Started
- Visual Studio Headlines

These sections contain a lot of information on the important features of Visual Studio 2005. The Start Page also contains a menu and toolbars at the top of its window, which you can use in writing code and building your applications.

13-2 **Starting a New Application**

Visual Studio saves applications in the form of *solutions*, which may consist of one or more *projects*.

To start a new application, do the following:

1. Open the **File** menu.

2. Select **New**.

3. Select **Project**.

The New Project window shown in Figure 13-1 opens on your screen.

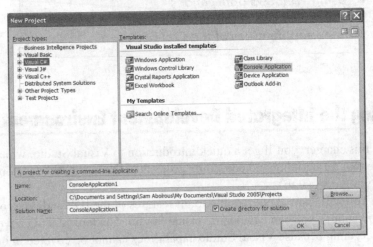

Figure 13-1: Starting a new project.

4. In the New Project window, select the project type from the Project types pane. Also select the template you are going to use from the Templates pane. As you can see in the figure above, **Visual C#** is chosen as a project type.

The templates indicate the types of applications available in Visual Studio, which are:

- Windows Application
- Class Library
- Windows Control Library
- Console Application
- Crystal Reports Application
- Device Application
- Excel Workbook
- Outlook Add-in

If you are familiar with the previous version of Visual Studio, you will notice the new options added to the templates. These templates are called the standard templates. When you expand the C# item in the Project types pane, you will see more templates. Some of these templates are explained in the following sections.

⊃ **Note** The programs used in this book can be compiled and run either in the command-line environment or as console applications in the IDE.

13-3 **Creating and Using Console Applications**

To create a console application project, do the following:

1. Select **Console Application** from the Templates pane of the New Project window.
2. Before you press **Enter** (or click **OK**), notice the following:
   a. The default name of the application is *ConsoleApplication* (followed by 1, 2, 3, etc.). You can change it by typing a new name in the **Name** text box.
   b. The default location of the application is: "C:\Documents and Settings\<user-name>\My Documents\Visual Studio 2005\Projects." You can change this by typing a new path in the **Location** text box.
   c. The default name of the solution is the same as the project name. You can give the solution a different name by changing the text in the **Solution Name** text box.
3. Click **OK** after you accept or change the default settings.
4. After clicking OK, you are transferred to the Code Editor, which contains the machine-generated code as shown in Figure 13-2.

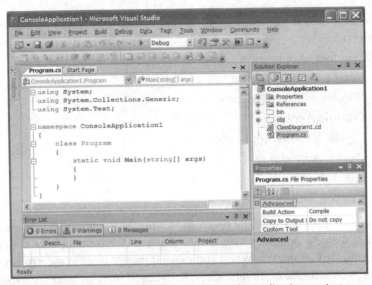

Figure 13-2: The Code Editor for a new console application project.

The machine-generated code includes:

- The **using** directives for the following namespaces:
  - System
  - System.Collections.Generic
  - System.Text
- The *ConsoleApplication1* namespace (assuming that you accepted the default project name).
- The *Program* class (you can change this name as appropriate).
- The Main method (empty).

You can compile and run this "empty" project just for testing (compilation is explained in Section 13-5, "Compiling and Running Projects") and, of course, you might modify it by adding your code to it. It is also possible to replace the entire content with a new C# program written in Notepad. Notice that when you use Notepad to write a program, however, you will miss out on the Code Editor's useful *IntelliSense* feature, which is explained later in this chapter.

13-4 The Main Features of the IDE

In Figure 13-2, you can see the default windows and tabs of the IDE:

- The Code Editor tab in the upper-left window, which is used for writing the program code. It contains the current code file, which is Program.cs in this case. Notice that there is a second tab in this window for the Start Page, from which you started.
- The Error List window at the bottom of the screen.
- The Solution Explorer window in the upper-right portion of the screen.
- The Properties window in the lower-right corner.

These are explained in more detail in the following sections.

13-4-1 The Solution Explorer

The Solution Explorer window shares space with the Class View window. Solution Explorer shows the folders and files of the project, while Class View shows the same details in the form of classes and class members. Both windows are shown in Figure 13-3.

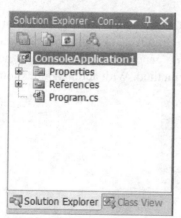
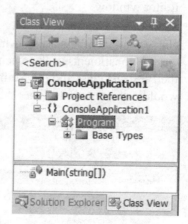

Figure 13-3: The Solution Explorer and the Class View windows.

The Solution Explorer window contains several toolbar buttons, as shown in Figure 13-4.

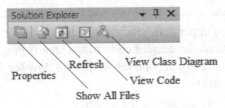

Figure 13-4: Toolbar buttons of Solution Explorer.

Following is a description of each toolbar button in the Solution Explorer window:

- **Properties:** Shows the properties of the selected object in the Properties window.
- **Show All Files:** Displays the hidden files of the project.
- **Refresh:** Refreshes the current view.
- **View Code:** Displays the source code of the current project in the Code Editor window.
- **View Class Diagram:** Displays the project graphically in the form of classes and members, as shown in Figure 13-5. The figure shows the current constituents of the machine-generated code, which consists of the *Program* class and the **Main** method. With actual applications you would expect more details.

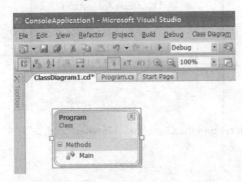

Figure 13-5: The class diagram.

Note There are no major changes in the IDE features when running console applications, but more features are added to other application types such as Windows and web applications.

13-4-2 **The Properties Window**

The Properties window is below the Solution Explorer window. If it is not open, you can display it by choosing **Properties Window** from the **View** menu. This window shows information about the currently selected item in the Solution Explorer. For example, in the following figure the file Program.cs is selected and the Properties window displays its properties (name, path, and so forth). With some applications, such as Windows applications, changing the properties directly affects your code.

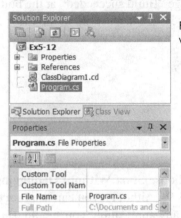

Figure 13-6: The Properties window.

13-4-3 **The Error List Window**

This portion of the screen is shared by other windows such as the Output and Task List windows. If the Error List window is not open, you can display it by choosing **Error List** from the **View** menu. As you can see in the following figure, this window shows the errors and warnings that resulted from compiling the code file of Example 5-12 (some errors and warnings are added deliberately). The errors are indicated by the red circular icon, while the warnings are indicated by the yellow triangular icon.

	Description ▲	File	Line	Column	Project
2	; expected	Program.cs	28	21	Ex5-12
1	Field 'Employee.companyID' is never assigned to, and will always have its default value null	Program.cs	28	12	Ex5-12

Error List — 1 Error, 1 Warning, 0 Messages

Figure 13-7: The Error List window.

13-5 **Compiling and Running Projects**

You can compile and execute all kinds of applications in this environment, except for library projects, which can only be compiled. Library projects are referenced and used in other projects.

To compile and run a project, do the following:

1. To only compile a project, choose **Build ConsoleApplication1** from the **Build** menu (see Figure 13-8). Unless there are errors in your code, you should see the message "Build succeeded" at the bottom of the screen. If there are errors, they would show up in the Error List window.

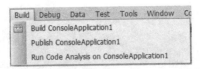

Figure 13-8: The Build menu options.

2. To compile and run a project, choose **Start Without Debugging** from the **Debug** menu (see Figure 13-9). Although you can use **Start Debugging** to compile and run any application, you should use **Start Without Debugging** for console applications. This option keeps the Console screen open until you press any key to continue. You might also use the shortcut keys **F5** and **Ctrl+F5** to access these commands.

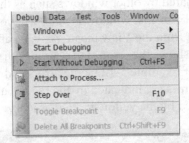

Figure 13-9: The Debug menu options.

➲ **Note**   You can also click the menu button to the left of an option, such as the ▶ button to compile and execute programs. This button is equivalent to the Start Debugging option.

13-6 **Using an Existing Application**

To open an application that already exists on the hard disk, do the following:

1. Open the **File** menu.
2. Select **Open**.
3. Select **Project/Solution**. When the Open Project window appears, you should see the solution file (with the extension .sln) in the target folder.
4. Double-click the solution file to open the solution.

In Figure 13-10, the code of the file Ex5-12.cs is displayed in the Code Editor.

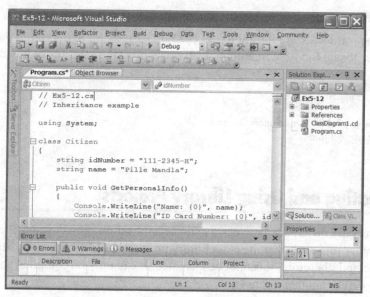

Figure 13-10: Example 5-12 in the Code Editor window.

You can also use Class View to see the inheritance hierarchy, as shown in Figure 13-11.

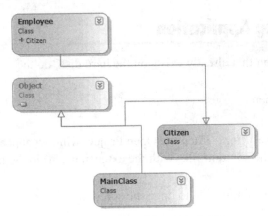

Figure 13-11: Class View of Example 5-12.

As an alternative to opening the solution file, you can open the project file (.csproj) located in the subfolder (Ex5-12), as shown in the following figure. Visual Studio will automatically recognize the solution and load it.

Figure 13-12: The solution file and the project folder.

13-7 Creating and Using Library Projects

The only difference between a console application project and a class library project is that the class library project doesn't contain the **Main** method; therefore, it cannot be executed. It can only be compiled and used as part of another application.

To create a library project, do the following:

1. Open the **File** menu.
2. Select **New**.
3. Select **Project**.
4. Select **Class Library** from the Templates window, and then accept the default name (*ClassLibrary* followed by 1, 2, and so forth) or enter a new name for the library. You might also change the Location at this step, if you so wish.

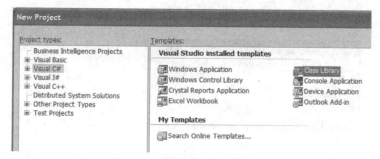

Figure 13-13: Starting a class library project.

5. Clicking the **OK** button transfers you to the Code Editor where you can start writing your code or paste previously created code in the Code Editor window.

The following figure shows the Code Editor for the class library named *ClassLibrary1*. The code represents a method that returns the *factorial* of a number (see Example Ex4-5a.cs).

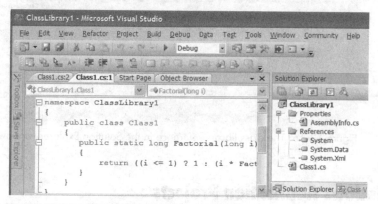

Figure 13-14: Writing the code for a class library.

To use this class library, start a console application, such as *ConsoleApplication2*, and write the code that will use the *factorial* method (you can use the file Ex4-5b.cs for this purpose).

To link your code to the class library, do the following:

1. Open the **Project** menu.
2. Select **Add Reference**. The Add Reference window appears.
3. Select the **Browse** tab and open the **Debug** folder of ClassLibrary1.

4. Select the **ClassLibrary1.dll** as shown in Figure 13-15.

Figure 13-15: Adding a reference to the project.

5. Click **OK** and ClassLibrary1 appears in the Solution Explorer window under the References node. The project screen should look something like the following figure. Notice that the fully qualified name is ClassLibrary1.Class1.Factorial.

6. Run the project by choosing **Start Without Debugging** or pressing **Ctrl+F5**.

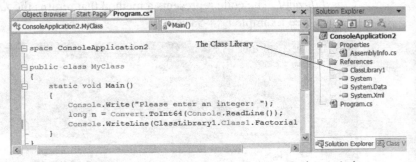

Figure 13-16: The class library reference in the Solution Explorer window.

13-8 **Windows Application Projects**

Although Windows applications are not covered in this book, in this section we take a quick look at how they are created.

To start a Windows forms application, do the following:

1. Open the **File** menu.

2. Select **New**.

3. Select **Project**.

4. Select **Windows Application**.

You will then be transferred to the design view (Form1.cs[Design]), which contains the Windows form (Form1), as shown in Figure 13-17. You can build the form by dragging control elements from the Toolbox and dropping them on the form. Visual Studio will then record your actions and generate the necessary code in the background.

The following figure shows the main features of the Windows Application environment. Notice also the form file (Form1.cs) in the Solution Explorer window. This file contains the form and the machine-generated code. You can switch between the form in the design view and the machine-generated code in the code view, as explained in the next section. You can add your code to the machine-generated code as you build your application.

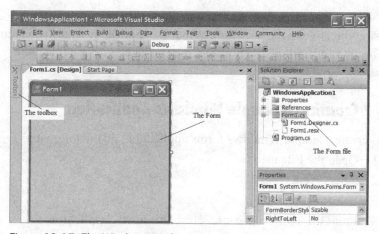

Figure 13-17: The Windows Application environment.

When you click the Toolbox, it opens to reveal its list of controls, which are grouped in categories as shown in Figure 13-18. By expanding a category you can see the controls it contains.

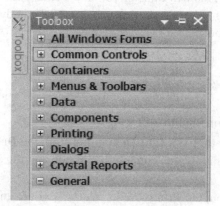

Figure 13-18: The Toolbox categories.

13-8-1 **Switching between Design and Code Views**

To switch to the code view, do the following:

1. Double-click the surface of **Form1** or right-click it and select **View Code**. You can also select **Code** from the **View** menu, or press **F7**. When you switch to the code view, you see the Form1.cs tab at the top of the Code Editor.

2. To go back to the design view, click the **Form1.cs [Design]** tab, or select **Designer** from the **View** menu.

The machine-generated code for an empty project contains all the common **using** directives necessary for a Windows application. It also contains the *WindowsApplication1* namespace, the partial class *Form1*, and the *Form1_Load* method.

13-8-2 **Creating a Simple Windows Application**

To create a simple Windows forms application, do the following:

1. Open the **File** menu.

2. Select **New**.

3. Select **Project**.

4. From the Templates pane, select **Windows Application**.

5. Type the application name and location or accept the defaults (the default name is *Windows Application1*, 2, or 3, and so forth).

6. Drag a **TextBox** and a **Button** and drop them on the form's surface. This will create a text box with the default name *textBox1* and a button with the default name *button1*.

7. Double-click the button. This will transfer you to the code page (Forms1.cs). Add the highlighted code shown below to the body of the **button1_Click** method:

```
private void button1_Click(object sender, EventArgs e)
{
    textBox1.Text = "Hello, World!";
}
```

To run the Windows application, do the following:

1. Press **Ctrl+F5** or select **Start Without Debugging** from the **Debug** menu. You will see the window that contains the button and the empty text box.

2. When you click the button, the string "Hello, World!" will be displayed in the text box, as shown in Figure 13-19.

Figure 13-19: Running the simple Windows forms application.

13-8-3 Using More Than One Form in the Windows Application

You can use more than one form in the same application. To do that, follow these steps:

1. Open the **Project** menu.

2. Click **Add Windows Form** (or **Add New Item**). The Add New Item dialog box appears.

3. Select **Windows Form** from the Add New Item dialog box.

The following figure shows a project that contains two forms. The second form is called Form2.

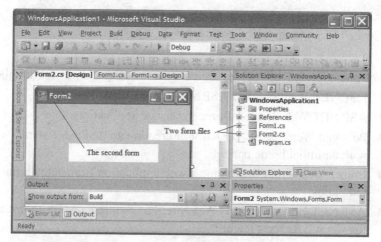

Figure 13-20: A Windows application project with two forms.

13-9 **Web Site Applications**

Although web site applications are not covered in this book, let's take a quick look at how such applications are created.

To create a web site application, do the following:

1. Open the **File** menu.
2. Select **New**.
3. Select **Web Site**.

The dialog box shown in Figure 13-21 opens on your screen. The screen shows the templates for various types of web site applications in addition to the Language, the Location, and the path of the project. The default name for the application is *WebSite1, 2, 3,* and so forth. You can accept the default or change it as you like.

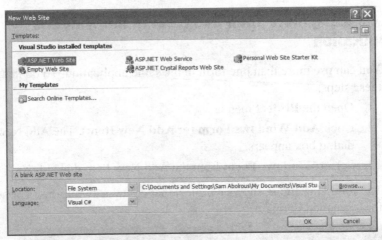

Figure 13-21: Starting a web site application.

Web site applications can be created from the installed project templates:

- ASP.NET Web Site: For ASP.NET applications.
- ASP.NET Web Service: For web service applications.
- Personal Web Site Starter Kit: For creating an ASP.NET starter web site with an initial home page.
- Empty Web Site: For creating a web application from scratch (no templates).
- ASP.NET Crystal Reports Web Site: For creating a web site that uses the Crystal Reports feature.

When you start an ASP.NET web site application, Visual Studio creates three files for you:

- Default.aspx: An HTML file that represents the web form.
- Default.aspx.cs: A C# file that contains the **Page_Load** method.
- Web.config: An XML file used to configure your application.

13-9-1 Creating a Simple Web Site Application

To create a simple web site application, do the following:

1. Open the **File** menu.
2. Select **New**.
3. Select **Web Site**.
4. From the Templates area, select **ASP.NET Web Site**. Select a name and location for the project or accept the defaults.
5. The program starts with the HTML file shown in Figure 13-22. To switch to the design view that contains the web form, click the **Design** tab below the code area.

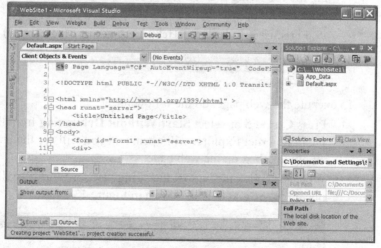

Figure 13-22: The file Default.aspx in a web site application.

6. When you switch to design view, the web form will be totally empty. Drag a **Button** and a **TextBox** from the Toolbox and drop them on the web page. The web page will look similar to Figure 13-23.

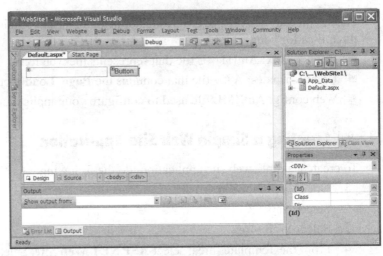

Figure 13-23: The web page after adding the controls.

7. Double-click the button to be transferred to the body of the method **button1_Click** in the file Default.aspx.cs. Modify the method by adding the following highlighted code to its body (notice that the method is initially empty):

```
protected void button1_Click(object sender, EventArgs e)
{
    TextBox1.Text = "Hello, World!";
}
```

To execute the web page, do the following:

1. Press **Ctrl+F5** or select **Start Without Debugging** from the **Debug** menu. Internet Explorer will open, and you will see the button and the empty text box on the web page.

2. When you click the button, the string "Hello, World!" will be displayed in the text box, as shown in Figure 13-24.

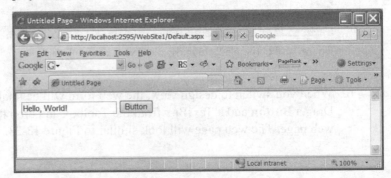

Figure 13-24: Running the web site application.

13-10 **Other Project Templates**

In addition to standard projects and web site projects, you can select other project templates such as:

- Smart Device Application: Includes templates for the Smartphone and Pocket PC.
- SQL Server Project: For creating database applications using SQL Server 2005.
- Starter Kit Project: Includes a complete application ready for you to load, build, and customize. This might be a good place to start.

13-11 **Features of the Code Editor**

The Code Editor of Visual Studio 2005 includes new features and enhancements. In this section, we'll discuss the most important features that can help you in building your console projects.

13-11-1 **IntelliSense**

IntelliSense helps developers speed up the typing process by providing a completion list that contains types, members, keywords, and so forth. For example, when you type the word "new" and press the Spacebar, a drop-down list appears containing all the expected items that can follow the word "new," as you can see in Figure 13-25. Notice in this specific example that IntelliSense is also smart, as it highlighted the most expected text (Employee). When you press Tab or Enter, the selected word is added for you.

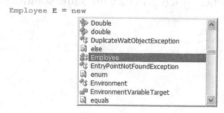

Figure 13-25: The drop-down list.

When you write a method from the .NET class library such as **Write** or **WriteLine**, the IntelliSense feature provides you with *parameter info* when you type the left parenthesis (as shown in Figure 13-26). Parameter info for a method contains the different signatures and method overloads. Use the arrows to see all the overloads.

```
Console.Write (|
```
```
▲ 1 of 18 ▼   void Console.Write (bool value)
value: The value to write.
```

Figure 13-26: The parameter info.

Sometimes you may forget to add a **using** directive or to qualify a member. When you hover over the underlined item that generated the error, you see the text of the error message, as shown in Figure 13-27.

```
Console.WriteLine("Citizen's Information:");
```
```
The name 'Console' does not exist in the current context
```

Figure 13-27: The error message.

IntelliSense provides a quick way to fix these errors without being distracted from the original task you were doing. Right-click the underlined item and select **Resolve** from the shortcut menu. The Resolve option provides two solutions in this particular case: either to add the **using** directive (**using System** here) to the file or to qualify the name by adding **System** to the method name.

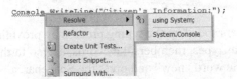

Figure 13-28: The Resolve menu options.

You can also use the *smart tag* menu, which is accessed by clicking the little red box that follows the unbound type. When you click the smart tag you will see the smart tag menu, which provides the same solutions.

```
The name 'Console' does not exist in the current context
Console.WriteLine("Citizen's Information:");
```
```
⌖ using System;
  System.Console
```

Figure 13-29: The smart tag menu.

13-11-2 Code Snippets

This feature saves programmers a lot of time they would otherwise spend typing, by allowing the reuse of previously written code. You can choose from three available options when you right-click the Code Editor window:

- Insert Snippet
- Surround With
- Refactor

These three options are explained below.

13-11-2-1 Insert Snippet

This option is used to insert one of the common snippets used by developers, such as the conditional or iteration statements. When you choose **Insert Snippet** from the shortcut menu, you get two choices:

- Office Development
- C#

By selecting C#, you see the drop-down list shown in Figure 13-30, which contains the snippet names.

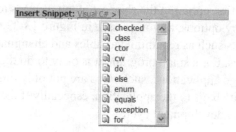

Figure 13-30: The snippet drop-down list.

When you click the name of the snippet, the code is inserted at the cursor position, as shown in Figure 13-31.

```
for (int i = 0; i < length; i++)
{

}
```

Figure 13-31: The for snippet.

As you can see in Figure 13-31, the snippet contains the syntax of the **for** loop, but you have to provide the *length* value and you may also want to change the name of the counter variable.

13-11-2-2 Surround With

The Surround With feature is another way to insert a snippet. For example, if you already have the statement:

```
Console.WriteLine ("Hello!");
```

you can surround it with a **for** loop by highlighting the statement and selecting the menu option **Surround With**. The statement will be surrounded by the **for** loop, as shown in Figure 13-32.

```
for (int i = 0; i < length; i++)
{
    Console.WriteLine ("Hello!");
}
```

Figure 13-32: Surrounding with for.

13-11-2-3 Refactor

The Refactor option is the first option in the shortcut menu. It leads to a submenu that contains many options, as you can see in Figure 13-33.

Refactoring include tasks such as renaming variables and changing method names or signatures. For a small program, it is okay to do these tasks manually. But for large applications, such tasks are not only time-intensive but they also invite bugs to the application, especially if the product is close to the end of the development cycle.

Figure 13-33: The Refactor submenu.

For the purpose of this chapter, we are not going to cover everything in the Refactor menu, but here is one example of how it works. Assume that you have a private field like this:

```
private string companyName;
```

To use the Encapsulate Field option, do the following:
1. Highlight the field and right-click to display the Refactor menu.
2. Select **Encapsulate Field**. The following window appears.

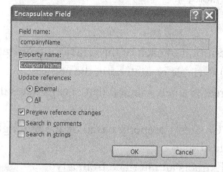

Figure 13-34: The Encapsulate Field window.

3. By clicking **OK**, the changes shown in Figure 13-34 will be made to the code.

Figure 13-35: The Preview Reference Changes window.

4. Review the code changes and click **Apply**.

The following code will replace the field declaration in your program:

```
public string CompanyName
{
    get { return companyName; }
    set { companyName = value; }
}
```

Following is a brief description of each of the refactoring operations:

- **Rename:** Renames a variable or method in the application.
- **Extract Method:** Creates a new method that encapsulates the highlighted code.
- **Encapsulate Field:** Creates a property based on the highlighted private field (see the example above).
- **Extract Interface:** Extracts an interface from a type.
- **Promote Local Variable to Parameter:** Converts a local variable to a parameter of the current method.
- **Remove Parameters:** Removes a method parameter. The Remove Parameters window opens, which allows you to preview and apply the changes.
- **Reorder Parameters:** Reorders the parameters of a method. The Reorder Parameters window opens, which allows you to preview and apply the changes.

Summary

In this chapter:

- You learned enough about the IDE to build and run the applications introduced in this book.
- You learned how to use the Code Editor to write code, and how to build an application and check the compilation result.
- You also learned about the main features of Windows and web site applications.
- Finally, you learned about some features that can speed up your application development when you use the IDE, such as IntelliSense and Code Snippets.

Chapter 14

C# 3.0 Features

Contents:

- Implicitly typed local variables
- Object initializers
- Extension methods
- Anonymous types
- Implicitly typed arrays
- Lambda expressions
- Func delegate types
- Query expressions
- Expression trees

14-1 Installing C# 3.0

This chapter discusses the features of the upcoming release of C# that was published with the Community Technology Preview (CTP) of Microsoft Visual Studio Code Name "Orcas." Orcas is the next-generation development tool for Windows Vista, the 2007 Office System, and the web.

In order to get started with the new compiler, you can install the Language Integrated Query (LINQ) features included with the C# 3.0 compiler from:

```
http://go.microsoft.com/fwlink/?LinkId=88254
```

When you install the LINQ features, it will add a new node (LINQ Preview) to the Visual Studio IDE as shown in Figure 14-1.

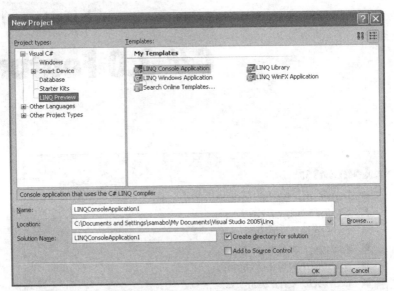

Figure 14-1: The LINQ features added to the C# compiler in Visual Studio.

To start a new project in C# 3.0 you can select one of the available project types:

- LINQ Console Application
- LINQ Library
- LINQ Windows Application
- LINQ WinFX Application

In this chapter's examples, we use the LINQ Console Application option to create the projects. We also use LINQ Library in one example. When you create a LINQ console application, you will see a new set of namespaces in your project:

```
using System;
using System.Collections.Generic;
using System.Text;
using System.Query;
using System.Xml.XLinq;
using System.Data.DLinq;
```

14-1-1 **Using the Command Line**

To compile a program using the command-line environment, use the following command:

```
C:\Program Files\LINQ Preview\Bin\Csc.exe
    /reference:"C:\Program Files\LINQ Preview\Bin\System.Data.DLinq.dll"
    /reference: System.dll
    /reference:"C:\Program Files\LINQ Preview\Bin\System.Query.dll"
    /target:exe Program.cs
```

where:

Program is the name of the C# file to compile.

To compile a library, use the switch /target:library instead of /target:exe.

14-1-2 **Installing Visual Studio (Orcas)**

You can also read about Orcas and download the Visual Studio CTP from the web site:

```
http://go.microsoft.com/fwlink/?LinkId=88253
```

It is recommended in this case to use Virtual PC.

➲ **Note**   The examples in this chapter are provided as C# text files (.cs). The easiest way to compile an example is to paste its text file into a LINQ console application and run it by using the menu option Start Debugging or Start Without Debugging.

14-2 **Implicitly Typed Local Variables**

You can declare a variable with the **var** keyword and let the compiler infer the type from the expression used to initialize the variable. For example:

```
var myVariable = 1.25;
var yourVariable = "Hello, World!";
var myArray = new int[] { 1, 2, 4, 8, 64 };
```

The C# compiler can infer that the type of myVariable is **double**, the type of yourVariable is **string**, and that of myArray is **int**. In other words, the three statements above generate the same result as the following statements:

```
double myVariable = 1.25;
string yourVariable = "Hello, World!";
int myArray = new int[] { 1, 2, 4, 8, 64 };
```

There are a few restrictions on using implicitly typed local variables though:

- You must initialize the variables. For example:

```
var myVariable;                    // error: not initialized
```

- The variable initializer cannot be null. For example:

```
var yourVariable = null;      // error: null value
```

- You cannot use object or collection initializers (explained in Section 14-3). For example:

```
var myArray = { 1, 2, 4, 8, 64 };
```

> **Note** It is obvious that if there is a type called var in the same scope, this type will be used in the declaration.

Example 14-1

```
// Example 14-1.cs
// Implicitly typed local variables

using System;
using System.Collections.Generic;
using System.Text;
using System.Query;
using System.Xml.XLinq;
using System.Data.DLinq;

namespace ImplicitlyTypedVariables
{
    class MyClass
    {
        static void Main(string[] args)
        {
            var myVariable = 1.25;
            var yourVariable = "Hello, World!";
            var myArray = new int[] { 1, 2, 4, 8, 64 };

            Console.WriteLine(myVariable);
            Console.WriteLine(yourVariable);
            foreach (var x in myArray)
            Console.WriteLine(x);
        }
    }
}
```

Output:

```
1.25
Hello, World!
1
2
4
8
64
```

14-2-1 Examine the Assembly

It is interesting at this point to see what the compiler has created for you in the background. Run ILDASM on the executable file generated from the compilation (ImplicitlyTyped.exe) by using the following command line:

```
ILDASM AnonTypes.exe
```

Notice that you have to issue this command from the directory in which the executable file exists.

You can then see the compiled assembly tree, as shown in the following figure.

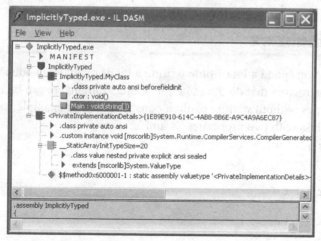

Figure 14-2: The class tree of the file ImplicitlyTyped.exe.

If you double-click the Main node, shown highlighted in the figure above, you will display the IL language of the **Main** class. Here you can see that the appropriate types were actually created, that is, **float 64**, **string**, and **int32[]**.

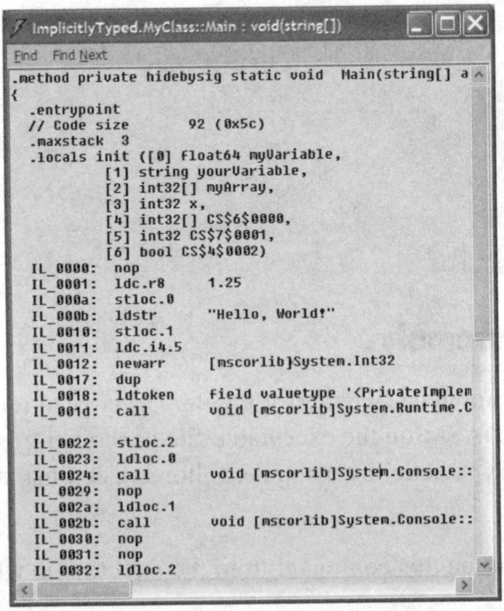

Figure 14-3: The generated IL for the Main class.

14-3 Object Initializers

Sometimes you spend a lot of time writing a lot of redundant code to declare constructors that do the same job. Object initializers can be used to initialize types without writing explicit constructors. For example, consider the **Point** class with two properties, X and Y:

```
class Point
{
    int x, y;
    public int X
    {
        get { return x; }
        set { x = value; }
    }
    public int Y
    {
        get { return y; }
        set { y = value; }
    }
}
```

When you instantiate this class you normally write the following code:

```
Point p = new Point();
p.X = 10;
p.Y = 20;
```

Instead, you can create and initialize a Point object like this:

```
Point p = new Point { X = 10, Y = 20 };      // object initializer
```

Or even like this:

```
var p = new Point { X = 10, Y = 20 };        // object initializer
```

With complex fields, such as a square or a rectangle whose corners are located at the points p1 and p2, you can create the **Rectangle** class as follows:

```
public class Rectangle
{
    Point p1; Point p2;
    public Point ULcorner { get { return p1; } set { p1 = value; } }
    public Point LRcorner { get { return p2; } set { p2 = value; } }
}
```

You can create and initialize the Rectangle object like this:

```
var rectangle = new Rectangle {
    ULcorner = new Point { X = 0, Y = 0 },
    LRcorner = new Point { X = 10, Y = 20 }
};
```

➲ **Note**   Notice the semicolon at the end of the object initializer block.

Example 14-2

```
// Example 14-2.cs
// Object initializers

using System;
using System.Collections.Generic;
using System.Text;
using System.Query;
using System.Xml.XLinq;
using System.Data.DLinq;

namespace ObjectInitializer
{
    public class Point
    {
        int x, y;
        public int X
```

```
        {
            get { return x; }
            set { x = value; }
        }
        public int Y
        {
            get { return y; }
            set { y = value; }
        }
        public class Rectangle
        {
            Point p1; Point p2;
            public Point ULcorner { get { return p1; } set { p1 = value; } }
            public Point LRcorner { get { return p2; } set { p2 = value; } }
        }

        static void Main(string[] args)
        {
            // Point object initializer:
            var p = new Point { X = 10, Y = 20 };

            // Rectangle object initializer:
            var rectangle = new Rectangle
            {
                ULcorner = new Point { X = 0, Y = 0 },
                LRcorner = new Point { X = 10, Y = 20 }
            };

            Console.WriteLine("Objects created successfully.");
        }
    }
}
```

Output:

```
Objects created successfully.
```

14-3-1 Initializing Collections

A collection such as a generic List can be initialized like this:

```
List<string> names = new List<string> { Dylan, Angelina, Isabella };
```

This initialization has the same effect as using the **Add** method with each collection element. Consider the following C# 2.0 example:

Example 14-3

```csharp
// Example 14-3.cs
// Initializing collections - C# 2.0

using System;
using System.Collections;
using System.Collections.Generic;
using System.Text;

namespace InitCollections
{
    public class Authors
    {
        string author;
        List<string> booksInPrint = new List<string>();
        public string Author { get { return author; } set { author =
                            value; } }
        public List<string> BooksInPrint { get { return booksInPrint; } }
    }

    class MyClass
    {
        static void Main(string[] args)
        {
            List<Authors> authorsList = new List<Authors>();
            Authors c1 = new Authors();
            c1.Author = "Dylan Combel";
            c1.BooksInPrint.Add("ISBN: 555-62280-58");
            c1.BooksInPrint.Add("ISBN: 555-71180-59");
            authorsList.Add(c1);
            Authors c2 = new Authors();
            c2.Author = "Isabella Abolrous";
            c2.BooksInPrint.Add("ISBN: 555-72390-88");
            c2.BooksInPrint.Add("ISBN: 555-65412-77");
            authorsList.Add(c2);
            Console.WriteLine(c1.Author + ":\n" + c1.BooksInPrint[0] +
                        "\n" + c1.BooksInPrint[1]);
            Console.WriteLine(c2.Author + ":\n" + c2.BooksInPrint[0] +
                        "\n" + c2.BooksInPrint[1]);
        }
    }
}
```

Output:

```
Dylan Combel:
ISBN: 555-62280-58
ISBN: 555-71180-59
Isabella Abolrous:
ISBN: 555-72390-88
ISBN: 555-65412-77
```

In C# 3.0, you can write less code to express the same concept:

```
static void Main(string[] args)
{
    var authorsList = new List<Authors> {
    new Authors { Author = "Dylan Combel",
        BooksInPrint = { "ISBN: 555-62280-58", "ISBN: 555-71180-59" } },
    new Authors { Author = "Isabella Abolrous",
        BooksInPrint = { "ISBN: 555-72390-88", "ISBN: 555-65412-77" }
    };
}
```

The following is the complete C# 3.0 example, which outputs the same result as that of Example 14-3.

Example 14-4

```
// Example 14-4.cs
// Initializing collections - C# 3.0

using System;
using System.Collections.Generic;
using System.Text;
using System.Query;
using System.Xml.XLinq;
using System.Data.DLinq;


namespace InitCollections
{
    public class Authors
    {
        string author;
        List<string> booksInPrint = new List<string>();
        public string Author { get { return author; } set { author =
                            value; } }
        public List<string> BooksInPrint { get { return booksInPrint; } }

        static void Main(string[] args)
        {
            var authorsList = new List<Authors> {
            new Authors { Author = "Dylan Combel",
                BooksInPrint = { "ISBN: 555-62280-58", "ISBN: 555-71180-59" }
```

```
        },
        new Authors {Author = "Isabella Abolrous",
            BooksInPrint = { "ISBN: 555-72390-88", "ISBN: 555-65412-77" }
        }
    };

    // Display the first author and his books:
    Console.WriteLine(authorsList[0].Author + ":\n" +
        authorsList[0].BooksInPrint[0] + "\n" +
        authorsList[0].BooksInPrint[1]);

    // Display the second author and her books:
    Console.WriteLine(authorsList[1].Author + ":\n" +
        authorsList[1].BooksInPrint[0] + "\n" +
        authorsList[1].BooksInPrint[1]);
    }
  }
}
```

Output:

```
Dylan Combel:
ISBN: 555-62280-58
ISBN: 555-71180-59
Isabella Abolrous:
ISBN: 555-72390-88
ISBN: 555-65412-77
```

14-4 Extension Methods

You can extend both regular types and constructed types by adding additional static methods, which can be invoked in the same way you invoke instance methods.

To create an extension method, declare it as a static method in a static class. The first parameter of an extension method must be the keyword **this**. The following is an example of an extension method to convert the temperature from Fahrenheit to Celsius.

```
namespace MyNameSpace
{
    public static class MyClass
    {
        public static double ConvertToCelsius(this double fahrenheit)
        {
            return ((fahrenheit – 32) / 1.8);
        }
    }
```

Compile the code above as a library by using the option LINQ Library in Visual Studio or by using the command line with the switch /target:library.

In order to use an extension method, reference its library and import its namespace by using the **using** directive. In the current example, you must import MyNameSpace:

```
using MyNameSpace;
```

Now it is possible to invoke the extension method, **ConvertToCelsius**, as if it is an instance method:

```
double fahrenheit = 98.7;
double Celsius = fahrenheit.ConvertToCelsius();
```

which is the same as using the static method:

```
double Celsius = MyClass.ConvertToCelsius(fahrenheit);
```

Notice that instance methods have precedence over extension methods. Notice also, in nested namespaces, the extension methods in the inner namespace have higher precedence over the ones in the outer namespace.

> **Note** Using extension methods is not recommended except in cases where instance methods are not available.
> Extension members such as properties, events, and operators are not currently supported.

14-5 Anonymous Types

The C# compiler can create an anonymous type by using the properties in an object initializer. For example, consider the following declaration:

```
var book1 = new { Title = "Organic Babies", ISBN = "5-1234-5678-x" };
```

This declaration creates and initializes an object with the values of the two properties, **Title** and **ISBN**. The compiler automatically creates an anonymous type and infers the types of the properties from the object initializer. It also creates the private fields associated with these properties and the necessary **set** and **get** accessors. When the object is instantiated, the properties are set to the values specified in the object initializer.

The following example declares one anonymous type and displays its contents.

Example 14-5

```
// Example 14-5.cs
// Anonymous types

using System;
using System.Collections.Generic;
using System.Text;
using System.Query;
using System.Xml.XLinq;
using System.Data.DLinq;

namespace AnonTypes
{
   class MyClass
   {
      static void Main(string[] args)
      {
         // Declare an anonymous type:
         var obj1 = new { Title = "Organic Babies", ISBN =
                          "5-1234-5678-x" };

         // Display the contents:
         Console.WriteLine("Title: {0}\nISBN: {1}", obj1.Title,
                          obj1.ISBN);
         Console.ReadLine();
      }
   }
}
```

Output:

```
Title: Organic Babies
ISBN: 5-1234-5678-x
```

In order to see the class tree, run ILDASM on the executable file generated from the compilation (AnonTypes.exe) by using the following command line:

```
ILDASM AnonTypes.exe
```

Notice that you have to issue this command from the directory in which the executable file exists. You will then see the compiled assembly tree, as shown in the following figure.

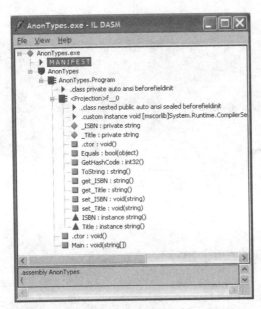

Figure 14-4: The class generated by an anonymous type in Example 14-5.

When you examine Figure 14-4, you can see the class **<Projection>f__0** that was created as well as the private fields _ISBN and _Title. You will also notice the two properties ISBN and Title along with their **set** and **get** accessors. If you double-click one of the properties, you will reveal the code behind it. For example, double-clicking the Title property displays the code shown in Figure 14-5.

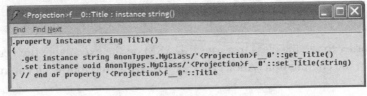

Figure 14-5: The code behind the Title property in Example 14-5.

14-5-1 **Using Multiple Anonymous Types**

Now consider the following change to Example 14-5, where you create two similar types:

```
static void Main(string[] args)
{
    // Declare two similar anonymous types:
    var book1 = new { Title = "Organic Babies", ISBN = "5-1234-5678-x" };
    var book2 = new { Title = "Best Games for Kids", ISBN =
                    "6-1234-5678-y" };
    // Display the contents:
    Console.WriteLine("Title = {0}\nISBN = {1}", book1.Title, book1.ISBN);
    Console.WriteLine("Title = {0}\nISBN = {1}", book2.Title, book2.ISBN);
}
```

This code would display the following output:

```
Title = Organic Babies
ISBN = 5-1234-5678-x
Title = Best Games for Kids
ISBN = 6-1234-5678-y
```

By examining the compiled assembly for this code, you will get the same result shown in Figure 14-4 because the two types are identical. If you created two different types, however, you will notice that the compiler will create two classes. For example, the following code declares two different anonymous types:

```
static void Main(string[] args)
{
    // Declare two different anonymous types:
    var book1 = new { Title = "Organic Babies", ISBN = "03-56789-xxx" };
    var book2 = new { Title = "Best Games for Kids", Price = 34.99 };

    // Display the contents:
    Console.WriteLine("Title: {0}\nISBN: {1}", book1.Title, book1.ISBN);
    Console.WriteLine("Title: {0}\nPrice: {1}", book2.Title, book2.Price);
}
```

The expected output from this code is:

```
Title: Organic Babies
ISBN: 03-56789-xxx
Title: Best Games for Kids
Price: 34.99
```

Now examine the compiled assembly shown in Figure 14-6 and notice that there are two classes: one contains the ISBN and Title properties, and the other contains the Price and Title properties.

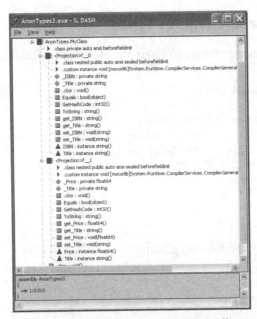

Figure 14-6: Two classes created by two different anonymous types.

14-6 **Implicitly Typed Arrays**

The implicitly typed local variables can be extended to declaring arrays. By examining the members of an array in the initialization expression, the compiler can infer the type of the array elements.

The following is the regular C# 2.0 code to declare variables of different types:

```
int a = new[] { 1, 2, 4, 8, 16, 32, 64 };
double b = new[] { 3, 3.14, 2.7 };
bool c = new [] { true, false };
string d = new[] { "Hello,", "world!" };
```

In C# 3.0, you don't have to declare the array types explicitly. Just use the keyword **var** and let the compiler infer the type of the array elements:

```
var intArray = new[] { 1, 2, 4, 8, 16, 32, 64 };
var doubleArray = new[] { 3, 3.14, 2.7 };
var boolArray = new[] { true, false };
var stringArray = new[] { "Hello,", "world!" };
```

Example 14-6

```
// Example 14-6.cs
// Implicitly typed arrays

using System;
using System.Collections.Generic;
using System.Text;
using System.Query;
using System.Xml.XLinq;
using System.Data.DLinq;

namespace ImplicitlyTypedArrays
{
    class MyClass
    {
        static void Main(string[] args)
        {
            // Declare some implicitly typed arrays:
            var intArray = new[] { 1, 2, 4, 8, 16, 32, 64 };
            var doubleArray = new[] { 3, 3.14, 2.7 };
            var boolArray = new[] { true, false };
            var stringArray = new[] { "Hello,", "world!" };

            // Display array elements:
            foreach(var x in intArray) Console.Write(x + " ");
                Console.WriteLine();
            foreach(var x in doubleArray) Console.WriteLine(x);
            foreach(var x in boolArray) Console.Write(x + " ");
                Console.WriteLine();
            foreach(var x in stringArray) Console.Write(x);
        }
    }
}
```

Output:

```
1 2 4 8 16 32 64
3
3.14
2.7
True False
Hello, world!
```

14-7 **Lambda Expressions**

Lambda expressions provide a concise syntax for writing anonymous methods. The C# 3.0 specification describes lambda expressions as a superset of anonymous methods.

14-7-1 **Using Anonymous Methods in C# 2.0**

In Chapter 10, you used delegates that encapsulate a block of code, which is called an anonymous method.

In C# 2.0, you can write a delegate using an anonymous method, as shown in this example:

```
public delegate int MyDelegate(int n);
class MyClass
{
    static void Main()
    {
        // Anonymous method that returns the argument multiplied by 5:
        MyDelegate delegObject1 = new MyDelegate(
            delegate(int n) { return n * 5; }
        );
        // Display the result:
        Console.WriteLine("The value is: {0}", delegObject1(5));
    }
}
```

This program outputs the value 25.

14-7-2 **Using Lambda Expressions in C# 3.0**

In C# 3.0 this feature is extended to lambda expressions, which are used in many functional languages such as Lisp.

Note For more information on functional languages, see http://en.wikipedia.org/wiki/Functional_programming_language.

Using a lambda expression you can use a simpler syntax to achieve the same goal:

```
// Lambda expression that returns the argument multiplied by 5:
MyDelegate delegObject2 = (int n) => n * 5;
```

The token "=>" used in this syntax is called the *lambda operator*. You can also use an abbreviated form like this:

```
MyDelegate delegObject2 = n => n * 5;
```

The following example demonstrates the two approaches (the anonymous method and the lambda expression) to return the argument multiplied by 5.

Example 14-7

```
// Example 14-7.cs
// Lambda expressions

using System;
using System.Collections.Generic;
using System.Text;
using System.Query;
using System.Xml.XLinq;
using System.Data.DLinq;

namespace Lambda
{
    public delegate int MyDelegate(int n);

    class MyClass
    {
        static void Main()
        {
            // Anonymous method that returns the argument multiplied by 5:
            MyDelegate delegObject1 = new MyDelegate(
                delegate(int n) { return n * 5; }
            );

            // Display the result:
            Console.WriteLine("The value using an anonymous method is: {0}",
                              delegObject1(5));

            // Using lambda expression to do the same job:
            MyDelegate delegObject2 = (int n) => n * 5;
            // or:
            // MyDelegate delegObject2 = n => n * 5;

            // Display the result:
            Console.WriteLine("The value using a lambda expression is: {0}",
                              delegObject2(5));
            Console.ReadLine();
        }
    }
}
```

Output:

```
The value using an anonymous method is: 25
The value using a lambda expression is: 25
```

14-7-3 **Using Two Arguments in a Lambda Expression**

A lambda expression can use two arguments, especially when you are using the *Standard Query Operators*. Let us start by declaring the following delegate that uses two arguments:

```
public delegate int MyDelegate(int m, int n);
```

You can instantiate the delegate by using a lambda expression like this:

```
MyDelegate myDelegate = (x, y) => x * y;
```

You can then invoke the delegate and display the result as follows:

```
Console.WriteLine("The product is: {0}", myDelegate(5, 4));
    // output: 20
```

➔ **Note**   The Standard Query Operators is an API used to query .NET arrays and collections. The API contains methods declared in the System.Query.Sequence static class in the assembly System.Query.dll. Examples of Standard Query Operators are Average and Count.

   This feature is enhanced with languages that support extension methods, lambda expressions, and native query syntax, such as C# 3.0.

   You can find more information on the Standard Query Operators as well as the Microsoft specification on the web site: http://www.hookedonlinq.com/StandardQueryOperators.ashx.

In the next section, we discuss a simpler way of using delegates and compare it to using lambda expressions.

14-8 **Func Delegate Types**

Language Integrated Query (LINQ) defined a number of parameterized generic delegate types in the **System.Query.Func** namespace. Those generic delegate types can be used to construct delegates without the need to explicitly declare a delegate. These generic delegates are:

```
public delegate TR Func<TR>();
public delegate TR Func<T0, TR>(T0 a0);
public delegate TR Func<T0, T1, TR>(T0 a0, T1 a1);
public delegate TR Func<T0, T1, T2, TR>(T0 a0, T1 a1, T2 a2);
public delegate TR Func<T0, T1, T2, T3, TR>(T0 a0, T1 a1, T2 a2, T3 a3);
```

When a single type parameter is used, as in the first delegate, this type parameter (TR) represents the return type of the delegate. In all the other delegates, the type parameters (T0, T1, and so forth) are the types of the arguments, while the last type parameter (TR) is the return type of the delegate. These delegate types are used in the Standard Query Operators.

You can use these types to declare and instantiate a delegate, like this:

```
Func<int, int, int> myFuncDelegate = (a, b) => a * b;
```

In the following example, a lambda expression and a Func delegate are used to multiply two arguments. They both output the same result, but the latter doesn't use the explicit delegate declaration.

Example 14-8

```
// Example 14-8.cs
// Comparison between lambda expressions and Func delegates.

using System;
using System.Collections.Generic;
using System.Text;
using System.Query;
using System.Xml.XLinq;
using System.Data.DLinq;

namespace LambdaAndFunc
{
    // Declare a delegate:
    public delegate int MyDelegate(int m, int n);

    class MyClass
    {
        static void Main(string[] args)
        {
            // Instantiate the delegate using a lambda expression:
            MyDelegate myDelegate = (x, y) => x * y;

            // Invoke the delegate and display the result:
            Console.WriteLine("The product from the lambda expression is:
                        {0}", myDelegate(5, 4));

            // Using the Func delegate type.
            // Notice that no delegate declaration is needed:
            Func<int, int, int> myFuncDelegate = (a, b) => a * b;
            Console.WriteLine("The product from the Func delegate is: {0}",
                        myFuncDelegate(5, 4));
        }
    }
}
```

Output:

```
The product from the lambda expression is: 20
The product from the Func delegate is: 20
```

14-9 Query Expressions

The main goal of LINQ is to bridge the gap between programming languages and databases. With the LINQ extensions it is possible to write SQL or XML queries in your C# code.

➔ **Note** At the time this book was written, LINQ was still under development, and it is expected to undergo more changes in the final version.

The following example demonstrates a query expression that uses a **string** array called names.

Example 14-9

```csharp
// Example 14-9.cs
// Query Expressions

using System;
using System.Collections.Generic;
using System.Text;
using System.Query;
using System.Xml.XLinq;
using System.Data.DLinq;

namespace QueryExpressions
{
    class MyClass
    {
        static void Main()
        {
            string[] names = { "Hazem", "Pille", "Isabella", "Angelina",
                "Sally", "Craig", "Dylan" };

            IEnumerable<string> myVariable = from name in names
                                            where name.Length > 5
                                            orderby name
                                            select name;

            foreach (string item in myVariable)
                Console.WriteLine(item);
                Console.ReadLine();
        }
```

```
        }
    }
```

Output:

```
Angelina
Isabella
```

Consider the following statement, which contains a query expression:

```
IEnumerable<string> myVariable = from name in names
                                 where name.Length > 5
                                 orderby name
                                 select name;
```

A query expression starts with the **from** clause and ends with either a
select or **group** clause. The variable myVariable, in this example, is
referred to as the *range variable*. This variable is never explicitly declared.
Its type, which is **string** in this case, is inferred from the context. This variable
goes out of scope after the query expression has been executed.

The names array is called the *source collection*. It should implement
either the **IEnumerable** or **IQueryable** interface. In this example, the
string array implements **IEnumerable**.

The query expression is in fact translated to explicit syntax, which is:

```
IEnumerable<string> expr = names
                           .Where(s => s.Length >= 5)
                           .OrderBy(s => s)
                           .Select(s => s);
```

You can use this syntax instead and you would get the same result.

In some cases, the underlying method calls include a chain of query
operators that use extension methods, lambda expressions, and *expression
trees*. Therefore, the syntax of the query expression hides this complex
code in the background and gives you syntax that is easy to understand and
use.

14-10 **Expression Trees**

By using expression trees, you can represent a lambda expression as data
instead of code. That is, if a lambda expression can be converted to a delegate
of the type "D", it can also be converted to an expression tree of type
System.Query.Expression<D>.

The following two lines represent a lambda expression, once as code and once as data:

```
Func<int,int> fnDel = n => n * 5;                    // Code
Expression<Func<int,int>> expTree = n => n * 5;   // Data
```

In the first statement, the delegate fnDel references a method that returns the argument multiplied by 5. In the second statement, the expression tree expTree references a data structure that describes the expression "n * 5."

 Note   The specification of the expression trees was not finished at the time of this book's publication and was not available for the Community Technology Preview.

Summary

In this chapter:

- You took a tour of the new C# 3.0 features and the LINQ project that was introduced in the Community Technology Preview.
- You learned how to add the C# 3.0 compiler to Visual Studio. You also learned that you can use the command line for compiling programs or installing the new Visual Studio CTP from the Microsoft web site.
- Using C# 3.0, you learned how to declare implicitly typed variables by using the keyword **var**.
- You also learned how to initialize objects and collections without repeating the details of constructors.
- You learned that the C# compiler can create an anonymous type by using the properties in an object initializer. The compiler can also infer the type of the array elements by examining the members of an array in the initialization expression.
- You used lambda expressions to declare and invoke delegates in a simpler syntax than that used in anonymous methods.
- You also learned about generic delegate types that can be used to construct delegates without the need to explicitly declare a delegate.
- Finally, you took a quick tour of query expressions and expression trees. Both help to bridge the gap between programming languages and databases.

Answers to Drills

```csharp
// Drill 2-1.cs
// WriteLine and Write

using System;

class HelloWorld
{
   static void Main()
   {
      // Using WriteLine:
      Console.WriteLine("Hello, World!");
      Console.WriteLine("Hello, C# user!");

      // Using Write:
      Console.Write("Hello, World!");
      Console.Write("Hello, C# user!");
   }
}

/*
Output:
Hello, World!
Hello, C# user!
Hello, World!Hello, C# user!
*/
```

```csharp
// Drill 2-2.cs
// Adding two integers

using System;

class MyClass
{
   static void Main()
   {
      int myInt = 123;
```

```
        int yourInt = 123;
        int sum = myInt + yourInt;

        Console.Write("The sum = "+ sum.ToString());
    }
}

/*
Output:
The sum = 246
*/
```

```
// Drill 3-1.cs
// Increment operator

using System;

class ArithmeticOperators
{
    public static void Main()
    {
        int x = 10;
        int y = 100;
        int z = y;
        y = y++ + x;
        Console.WriteLine(y);
        z = ++z + x;
        Console.WriteLine(z);
    }
}

/*
Output:
110
111
*/
```

```
// Drill 3-2.cs
// Get types 1

using System;

class MyTypes
{
    static void Main()
    {
        Console.WriteLine(123.GetType());
        Console.WriteLine(3.14.GetType());
    }
```

```
}

/*
Output:
System.Int32
System.Double
*/
```

```
// Drill 3-3.cs
// Get types 2

using System;

class MyTypes
{
   static void Main()
   {
      decimal myDc = 23.4M;
      float myFl = 23.4F;
      double myDb = 23.4;

      Console.Write("myDc ={0}\nmyFl ={1}\nmyDb ={2}",
         myDc.GetType(), myFl.GetType(), myDb.GetType());
   }
}

/*
Output:
myDc = System.Decimal
myFl = System.Single
myDb = System.Double
*/
```

```
// Drill 3-4.cs
// Get types 3

using System;

class MyClass
{
   static void Main()
   {
      Console.WriteLine(9223372036854775808L.GetType());
      Console.WriteLine(123UL.GetType());
      Console.WriteLine(4294967296L.GetType());
      Console.WriteLine(4294967290U.GetType());
   }
}
```

```
/*
Output:
System.UInt64
System.UInt64
System.Int64
System.UInt32
*/
```

```csharp
// Drill 3-5.cs
// Strings

using System;

class UnicodeChars
{
    static void Main()
    {
        string a = "\u0041";
        string b = "\u0042";
        string c = "\u0043";

        Console.WriteLine("{0}, {1}, and {2} are the first three letters.",
                          a, b, c);
    }
}

/*
Output:
A, B, and C are the first three letters.
*/
```

```csharp
// Drill 4-1.cs
// Character Tester

using System;

public class CharTester
{
    public static void Main()
    {
        Console.Write("Please enter a character: ");
        char yourChar = (char) Console.Read();
            if (Char.IsLower(yourChar))
                Console.WriteLine("The letter {0} is lowercase.", yourChar);
            else if (Char.IsUpper(yourChar))
                Console.WriteLine("The letter {0} is uppercase.", yourChar);
            else
                Console.WriteLine("The character {0} is not alphabetic.",
                                  yourChar);
```

```
    }
}

/*
Sample Run 1:
Please enter a character: a
The letter a is lowercase.

Sample Run 2:
Please enter a character: A
The letter A is uppercase.

Sample Run 3:
Please enter a character: 3
The character 3 is not alphabetic.

Sample Run 4:
Please enter a character: #
The character # is not alphabetic.
*/
```

```
// Drill 4-2.cs
// Computing the power

using System;

public class Power
{
    static void Main(string[] args)
    {
        // Enter the first number:
        Console.Write("Please enter the number: ");
        string stringNumber = Console.ReadLine();
        int number = Int32.Parse(stringNumber);
        // Enter the second number:
        Console.Write("Please enter the power: ");
        string stringPower = Console.ReadLine();
        int power = Int32.Parse(stringPower);
        int result = 1;
        for (int i = 1; i <= power; i++)
            result = result * number;
        Console.WriteLine("The number {0} raised to the power {1} = {2}",
                        number, power, result);
    }
}

/*
Sample Run 1:
Please enter the number: 4
```

```
Please enter the power: 3
The number 4 raised to the power 3 = 64

Sample Run 2:
Please enter the number: 2
Please enter the power: 3
The number 2 raised to the power 3 = 8
*/
```

```
// Drill 4-3.cs
// Two-dimensional arrays example

using System;

class JaggedClass
{
   static void Main ()
   {
      // Two dim array:
      string[,] grades = new string[2,4]
         { {"Pass", "Good", "VeryGood", "Distinct"},
           {"55%", "65%", "75%", "85%"} };
      for (int j = 0; j <= 3; j++)
      {
         Console.Write("Grade={0}\t", grades[0,j]);
         Console.WriteLine("Score={0}", grades[1,j]);
      }
   }
}

/*
Output:
Grade=Pass              Score=55%
Grade=Good              Score=65%
Grade=VeryGood          Score=75%
Grade=Distinct          Score=85%
*/
```

```
// Drill 4-4.cs
// Computing the power, version 2

using System;

public class ConvertMethod

{
   static void Main(string[] args)
   {
      int number = Int32.Parse(args[0]);
```

```
        int power = Int32.Parse(args[1]);
        int result = 1;
        for (int i = 1; i <= power; i++)
            result = result * number;
        Console.WriteLine(
            "The number {0} raised to the power {1} = {2}",
                    number, power, result);
    }
}

/*
Sample Run 1:
>power 4 2
The number 4 raised to the power 2 = 16

Sample Run 2:
>power 4 3
The number 4 raised to the power 3 = 64
*/
```

```
// Drill 4-5.cs
// Using array methods

using System;

class MyClass
{
    static void Main()
    {
        int[] myArray = {1, 4, 25, 3};

        // Display the array:
        foreach (int i in myArray)
            Console.Write(i + " ");
        Console.WriteLine("Original");

        // Sort, then display:
        Array.Sort(myArray);
        foreach (int i in myArray)
            Console.Write(i + " ");
        Console.WriteLine("Sorted");

        // Reverse, then display:
        Array.Reverse(myArray);
        foreach (int i in myArray)
            Console.Write(i + " ");
        Console.WriteLine("Reversed");
    }
}
```

```
/*
Output:
1 4 25 3 Original
1 3 4 25 Sorted
25 4 3 1 Reversed
*/
```

```
// Drill 5-2.cs
// Private constructors

using System;

public class MyClass
{
    /* Remove the comment characters from the next line to see the
       compiler error */
    // private MyClass() {}
    public string companyName = "Microsoft";
    public string employmentDate = "5/12/2006";
}

public class TestingPrivateCtor
{
    public static void Main()
    {
        MyClass mc = new MyClass();
        // Displayed only if compilation succeeded:
        Console.WriteLine(mc.companyName +"\n" + mc.employmentDate);
    }
}

/*
Compilation error:
error CS0122: 'MyClass.MyClass()' is inaccessible due to its protection
level
drill5-2.cs(7,12): (Location of symbol related to previous error)
*/
```

```
// Drill 5-3 - file1.cs
// Compilation command: csc/out:Drill5-3.exe file1.cs file2.cs

using System;

public class Citizen
{
    private int age = 36;
    private string ssn = "555-55-5555";

    public void GetPersonalInfo()
```

```
    {
      Console.WriteLine("SSN: {0}", ssn);
      Console.WriteLine("Age: {0}", age);
    }
}

public partial class Employee
{
    private string name = "Pille Mandla";
    private string id = "123-WxYz";
}
```

```
// Drill 5-3 - file2.cs
// Compilation command: csc/out:Drill5-3.exe file1.cs file2.cs

using System;

public partial class Employee: Citizen
{
    public void GetInfo()
    {
      // Calling the base class GetPersonalInfo method:
      Console.WriteLine("Citizen's Information:");

      GetPersonalInfo();

      Console.WriteLine("\nJob Information:");
      Console.WriteLine("Company Name: {0}", name);
      Console.WriteLine("Company ID: {0}", id);
    }
}

class MyClass
{
    static void Main(string[] args)
    {
      // Create object:
      Employee emp = new Employee();

      // Display information:
      emp.GetInfo();
    }
}

/*
Output:
Citizen's Information:
SSN: 555-55-5555
Age: 36
```

```
Job Information:
Company Name: Pille Mandla
Company ID: 123-WxYz
*/
```

```csharp
// Drill 6-1.cs
// using override and virtual

using System;

class Citizen
{
    string idNumber = "DAC-2345-A";
    string name = "Dylan Alexander Combel";

    public virtual void GetInformation()
    {
        Console.WriteLine("Name: {0}", name);
        Console.WriteLine("ID Card Number: {0}", idNumber);
    }
}
class Employee: Citizen
{
    string companyName = "Technology Group Inc.";
    string companyID = "ENG-RES-101-C";

    public override void GetInformation()
    {
        // Calling the base class GetInformation method:
        base.GetInformation();

        Console.WriteLine("\nJob Information:");
        Console.WriteLine("Company Name: {0}", companyName);
        Console.WriteLine("Company ID: {0}", companyID);
    }
}
class MainClass
{
    public static void Main()
    {
        Employee E = new Employee();
        E.GetInformation();
    }
}

/*
Output:
Name: Dylan Alexander Combel
```

```
ID Card Number: DAC-2345-A

Job Information:
Company Name: Technology Group Inc.
Company ID: ENG-RES-101-C
*/
```

```
// Drill 6-2.cs
// Abstract classes

using System;

abstract class MyBaseClass
{
    // Fields:
    protected int number = 100;
    protected string name = "Dale Sanders";

    // Abstract method:
    public abstract void MyMethod();

    // Abstract properties:
    public abstract int Number
    { get; }
    public abstract string Name
    { get; }
}

// Inheriting the class:
class MyDerivedClass: MyBaseClass
{
    // Overriding properties:
    public override int Number
    {
        get { return number; }
    }
    public override string Name
    {
        get { return name; }
    }

    // Overriding the method:
    public override void MyMethod()
    {
        Console.WriteLine("Number = {0}", Number);
        Console.WriteLine("Name = {0}", Name);
    }
}
```

```csharp
class MySecondDerivedClass: MyDerivedClass
{
   public override void MyMethod()
   {
      // Implementation
      Console.Write("Hello...");
      Console.WriteLine("again!");
   }
}

class MainClass
{
   public static void Main()
   {
      MyDerivedClass myObject1 = new MyDerivedClass();
      MySecondDerivedClass myObject2 = new MySecondDerivedClass();
      myObject1.MyMethod();
      myObject2.MyMethod();
   }
}

/*
Output:
Number = 100
Name = Dale Sanders
Hello...again!
*/
```

```csharp
// Drill 6-3.cs
// Overloading methods with different number of parameters

using System;

class MyClass
{
   // Using an integer parameter:
   static void MyMethod(int m1)
   {
      Console.WriteLine(m1);
   }

   // Using two integer parameters:
   static void MyMethod(int m1, int m2)
   {
      Console.WriteLine("{0}, {1}", m1, m2);
   }

   static void Main()
   {
```

```
        int m = 134, n = 155;
        MyMethod(m);
            MyMethod(m, n);
    }
}

/*
Output:
134
134, 155
*/
```

```
// Drill 6-4.cs
// Swapping two strings

using System;

class MyClass
{
    static void Swap(ref string s1, ref string s2)
    {
        string temp = s1;
        s1 = s2;
        s2 = temp;
        Console.WriteLine("Inside the swap method: " +
                          "s1 = {0}, s2 = {1}", s1, s2);
    }
    public static void Main()
    {
        string s1 = "John";
        string s2 = "Smith";
        Console.WriteLine("Before swapping: "+
                    "s1 = {0}, s2 = {1}", s1, s2);
        Swap(ref s1, ref s2);
        Console.WriteLine("After swapping: "+
                    "s1 = {0}, s2 = {1}", s1, s2);
    }
}

/*
Output:
Before swapping: s1 = John, s2 = Smith
Inside the swap method: s1 = Smith, s2 = John
After swapping: s1 = Smith, s2 = John
*/
```

```
// Drill 6-5.cs
// Overloading Example

using System;

public class MyClass
{
   public void MyMethod(out int x, out int y, out int z)
   {
     x = 1945;
     y = 1966;
     z = 1987;
   }

   public void MyMethod(ref int x, ref int y)
   {
     x++;
     y++;
   }
}

class MainClass
{
   public static void Main()
   {
     int d1, d2, d3;
     int m = 100, n = 200;

     MyClass mc = new MyClass();

     mc.MyMethod(out d1, out d2, out d3);
     mc.MyMethod(ref m, ref n);

     Console.Write("My dates are: {0}, {1}, {2}\n", d1, d2, d3);
     Console.WriteLine ("My numbers are: {0}, {1}", m, n);
   }
}

/*
Output:
My dates are: 1945, 1966, 1987
My numbers are: 101, 201
*/
```

```
// Drill 6-6.cs
// Using params

using System;
```

```csharp
public class MyClass
{
    // Declare MyMethod that uses object parameters:
    public void MyMethod(params object[] myObjArray)
    {
        for(int i = 0; i< myObjArray.Length; i++)
            Console.WriteLine(myObjArray[i]);
        Console.WriteLine();
    }
}

class MainClass
{
    static void Main()
    {
        MyClass mc = new MyClass();
        mc.MyMethod(11, 22, 33);
        mc.MyMethod(45.33, 'A', "My string");
    }
}

/*
Output:
11
22
33

45.33
A
My string
*/
```

```csharp
// Drill 6-7.cs
// Overloading operators

using System;

public class CompNum
{
    public int real;
    public int imag;

    // Constructor:
    public CompNum(int r, int i)
    {
        real = r;
        imag = i;
    }
```

```csharp
      // The overloaded operator:
      public static CompNum operator+(CompNum c1, CompNum c2)
      {
         // Return the sum as a complex number:
         return new CompNum(c1.real + c2.real, c1.imag + c2.imag);
      }

      // Override ToString():
      public override string ToString()
      {
         return (String.Format("{0} + {1}i", real, imag));
      }

      static void Main()
      {
         CompNum n1 = new CompNum (15, 33);
         CompNum n2 = new CompNum (10, 12);

         // Add two complex numbers using the overloaded + operator:
         CompNum sum = n1 + n2;

         // Display the objects:
         Console.WriteLine("Num1 = {0}", n1);
         Console.WriteLine("Num2 = {0}", n2);
         Console.WriteLine("Sum  = {0}", sum);
      }
   }

/*
Output:
Num1 = 15 + 33i
Num2 = 10 + 12i
Sum  = 25 + 45i
*/
```

```csharp
// Drill 7-1.cs
// Struct properties

using System;

struct Color
{
   // Fields:
   private int r;
   private int g;
   private int b;

   // Constructor:
   Color(int r, int b, int g)
```

```
        {
            this.r = r;
            this.b = b;
            this.g = g;
        }

        // Properties:
        public int R
        {
            get { return r; }
            set { r = value; }
        }

        public int B
        {
            get { return b; }
            set { b = value; }
        }

        public int G
        {
            get { return g; }
            set { g = value; }
        }

        // Override the method ToString():
        public override string ToString()
        {
            return (String.Format("Red = {0}, Green = {1}, Blue = {2}",
                    R, B, G));
        }
        static void Main()
        {
            // Declare objects:
            Color c1 = new Color();
            Color c2 = new Color(100, 100, 0);

            // Display objects:
            Console.WriteLine("The first object:");
            Console.WriteLine("The colors are: {0}", c1);
            Console.WriteLine("The second object:");
            Console.WriteLine("The colors are: {0}", c2);
        }
}

/*
Output:
The first object:
The colors are: Red = 0, Green = 0, Blue = 0
```

```
The second object:
The colors are: Red = 100, Green = 100, Blue = 0
*/
```

```csharp
// Drill 7-2.cs
// Passing struct & class objects

using System;

class MyClass
{
    public string classField;
}

struct MyStruct
{
    public string structField;
}

class MainClass
{
    public static void MyMethod1(MyStruct s)
    {
        s.structField = "New Value";
    }
    public static void MyMethod2(MyClass c)
    {
        c.classField = "New Value";
    }

    static void Main()
    {
        // Create class and struct objects:
        MyStruct sObj = new MyStruct();
        MyClass cObj = new MyClass();

        // Initialize the values of struct and class objects:
        sObj.structField = "Original Value";
        cObj.classField = "Original Value";

        // Print results:
        Console.WriteLine("Results before calling methods:");
        Console.WriteLine("Struct member = {0}", sObj.structField);
        Console.WriteLine("Class member = {0}\n", cObj.classField);

        // Change the values through methods:
        MyMethod1(sObj);
        MyMethod2(cObj);
```

```
      // Print results:
      Console.WriteLine("Results after calling methods:");
      Console.WriteLine("Struct member = {0}", sObj.structField);
      Console.WriteLine("Class member = {0}", cObj.classField);
   }
}

/*
Output:
Results before calling methods:
Struct member = Original Value
Class member = Original Value

Results after calling methods:
Struct member = Original Value
Class member = New Value
*/
```

```
// Drill 7-3.cs
// Using enum in a switch

using System;

// Declare the enum Color:
enum Color { Red = 1, Green, Blue }

class MyClass
{
   // A method that uses a Color parameter:
   static void SelectColor(Color c)
   {
      switch (c)
      {
         // The switch displays the appropriate message according to
            the color:
         case Color.Red:
            Console.WriteLine("The selected color is Red.");
            break;
         case Color.Green:
            Console.WriteLine("The selected color is Green.");
            break;
         case Color.Blue:
            Console.WriteLine("The selected color is Blue.");
            break;
         default:
            Console.WriteLine("Not a valid choice.");
            break;
      }
   }
```

```
    static void Main()
    {
        // Read a color from the keyboard:
        Console.Write("Please select a color: 1=Red, 2=Green, 3=Blue: ");

        // Convert the string to int:
        int myColor = Int32.Parse(Console.ReadLine());

        // Pass the color to the method SelectColor:
        SelectColor((Color)myColor);
    }
}

/*
Sample Run 1:
Please select a color: 1=Red, 2=Green, 3=Blue: 2 --> input
The selected color is Green.

Sample Run 2:
Please select a color: 1=Red, 2=Green, 3=Blue: 0 --> input
Not a valid choice.
*/
```

```
// Drill 7-5.cs
// Using PInvoke

using System;

using System.Runtime.InteropServices;

class PlatformInvokeTest
{
    [DllImport("msvcrt.dll")]
    static extern int puts(string c);

    static void Main()
    {
        string s = "This is an example of platform invoke.";
        puts(s);
    }
}

/*
Output:
This is an example of platform invoke.
*/
```

```csharp
// Drill 7-6.cs
// Emulating unions

using System;
using System.Runtime.InteropServices;

[type: StructLayout(LayoutKind.Explicit)]
struct UnionStruct
{
   [field: FieldOffset(0)]
   public long longVar;
   [field: FieldOffset(0)]

   public int byte1;
   [field: FieldOffset(4)]
   public int byte5;
}
class MyClass
{
   static void Main()
   {
      UnionStruct u = new UnionStruct();

      u.byte1 = 5;
      u.byte5 = 7;

      Console.WriteLine("The bytes of the first int number:
                        {0:x8}",u.byte1);
      Console.WriteLine("The bytes of the second int number:
                        {0:x8}",u.byte5);
      Console.WriteLine("The bytes of the long number:
                        {0:x16}",u.longVar);
   }
}

/*
Output:
The bytes of the first int number: 00000005
The bytes of the second int number: 00000007
The bytes of the long number: 0000000700000005
*/
```

```csharp
// Drill 8-1.cs
// Explicit interface implementation

using System;

public interface ITemp1
{
```

```
   double Convert(double d);
}

public interface ITemp2
{
   double Convert(double d);
}

public class TempConverter: ITemp1, ITemp2

{
   double ITemp1.Convert(double d)
   {
     // Convert to Fahrenheit:
     return (d * 1.8) + 32;
   }

   double ITemp2.Convert(double d)
   {
     // Convert to Celsius:
     return (d - 32) / 1.8;
   }
}

class MyClass
{
   public static void Main()

   {
     // Create a class instance:
     TempConverter cObj = new TempConverter();

     // Create instances of interfaces
     // Create a From-Celsius-to-Fahrenheit object:
     ITemp1 iCF = (ITemp1) cObj;
     // Create From-Fahrenheit-to-Celsius object:
     ITemp2 iFC = (ITemp2) cObj;

     String display = @"Please select a converter:
     1. From Celsius to Fahrenheit.
     2. From Fahrenheit to Celsius.
     :";
     Console.Write(display);

     double F = 0, C = 0;
     string selection = Console.ReadLine();
     switch(selection)
     {
       case "1":
```

```
            Console.Write("Please enter the Celsius temperature: ");
            C = Convert.ToDouble(Console.ReadLine());
            F = iCF.Convert(C);
            Console.WriteLine("Temperature in Fahrenheit: {0:F2}",F);
            break;

        case "2":
            Console.Write("Please enter the Fahrenheit temperature: ");
            F = Convert.ToDouble(Console.ReadLine());
            C = iFC.Convert(F);
            Console.WriteLine("Temperature in Celsius: {0:F2}",C);
            break;

        default:
            Console.WriteLine("Please select a converter.");
            break;
        }
    }
}

/*
Sample Run #1:
Please select a converter:
1. From Celsius to Fahrenheit.
2. From Fahrenheit to Celsius.
:1   --> Keyboard input
Please enter the Celsius temperature: 0    --> Keyboard input
Temperature in Fahrenheit: 32.00

Sample Run #2:
Please select a converter:
1. From Celsius to Fahrenheit.
2. From Fahrenheit to Celsius.
:2   --> Keyboard input
Please enter the Fahrenheit temperature: 32    --> Keyboard input
Temperature in Celsius: 0.00
*/
```

```
// Drill 8-3.cs
// The as operator

using System;

public class MyClass
{
    static void TestType(object o)
    {
        if (o as string != null)
            Console.WriteLine ( "The object \"{0}\" is a string.", o);
```

```
        else
            Console.WriteLine ( "The object \"{0}\" is not a string. It is
                                {1}.", o, o.GetType());
    }

    static void Main()
    {
        object o1 = "Hello, World!";
        object o2 = 123;
        object o3 = 12.34;
        TestType(o1);
        TestType(o2);
        TestType(o3);
    }
}

/*
Output:
The object "Hello, World!" is a string.
The object "123" is not a string. It is System.Int32.
The object "12.34" is not a string. It is System.Double.
*/
```

```
// Drill 8-4.cs
// Hiding interface members

using System;

interface IBase
{
    int M1 {set; get;}
}

interface IDerived: IBase
{
    // Declare a method that hides the property
    // on the IBase interface:
    new void M1();
}

class MyClass: IDerived
{
    private int x;

    // Explicit implementation of the property:
    int IBase.M1
    {
        get { return x; }
        set { x = value; }
```

```
    }

    // Regular implementation of the method:
    public void M1()
    {
        Console.WriteLine("Hi, I am the M1 method!");
    }
}

class MainClass
{
    static void Main()
    {
        // Create a class object:
        MyClass mc = new MyClass();

        // Create an IBase object:
        IBase mi = (IBase)mc;

        // Use the property:
        mi.M1 = 123;

        // Call the method:
        mc.M1();

        // Display the property:
        Console.WriteLine("I am the M1 property. My value is {0}.", mi.M1);
    }
}

/*
Output:
Hi, I am the M1 method!
I am the M1 property. My value is 123.
*/
```

```
// Drill 9-1.cs
// Exception hierarchy

using System;

class MyClass
{
    static void Main()
    {
        int x = 0;
        int y = 10;
        try
        {
```

```
        int z = y/x;
    }

    // The most specific exception:
    catch (DivideByZeroException e)
    {
        Console.WriteLine("Divide-by-zero Exception Handler: {0}", e);
    }

    // The less specific exception:
    catch (ArithmeticException e)
    {
        Console.WriteLine("Arithmetic Exception Handler: {0}", e);
    }

    // Catch the general exception:
    catch (Exception e)
    {
        Console.WriteLine("General Exception Handler: {0}", e);
    }

    // Continue the program:
    Console.WriteLine("Program continues...");
    }
}

/*
Output:
Divide-by-zero Exception Handler: System.DivideByZeroException:
Attempted to divide by zero.
at MyClass.Main()
Program continues...
*/
```

```
// Drill 9-2.cs
// Reading a text file

using System;
using System.IO;

class MyClass
{
    static void Main()
    {
        StreamReader myFile = null;
        try
        {
            myFile = new StreamReader("test.txt");
            string myString = myFile.ReadToEnd();
```

```
         Console.WriteLine(myString);
         myFile.Close();
      }
      catch (FileNotFoundException)
      {
         Console.WriteLine("The file you are trying to open is not
                           found.");
      }
      catch
      {
         Console.WriteLine("General catch statement.");
      }
   }
}

/*
Output:
The file you are trying to open is not found.
*/
```

```
// Drill 9-3.cs
// Processing files using finally

using System;
using System.IO;

class MyClass
{
   static void Main()
   {
      int counter = 0;
      string line;
      StreamReader file = null;

      try
      {
         file = new StreamReader("test.txt");
         while((line = file.ReadLine()) != null)
         {
            Console.WriteLine (line);
            counter++;
         }
      }

      catch (FileNotFoundException)
      {
         // If the file does not exist, you will get this message:
         Console.WriteLine("The file you are trying to open is not
                           found.");
```

```
         }

      catch
      {
         Console.WriteLine("General catch statement.");
      }

      finally
      {
         // If you opened a file with the name "test.txt" it will be
         closed here.
         if (file != null)
         {
            file.Close();
            Console.WriteLine("The file is closed.");
         }
      }
   }
}

/*
Sample Run 1 (if the file exists):
The file is closed.

Sample Run 2 (if the file does not exist):
The file you are trying to open is not found.

*/
```

```
// Drill 9-4.cs
// Fixing errors at run time

using System;

class MainClass
{
   static void Main()
   {
      MyClass mc = new MyClass();
      int x = 0;

      try
      {
         mc.MyMethod(x);
      }

      catch
      {
```

```
                Console.Write("Please enter the denominator of the
                            division 'x': ");
            x = Int32.Parse(Console.ReadLine());
            mc.MyMethod(x);
        }
    }
}

class MyClass
{
    public void MyMethod(int x)
    {
        int y = 10;
        int z = 0;

        try
        {
            z = y / x;
            Console.WriteLine("The division: {0} / {1} = {2}", y, x, z);
        }

        // Catch the exception:
        catch (DivideByZeroException ex)
        {
            Console.WriteLine("A divide-by-zero occurred:\n{0}",
                            ex.StackTrace);

            // Rethrow the exception:
            throw;
        }
    }
}

/*
Output:
A divide-by-zero occurred:
    at MyClass.MyMethod(Int32 x)
Please enter the denominator of the division 'x': 2
The division: 10 / 2 = 5
*/
```

```
// Drill 10-1.cs
// Using delegates

using System;

// Declare a delegate:
delegate void MyDelegate(int n, string s);
```

```csharp
class MainClass
{
   static void Main()
   {
      // Instantiate the class:
      MyClass obj = new MyClass();

      // Instantiate the delegate:
      MyDelegate d = new MyDelegate(obj.MyMethod);

      // Invoke the delegate:
      d(123, "Jane Doe");
   }
}

class MyClass
{
   // The encapsulated Method:
   public void MyMethod(int id, string name)
   {
      Console.WriteLine("ID = {0}\nName = {1}", id, name);
   }
}

/*
Output:
ID = 123
Name = Jane Doe
*/
```

```csharp
// Drill 10-2.cs
// Adding and removing delegates

using System;

// Declare a delegate:
delegate void MyDelegate();

class MyClass
{
   public static void MyMethod1()
   {
      Console.Write("MyMethod #1 ");
   }

   public static void MyMethod2()
   {
      Console.Write("MyMethod #2 ");
   }
```

```csharp
    public static void Main()
    {
        // Declare delegate object and reference MyMethod1:
        MyDelegate d1 = new MyDelegate(MyClass.MyMethod1);

        // Declare delegate object and reference MyMethod2:
        MyDelegate d2 = new MyDelegate(MyClass.MyMethod2);

        // Declare delegate d3 by adding d1 and d2.
        // This will invoke both MyMethod1 and MyMethod2:
        MyDelegate d3 = d1 + d2;

        // Declare delegate d4 by removing d1 from d3. This will invoke
          MyMethod2 only:
        MyDelegate d4 = d3 - d1;

        Console.Write("Invoking d1, referencing ");
        d1();
        Console.Write("\nInvoking d2, referencing ");
        d2();
        Console.Write("\nInvoking d3, referencing ");
        d3();
        Console.Write("\nInvoking d4, referencing ");
        d4();
    }
}

/*
Output:
Invoking d1, referencing MyMethod #1
Invoking d2, referencing MyMethod #2
Invoking d3, referencing MyMethod #1 MyMethod #2
Invoking d4, referencing MyMethod #2
*/
```

```csharp
// Drill 10-3.cs
// Right-button simulation

using System;

public delegate void RightButtonDown(object sender, EventArgs e);

public class MouseClass
{
    public static event RightButtonDown PressDown;

    public static void OnPressDown()
    {
```

```csharp
        if (PressDown != null)
        PressDown(new MouseClass(), new EventArgs());
    }
}

class MyClass
{
    public static void MouseHandler(object sender, EventArgs e)
    {
        Console.WriteLine("Message from the right button: 'Hey, you
                          pressed me down.' ");
    }

    static void Main()
    {
        MouseClass.PressDown += new RightButtonDown(MouseHandler);
        MouseClass.OnPressDown();
        MouseClass.PressDown -= new RightButtonDown(MouseHandler);
    }
}

/*
Output:
Message from the right button: 'Hey, you pressed me down.'
*/
```

```csharp
// Drill 11-1.cs
// Stack

using System;
using System.Collections;

public class MyClass
{
    public static void Main()
    {
        // Initialize a stack object:
        Stack myStack = new Stack();

        myStack.Push("One");
        myStack.Push("Two");
        myStack.Push("Three");
        myStack.Push("Four");

        // Display all:
        Console.Write("myStack elements are: ");
        foreach (object obj in myStack)
            Console.Write(obj + " ");
```

```csharp
      // Display first element:
      Console.WriteLine("\nFirst element: {0} ", myStack.Peek());

      // Pop one element:
      myStack.Pop();

      // Displays the count of elements:
      Console.WriteLine("Number of elements is now: {0}",
         myStack.Count);

      // Display first element:
      Console.WriteLine("First element: {0} ", myStack.Peek());

      // Check if the stack contains the value "Four":
      if(myStack.Contains("Four"))
         Console.WriteLine("The stack contains the element 'Four'");

      // Copy the contents to an array:
      object[] myArr = myStack.ToArray();

      // Display the array:
      Console.WriteLine("Elements of the array are: ");
      foreach (object obj in myArr)
         Console.Write(obj + " ");
   }
}

/*
Output:
myStack elements are: Four Three Two One
First element: Four
Number of elements is now: 3
First element: Three
Elements of the array are:
Three Two One
*/
```

```csharp
// Drill 11-2.cs
// Queue

using System;
using System.Collections;

public class MyClass
{
   public static void Main()
   {
      // Declare an int array:
      int[] myIntArr = { 1, 2, 3, 4, 5 };
```

```
            // Initialize a Queue collection with the array elements:
            Queue myQueue = new Queue(myIntArr);

            // Declare a string array:
            string[] myStrArr = { "one", "two", "three" };

            // Add some string elements to the Queue collection:
            foreach(string s in myStrArr)
                myQueue.Enqueue(s);

            // Display all:
            Console.WriteLine("myQueue elements are: ");
            foreach (object obj in myQueue)
                Console.Write(obj + " ");

            // Display the count of elements:
            Console.WriteLine("\nThe number of elements is: {0}",
                myQueue.Count);

            // Display first element:
            Console.WriteLine("The first element is: {0}",
                myQueue.Peek());

            // Remove one element:
            myQueue.Dequeue();
            Console.WriteLine("Removing one element...");

            // Display the count of elements:
            Console.WriteLine("The number of elements is now: {0}",
                myQueue.Count);

            // Copy the contents to an object array:
            object[] myArr = myQueue.ToArray();

            // Display the array:
            Console.WriteLine("Elements of the array are: ");
            foreach (object obj in myArr)
                Console.Write(obj + " ");
    }
}

/*
Output:
myQueue elements are:
1 2 3 4 5 one two three
The number of elements is: 8
The first element is: 1
Removing one element...
```

```
The number of elements is now: 7
Elements of the array are:
2 3 4 5 one two three
*/
```

```
// Drill 11-3.cs
// ArrayList

using System;
using System.Collections;

public class MyClass
{
    public static void Main()
    {
        // Creates an ArrayList:
        ArrayList myArrayList = new ArrayList();

        // Initializes the list with some elements:
        myArrayList.Add("SNL");
        myArrayList.Add("Mad TV");
        myArrayList.Add("Seinfeld");
        myArrayList.Add("Everybody Loves Raymond");
        myArrayList.Add("Married with Children");
        myArrayList.Add("SNL");

        // Displays the index of the first matching item starting at
            index 2:
        Console.WriteLine("The index of the first match for 'SNL' starting
                            at index 2: {0}",
        myArrayList.IndexOf("SNL", 2));
    }
}

/*
Output:
The index of the first match for 'SNL' starting at index 2: 5
*/
```

```
// Drill 11-4.cs
// SortedList

using System;
using System.Collections;

public class MyClass
{
    public static void Main()
    {
```

```csharp
        // Create an ArrayList:
        SortedList myList = new SortedList();

        // Initialize the list with some elements:
        myList.Add("003","SNL");
        myList.Add("002","Mad TV");
        myList.Add("004","Seinfeld");
        myList.Add("001","Married with Children");
        myList.Add("006","Everybody Loves Raymond");

        // Display the index of the key "004":
        Console.WriteLine("The index of the key \"004\" is: {0}",
            myList.IndexOfKey("004"));

        // Display the item that corresponds to key "004":
        Console.WriteLine("The item that corresponds to the key
                        \"004\": {0}", myList["004"]);

        // Search for "Seinfeld":
        Console.WriteLine("Is Seinfeld in the list?: {0}",
            myList.ContainsValue("Seinfeld"));
    }
}

/*
Output:
The index of the key "004" is: 3
The item that corresponds to the key "004": Seinfeld
Is Seinfeld in the list?: True
*/
```

```csharp
// Drill 11-5.cs
// Hashtable

using System;
using System.Collections;
public class MyClass
{
    public static void Main()
    {
        // Creates a Hashtable object:
        Hashtable ZipCodeHash = new Hashtable();

        // Initializes the Hashtable.
        ZipCodeHash.Add("98006", "Bellevue");
        ZipCodeHash.Add("98201", "Everett");
        ZipCodeHash.Add("98101", "Seattle");
        ZipCodeHash.Add("98501", "Olympia");
        ZipCodeHash.Add("98040", "Mercer Island");
```

```
      ZipCodeHash.Add("98033", "Kirkland");

      // Displays the contents of the Hashtable.
      DisplayIt(ZipCodeHash);

      // Display the city that corresponds to zip code "98006":
      Console.WriteLine("The city that corresponds to zip code
                  \"98006\": {0}",
      ZipCodeHash["98006"]);
   }

   public static void DisplayIt(Hashtable ZipCodeHash)
   {
      Console.WriteLine("Zip Code\tCity");
      foreach (string k in ZipCodeHash.Keys)
         Console.WriteLine("{0}\t\t{1}", k, ZipCodeHash[k]);
   }
}

/*
Output:
Zip Code        City
98501           Olympia
98101           Seattle
98006           Bellevue
98201           Everett
98040           Mercer Island
98033           Kirkland
The city that corresponds to zip code "98006": Bellevue
*/
```

```
// Drill 11-6.cs
// ListDictionary collection

using System;
using System.Collections;
using System.Collections.Specialized;

public class LDClass
{
   public static void Main(string[] args)
   {
      // Create an empty ListDictionary object:
      ListDictionary myLD = new ListDictionary();

      // Initialize the ListDictionary collection:
      myLD.Add("Learn Pascal", "$39.95");
      myLD.Add("Learn Pascal in Three Days", "$19.95");
      myLD.Add("Learn C in Three Days", "$19.95");
```

```csharp
        myLD.Add("Learn J#", "$35.95");
        myLD.Add("Learn C#", "$39.95");

        // Display Values and Keys:
        foreach (string key in myLD.Keys)
            Console.WriteLine("Key: {0}", key);
        Console.WriteLine();

        foreach (string value in myLD.Values)
            Console.WriteLine("Value: {0}", value);
        Console.WriteLine();

        // Display the collection:
        DisplayIt(myLD);
    }

    public static void DisplayIt(ListDictionary myLD)
    {
        string s = "\t\t\t\t";
        Console.WriteLine("Book{0}Price\n", s);
        foreach (string key in myLD.Keys)
            Console.WriteLine("{0, -32}{1}", key, myLD[key]);
    }
}

/*
Output:
Key: Learn Pascal
Key: Learn Pascal in Three Days
Key: Learn C in Three Days
Key: Learn J#
Key: Learn C#

Value: $39.95
Value: $19.95
Value: $19.95
Value: $35.95
Value: $39.95

Book                            Price

Learn Pascal                    $39.95
Learn Pascal in Three Days      $19.95
Learn C in Three Days           $19.95
Learn J#                        $35.95
Learn C#                        $39.95
*/
```

```
// Drill 11-7.cs
// Prime numbers iterator

using System;
using System.Collections;

class MyClass
{
   public IEnumerable MyIterator(int start, int end)
   {
      for (int i = start+1; i <= end; i++)
      {
         bool x = false;
         for (int j = start + 1; j <= i - 1; j++)
         {
            if (i % j == 0)  x = true;
         }
         if (x == false) yield return i;
            continue;
      }
   }
   static void Main(string[] args)
   {
      MyClass mc = new MyClass();

      // Display prime numbers:
      Console.WriteLine("Prime numbers between 1 and 10 are:");
      foreach (int item in mc.MyIterator(1,10))
      {
         Console.WriteLine(item);
      }
   }
}

/*
Output:
Prime numbers between 1 and 10 are:
2
3
5
7
*/
```

```
// Drill 12-1.cs
// List<T> example

using System;
using System.Collections.Generic;
```

```
class MyClass
{
   static void Main()
   {
      // Declare the list:
      List<string> myList = new List<string>();

      // Build the list from the array:
      myList.Add("Dylan");
      myList.Add("Isabella");
      myList.Add("Eve");
      myList.Add("Angelina");

      // Sorting the List:
      myList.Sort();

      // Display items:
      Console.WriteLine("The sorted List items:");
      DisplayIt(myList);

      // Copy items to an array:
      string[] myArray = myList.ToArray();

      // Display the array elements:
      Console.WriteLine("The array elements:");
      foreach (string s in myArray)
         Console.WriteLine(s + " ");
   }

   // Display the list:
   static void DisplayIt(List<string> myL)
   {
      foreach (string name in myL)
      {
         Console.WriteLine(name);
      }
      Console.WriteLine();
   }
}

/*
Output:
The sorted List items:
Angelina
Dylan
Eve
Isabella
```

```
The array elements:
Angelina
Dylan
Eve
Isabella
*/
```

```
// Drill 12-2.cs
// Dictionary collection

using System;
using System.Collections.Generic;

public class Example
{
    public static void Main()
    {
        // Create an empty Dictionary collection:
        Dictionary<string, double> myDictionary =
            new Dictionary<string, double>();

        // Add some elements to the dictionary.
        // Assume keys are fruit and values are prices.
        // Prices can be duplicates.
        myDictionary.Add("Apples", 0.30);
        myDictionary.Add("Oranges", 0.50);
        myDictionary.Add("Cherries", 0.44);
        myDictionary.Add("Peaches", 0.50);

        // Create the KeyCollections object:
        Dictionary<string, double>.KeyCollection kC =
            myDictionary.Keys;
        // List all keys (fruit types):
        Console.WriteLine("The fruit types in the store are:");
        foreach (string fruit in kC)
        {
            Console.WriteLine("{0}", fruit);
        }

        // Create the ValueCollections object:
        Dictionary<string, double>.ValueCollection vC =
            myDictionary.Values;
        // List all values (prices):
        Console.WriteLine("The fruit prices in the store are:");
        foreach (double price in vC)
        {
            Console.WriteLine("{0:C}", price);
        }
    }
```

```
}

/*
Output:
The fruit types in the store are:
Apples
Oranges
Cherries
Peaches
The fruit prices in the store are:
$0.30
$0.50
$0.44
$0.50
*/
```

```
// Drill 12-3.cs
// Generic LinkedList

using System;
using System.Collections.Generic;

public class LinkedList
{
   public static void Main()
   {
      string[] myArray = { "Paul", "John", "Mary" };
      LinkedList<string> myLinkedList = new LinkedList<string>(myArray);

      // Build the list:
      myLinkedList.AddLast("Tom");
      myLinkedList.AddLast("Dick");
      myLinkedList.AddLast("Harry");

      myLinkedList.AddBefore(myLinkedList.Last, "and");

      // Display the list:
      Display(myLinkedList);
   }

   // Display a LinkedList object:
   private static void Display(LinkedList<string> myLL)
   {
      foreach (string name in myLL)
      {
         Console.Write(name + " ");
      }
      Console.WriteLine();
```

```
      // Display the number of items:
      Console.WriteLine(
        "The number of nodes is {0}.", myLL.Count);
  }
}

/*
Output:
Paul John Mary Tom Dick and Harry
The number of nodes is 7.
*/
```

```
// Drill 12-4.cs
// Constraints

using System;
using System.Collections;
using System.Collections.Generic;

public class Employee
{
    private string name;
    private string id;

    public string Name
    {
        get { return name; }
        set { name = value; }
    }

    public string ID
    {
        get { return id; }
        set { id = value; }
    }
}

public class MyClass<T> where T: Employee
{
    Stack<string> s = new Stack<string>();
    public void MyMethod(T t)
    {
        s.Push(t.ID);
        s.Push(t.Name);

        for (int i = 0; i <= s.Count; i++)
            Console.WriteLine(s.Pop());
    }
}
```

```csharp
public class MainClass
{
   static void Main()
   {
      MyClass<Employee> mc = new MyClass<Employee>();
      Employee emp = new Employee();
      emp.Name = "Francis";
      emp.ID = "123ABC";
      mc.MyMethod(emp);
      Employee emp1 = new Employee();
      emp1.Name = "Donn";
      emp1.ID = "123XYZ";
      mc.MyMethod(emp1);
   }
}

/*
Output:
Francis
123ABC
Donn
123XYZ
*/
```

```csharp
// Drill 12-5.cs
// Generic delegates

using System;

// Declare a delegate:
public delegate void MyDelegate<T1, T2>(T1 id, T2 name);

class MyClass
{
   // Declare the encapsulated Method:

   public void MyMethod(int id, string name)
   {
      Console.WriteLine("ID number = {0}\nName = {1}", id, name);
   }
}

class MainClass
{
   static void Main()
   {
      // Instantiate the class:
      MyClass mc = new MyClass();
```

```
        //MyDelegate<int, string> delg =
        // new MyDelegate<int, string>(mc.MyMethod);
        // or:
        MyDelegate<int, string> delg = mc.MyMethod;

        // Invoke the delegate:
        delg.Invoke(911, "Angelina Abolrous");
    }
}

/*
Output:
ID number = 911
Name = Angelina Abolrous
*/
```

Index

Looking for more?

Check out Wordware's market-leading Applications Library featuring the following titles.

Recent Releases

Essential LightWave v9
1-59822-024-1 • $49.95
6 x 9 • 992 pp.

LightWave v9 Texturing
1-59822-029-2 • $44.95
6 x 9 • 648 pp.

LightWave v9 Lighting
1-59822-039-X • $44.95
6 x 9 • 616 pp.

Managing Virtual Teams:
Getting the Most From Wikis, Blogs, and Other Collaborative Tools
1-59822-028-4 • $29.95
6 x 9 • 400 pp.

Microsoft Excel Functi **& Formulas**
1-59822-011-X • $2!
6 x 9 • 416 pp.

Advanced SQL Functions in Oracle 10g
1-59822-021-7 • $36.95
6 x 9 • 416 pp.

SQL for Microsoft Access
1-55622-092-8 • $39.95
6 x 9 • 360 pp.

Word 2003 Document Automation with VBA, XML, XSLT and Smart Documents
1-55622-086-3 • $36.95
6 x 9 • 464 pp.

Access 2003 Programming by Example with VBA, XML, and ASP
1-55622-223-8 • $39.95
6 x 9 • 704 pp.

Excel 2003 VBA Progr **with XML and ASP**
1-55622-225-4 • $3
6 x 9 • 968 pp.

Don't Miss

Camtasia Studio 4: The Definitive Guide
1-59822-037-3 • $39.95
6 x 9 • 600 pp.

Introduction to Game Programming with C++
1-59822-032-2 • $44.95
6 x 9 • 392 pp.

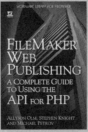

FileMaker Web Publishing: A Complete Guide to Using the API for PHP
1-59822-041-1 • $49.95
6 x 9 • 472 pp.

FileMaker Pro Business Applications
1-59822-014-4 • $49.95
6 x 9 • 648 pp.

Learn FileMaker Pro
1-59822-046-2 • $3
6 x 9 • 550 pp.

Visit us online at www.wordware.com for more information
Use the following coupon code for online specials: csharp0357